Michael W. Hill

The Impact of
Information on Society

An examination of its nature,
value and usage

K·G·Saur München 2001

Die Deutsche Bibliothek – CIP-Einheitsaufnahme

Hill, Michael W.:
The impact of information on society
/ Michael W. Hill. - München : Saur, 2001
ISBN 3-598-11546-6

Reprint of the first edition,
published by Bowker-Saur, East Grinstead, 1999

(∞)

Printed on acid-free paper

© 2001 K. G. Saur Verlag GmbH, München

Cover design by John Cole

Typesetting by Florence Production Ltd., Stoodleigh, Devon

Printed and Bound in Great Britain by Antony Rowe Ltd., Chippenham, Wiltshire

ISBN 3-598-11546-6

About the author

An Oxford educated chemist, Michael Hill spent the first half of his career in industrial research, production management and public relations. He then joined a team at the British Museum entrusted with establishing a national reference library for science and technology incorporating the Patent Office Library. By 1968 he had become Director (Keeper) of the library and remained in that post when the library was incorporated into the newly created British Library.

Michael has been a Director of the UK Chemical Information Service (UKCIS) and Chairman of the BL Committee which aided the spread of online services in the UK. He has been the Honorary Secretary and Chairman of the Aslib Council, and Chairman of the Circle of State Librarians. He is a Fellow of the IIS and of the RSA, an Honorary Fellow of FID, a member of the Royal Society of Chemistry and also of the Royal Institution. As UK delegate to FID for some 12 years, he was its President for six years and has also been a Vice-President of IATUL.

Michael is co-founder of the European Council of Information Associations and helped launch the journal *World Patent Information*. He has published and lectured extensively on the exploitation of information and of technical libraries, and more recently on national information policy and on ethical principles in information work. His books include *Patent Documentation, Michael Hill on Science, Invention and Information* and *National Information Policies and Strategies*. He is currently Joint Editor of the K.G. Saur *Guides to Information Sources* series.

To my wife Barbara, who has helped much
and put up with much more.

Contents

About the author   v

Preface   ix

1 Introduction   1

2 The nature of information and knowledge   11

3 The quality and reliability of information   42

4 Comprehending   60

5 Communicating   78

6 Some aspects of information, knowledge and
   document management   94

7 Information ethics: expectations and rights   111

8 Information ethics: duties and responsibilities   133

9 Information ethics: intellectual property and
   data protection   153

10 Some social and cultural issues   172

11 Economic factors   199

12 Information and the environment   225

13 Education now and in the next decade   232

14 Information in politics and government   251

15 The Information Society: are we now part of it and
    where is it heading?   274

Index   287

Preface

'Turned calmly and inquisitive, to scan
The licence and the limit, space and bound,
Allowed to Truth made visible in Man.'
Browning, *Pictor Ignotus*

Many endeavours start from lofty thoughts but are quickly brought down to reality by starting to work them out. This book is no exception. My aim has been, with all the talk of the Information Society, to take a hard look at what information really is, what are its licence and its limit, its space and bounds and where its dramatic growth is leading us. It has often been joked that the I has got lost in the IT.

Others, too, are intrigued by this curious material. In a January 1998 issue of the *New Scientist*, there is a report of a survey of a large sample of scientists, engineers and other researchers which asked them what big questions they were currently pondering. Among the responses which ranged widely and were often unrelated to their work was 'What is information and where did it originally come from?' Something of that sort was in my mind when I started on this book.

It is one which I have long felt ought to be written. Much has been published on information technology, the information society, global or otherwise, information policy, information management and so on but none, it seems to me, has concentrated on the basics, on looking at the scene from the point of view of information or, as it usually manifests itself, the content of the systems. So my principal aim has been to ask what is information, why does it have the role it does and is it merely increase or fundamental change in that role which makes some people claim that we are entering an information age.

Since so much has already been written from other viewpoints, the second of my aims has been to pull together the various strands, the views of many expert exponents of its usage and many examples that have emerged in recent years of what information can do for us, what has changed about it and our attitudes towards it, and what its manipulation and transmission by modern computers and telecommunications systems, especially the Internet, do to our ways of exploiting it.

It is probably my training as a chemist that has led me to structure the book into first the equivalent of 'preps and props' followed by 'applications'. The parallel is not exact but it is not far off.

This is not a book about computers and telecommunications. They are constantly referred to but they are not the principal focus of attention. Indeed, I start with the assumption that many readers will be much more familiar with them than I. There will be no account, therefore, of what is required to gain access to the Internet, the use of search engines, or of arranging or paying for access to particular sites. Rather, there will be a consideration of matters such as ethical aspects of one's rights to access and communicate any information one wants, whatever the source, of the problems encountered in ensuring that one does get across to an audience the information one wishes to convey, and of the political, social, economic and educational issues it creates.

I hope that this examination will provide a base from which others can progress further. I hope too that it will prove useful to those starting to work in the information sector of the economy, in libraries or in computer science as well as reminding my colleagues of many years standing what a curious field we have worked in and with what a strange material.

One of the fascinations of preparing this book has been that even as I was writing events were occurring which caused me to change or add to the text. Proposals for a Freedom of Information Bill were published; a decision was taken to incorporate the European Convention on Human Rights into British law; beef on the bone was banned on the strength of scientific evidence that a minute risk to health existed; in the USA the Communications Decency Act was overthrown in the Courts. It all added interest to the task, amendments to the text, time to complete and a test of the points I was making.

I must acknowledge my gratitude to the authors of all those books and articles which have influenced my thinking. Many are referred to but by no means all. Especially I must mention Michael Oakeshott's *The Voice of Liberal Learning*, Steven Pinker's *The Language Instinct*, Lord Annan's *Our Age*, Lady Warnock's *Imagination and Time* and Frank Webster's article 'What information society?' Several books by such differing authors as Isaiah Berlin, Peter Drucker and Bertrand Russell have also been very influential, as have many of the papers given at meetings of the Royal Society of Arts, Manufacturers and Commerce, the RSA. The news media, especially the *Daily Telegraph*, have been a very useful source despite my strictures about them.

In addition, much of the credit for whatever is good in this book should be given to those very many individuals from many areas of the information field and many countries who over the years have given me so generously of their knowledge and experience. My knowledge of the information field has been gained from them: I hope they approve of what they see in the text. They include colleagues in the Science Reference Library, BLR&DD (now the British Library Research and Innovation Centre), UCL, City University and several other schools of LIS, Aslib, the IIS and the LA, colleagues in FID, IATUL, ECIA, the EPO, WIPO, UNESCO's PGI, fellow conferees from many meetings, for example that at Cumberland Lodge in July 1996, and many many more. I only wish I had space to list them all. However, I must mention by name Roger Bowes who checked part of chapter 6, Robert Youngman, a former headmaster, who was very helpful with the chapter on education and John Owston, librarian of the United Oxford and Cambridge University Club for help with many of the references. I should also like to thank the staff of the publisher, Bowker-Saur, for being both very helpful and very patient. Nevertheless, none of these should be blamed if any of the opinions are unsound or the facts erroneous. The responsibility for them is entirely mine.

CHAPTER ONE
Introduction

The rather touching story is told that in 1934 the great Australian cricketer, Don Bradman, was struggling for his life in hospital in England after an emergency operation. His wife, Jessie, cabled him from Australia saying, 'It's all right, Don. I'm coming'. The surgeon said that from the moment he received that message, the information that she was on her way, Bradman turned the corner and started to recover. An unusual example, perhaps, but there are many others that could be quoted to show how the right information at the right moment does have considerable impact. It also serves to make a second point: that information and communication technologies (ICTs) play a very important part in making sure that the information can achieve its full impact. The same message sent by post rather than cable would have been useless because even if airmailed it would have arrived too late.

That is one example of information having an impact. Others range widely. In one patent case between two aircraft engine manufacturers, when many millions of pounds of business were at stake, the decision turned on whether a particular piece of technical information had been published in the obscure journal *Flugsport*. Recently a Minister's career depended on whether or not he had been given information about arms sales to a foreign country. A trial collapsed because information about the men who escaped from Whitemoor prison was published in a newspaper.

At a different level of importance, my being met at the station may depend on being able to get the information to my wife that I am travelling home on an earlier train. Watching a woodpecker on my lawn gives me fascinating information about the habits of that bird.

The examples show several very different types of impact, from a matter of life and death to mere personal benefit and increase of knowledge, from the profitability of an enterprise to the losses of a career or a criminal prosecution.

The nature of the information in each of these examples is so very different from the others that it is hardly surprising if, as was the case until recently, most people were unwilling to take seriously any proposal to manage or even discuss information as such. That was not so with specific categories of information, especially scientific and technical information (STI). Emphasis on the importance of managing and exploiting that resource was given by a Royal Society Conference held in 1948. For the next 20 years information work was largely concerned with STI and it was only when computers started to be used for printing journals, which led to searchable databases, that the information industry started to take off.

By 1981 the situation had advanced enormously. There was even, in the UK, a Minister for Information Technology. In that year, Lord Dainton, an eminent scientist, former Chairman of the Advisory Council for Scientific and Technical Information and at the time of the British Library Board, said in a lecture [1], 'The Information Revolution has consequences for employment, for leisure, for the nature and location of industry, for education, for the democratic process and for the further acquisition of knowledge. It beckons with opportunities for a better life and threatens dire consequences if wrong choices are made'. His words expressed a situation that was by then widely accepted.

Perhaps the most important change that has occurred in the last 50 years is that there is now a perception or realisation that information *per se* is something to be collected, stored, managed and exploited. It has become a resource. No longer is it regarded as something available free, as a right, merely for the asking.

That a change of attitude was necessary may be highlighted by the following. A survey was being carried out of the use by Canadian companies of information sources and services. From one managing director the researcher received the dusty response, 'If any member of this company goes outside for information, he's fired!'

The change of attitude has been caused by a number of factors, the most important being the great improvements in computers, microprocessors and telecommunications, equipment known as information and communication technologies (ICTs). Best selling books like Toffler's *Future Shock* [2] alerted the public to anticipated developments which have since then followed thick and fast.

Consider the following short list of a few of the facilities that the new technologies have brought:

* home computers;
* debit and credit cards;
* telebanking;
* worldwide financial transactions;
* online holiday and hotel bookings;
* countrywide databases of houses and cars for sale;
* just-in-time ordering systems;
* barcode check out systems;
* Internet discussion groups;
* radio-tagging to trace the whereabouts of animals, people or goods;
* distance learning;
* Ceefax and Oracle, information systems over the home TV;
* mobile telephones;
* automatic surveillance and security systems;

and there are so many more. In each case, information handling and/or communicating is at the the heart of the development.

At the institutional level, awareness of the impending developments was probably brought home to those in a position to influence events by Bell's epochal book *The Coming of the Post-Industrial Society* [3].

In the 1970s and early 1980s most attention was paid to the impact of computers. Since then, attention has switched to telecommunication systems. Most advanced countries have taken steps to ensure that they have a telecoms infrastructure to cope with all manner of systems requirements. Particular attention has been paid to wideband channels to ensure fast communication of large files and pictorial information. Looking beyond this stage in its 1996 report *Information Society: Agenda for Action in the UK* the House of Lords' Select Committee on Science and Technology writes [4], 'As the physical infrastructure [of the information superhighway] develops, the focus of attention needs to move on to what the superhighways will carry'. Most of what they will carry, indeed are already carrying and have been for some time, is information. It is that information, whether carried by networks, transmitted orally or even conveyed in writing, with which this book is concerned.

The interplay of a greater awareness of the value of information with the new ways of handling it which the ICTs provide, and the social, cultural, economic and political changes which are simultaneously occurring, give rise to many fascinating issues. Much has been written on the ICTs, on social changes and on economic developments. In this book the whole range will be surveyed from the point of view of the impact information has and the consequences there are for its generation and use.

To start with, the nature of information itself will be examined, how it is perceived, generated, managed and used. Factors involved in the process of communication between two human beings will be discussed including the ways we communicate, how we understand what each other is trying to tell us including hidden messages and the fact that, for example, we manage even to correct poorly expressed information. The book will cover many of the wide ranging issues which are arising in the information age including government policies, worldwide data flows, the use of information for commercial advantage, the sort of educational systems and environment needed for the immediate future, and the way new research gives rise to information which causes scares or changes to our lifestyle including changing our attitude to our physical environment. Personal, national and global aspects will be taken into account.

Other topics will include a range of ethical issues, not only data protection, personal privacy and copyright but also freedom of access to government information, censorship, the use of encryption and the availability of illegal material on the superhighways via the Internet. There is growing concern about some of the uses to which information is being put and the opportunities for crime that the technologies seem to be offering.

A glance at the background

It could be argued that, whereas the modern ICT era began with Babbage's design for a computer in 1835 and Morse's invention of the telegraph in 1844, the modern information era started at the Renaissance. Suddenly the truth of religious dogma and everyday observation had to stand up to comparison with that of scientific observation and experiment. From then on beliefs were subject to critical scrutiny, to testing and to rejection if they did not pass the test. Is it coincidence that Nostradamus, possibly the greatest prophet of the old era, died only two years after Galileo was born and three years before Tycho Brahe started his series of discoveries? It was not only religious beliefs that were challenged but also the common sense rules of everyday life. For example, experiment showed that bodies of different weights fall not at different speeds, as common sense might suggest, but with the same rate of acceleration, provided air resistance is insignificant.

In the centuries since the Renaissance information has steadily grown as explorations have revealed the nature of the surface of our globe, and especially as scientific research and technological development have progressed. Each has aided the other so that technological improvements have enabled new scientific discoveries to be made and those discoveries in turn have led to new technological developments. The development of high powered magnets with very homogeneous fields enabled research into the spin of atomic nuclei to be studied. At the outset this seemed to be pure curiosity research of no practical use whatever. However, it has led to the development by engineers and technologists of machines which scan human brains to reveal information about the presence of tumours. It is, of course, the subject known as NMR or nuclear magnetic resonance.

The interaction of science and technology has resulted in a steadily increasing rate of production of new information. So too has the immense amount of research carried out in other disciplines such as history, literature and economics and many more. The numbers of people attending universities and hence taking part in activities which add new information have grown steadily, with the combined result that the rate of growth of information has been increasing very rapidly. Now, instead of the handful of people involved in research in the 16th century there are several million worldwide. Information is difficult to quantify but if one takes inventions as some guide, there are over a hundred thousand applications each year for patents for new inventions.

Does information always have the impact it should?

The information that the Germans had invaded Poland was the signal for the start of the second World War. The information that at the heart of human cells is a large spiral molecule, DNA, unique to each of us, which controls the replication of cells has provided some dramatic instances of identifying people and animals from samples of their DNA, and has led eventually to the cloning of animals. Of course some information has impact. Most of it has much less dramatic results than those examples. Some has no effect at all.

The strength of the impact often depends on how it is presented. Public concern may cause the impact to be excessive, in some cases because information has not been fully assessed and verified. The theory that cot deaths of babies might be due to chemicals in the mattresses was a classic example. Thousands of mattresses were needlessly discarded.

Consider the sales technique some street traders use. They present a package of not one, not two, not three but four items as if it were a great bargain and there are people who fall for it. There is no real bargain. The price is set to produce a healthy profit on the package of four items and selling four at a time disposes of stock quickly.

Both these examples illustrate not just that some people are gullible but that the impact of information, or something proffered as if it were information, depends on the way it is presented. It follows that those giving information need to consider carefully how it is presented and those acquiring information to check that it is reliable, complete and properly understood.

On the other hand much information, even that proven and widely accepted, may have no impact at all on some of the population. Firmly held beliefs can be impossible to overcome. In addition to those who still cannot accept that two bodies will fall with the same acceleration irrespective of their mass or velocity at right angles to the direction of fall (try asking whether a bullet fired horizontally or one simultaneously dropped from the same position hits the ground first) there are also those who maintain, despite all evidence to the contrary, that the earth is flat. The capacity of individuals to understand and accept information is a facet of our subject that will be discussed in detail later.

Failure to heed information is far from uncommon. Two recent examples, one with tragic consequences, were the following: apparently, five warnings were given that car ferries were starting off from the quay while their doors were still open before one sank at Zeebrugge; and the letter from an employee at the Matrix Churchill company to the Foreign Secretary about munitions for Iraq was apparently ignored by the civil servants.

Of course only a very small portion of the information we meet has a dramatic effect or is difficult to accept. It is an everyday, common-or-garden phenomenon. We acquire a wide variety of new pieces of information every day of our lives. We select what we want, we use it or store it for future use, and we pass it on to others. It is not many years ago that the chief executive of a large organization said to his librarian, 'Don't waste my time talking about information sources and their management. When I want information I know where to get it'. While chief executives still have and use their private sources of information, the management of information has become one of the significant operations of organizations of all types and sizes, and especially of those that operate globally. Now even knowledge management is being attempted.

Information and social change

Frequently we are told by pundits and politicians that the information society will result in huge social, cultural, political and economic changes (I shall for the time being follow popular practice and use the term 'information society', though whether it is really the appropriate title to give the era of the present and next twenty years is a topic that will be discussed later). The analogy is the extent of the changes that occurred as western countries evolved from agrarian into industrial societies. But the comparison may be misleading not least because changes that have occurred during the first eighty years of this century, during the era of industrial society, have been far greater than those of any previous century. One has but to remember the emancipation of women, the changed attitudes to religion, the huge increase in wealth and lifestyle, foreign travel for all, sophisticated home entertainment, the changed relations between the generations and the changes in moral codes to realize this. All of these have been hastened by better and more widely disseminated information but their start preceded the arrival of the information society which, publicity implies, is only just upon us.

There has been, since the late 1950s, not only a growth in the consumption of reported information but also in that from first hand observation. Foreign holiday travel to remoter and yet remoter countries has brought home to most western people the great poverty in which many people in developing countries live. Television pictures of the consequences of famine have added to this realization. Travel, television and living and working with immigrants have together brought people to realize that the inhabitants of underdeveloped countries are not sub-human species, as was popularly believed in the last century, but in most respects just the same as ourselves. The only real differences are in culture and in social perceptions. The phrase 'brought to realize', or some variant of it, is commonly used in situations where unsound beliefs are not immediately dispelled by reliable information. Evidence of the unsoundness of a belief has to cumulate and time is needed for us to come to terms with, i.e. adjust our thinking and behaviour to, the new facts. The impact of information may be immediate in some circumstances, but it is gradual in others.

Nowadays the ease of communicating has created the concept of a global society. Information needs no passport to cross national borders. Broadcasts have been aimed at the inhabitants of foreign countries for a great many years. True they have been jammed by those Governments that did not want their peoples to be subverted by hostile propaganda, but such efforts have usually been ineffective. More importantly foreign broadcasts have been effective in contributing to the collapse of repressive regimes such as Soviet Communism by enabling the population to gain correct information and compare the situation in their own country with that in others.

Another major concern is that of social and cultural destabilization. As has been evident in the way the UK has adopted American ways, exposure of young people to other, economically richer, cultures can lead to a downgrading and even loss of one's own. With English gaining the status of a lingua franca, language is no longer the barrier it was and the global information society, not least through the Internet, is accelerating the spread of alien social and cultural changes from one country to another.

The ability to disseminate information widely through the media is used within countries as well as internationally. In modern society utilitarian attitudes urged on by single-issue pressure groups, such as those lobbying on behalf of the environment, the disabled or animal rights, are having a major impact on the political scene. The establishment of discussion groups on the networks is giving rise to the possibility of a new type of democracy nearer the old Athenian model. An investigation is underway into the feasibility of both electronic voting and of undertaking surveys of opinion via the Internet.

It is obvious that nowadays we live in a much more open society. Part of this is that we are much more open with information than before. As recently as the 1950s most people kept details of what they earned to themselves. This secrecy vanished in the 1960s so that pressure could be put on employers to give equal wages for equal work.

However open society becomes, the need to be able to communicate securely highly sensitive information, such as financial transactions between banks, will remain. The activities of hackers have been made illegal as have those of people who use confidential information, gained in the course of their work, for personal gain (insider trading). The House of Lords Paper [5] advocated strong end-to-end encryption to enable commercial transactions to be performed securely. Governments are being very cautious not to lose the possibility of monitoring the use of public networks, should it prove necessary. Considerable attention continues to be given to the misuse of both information and of the ICTs. There are many issues to examine.

The information society that is developing around us is full of exciting possibilities, uncertainties and conflicting ideas and practices. It is time to explore them, to examine the strange and extensive set of laws, customs and taboos which surrounds its use, non-use and misuse, to try to establish a foundation for their better understanding and to examine the factors that will play a role in determining how the information culture will affect the future. First, and to provide a basis, let us examine the nature of information itself and its relation to knowledge and to beliefs, theories and even imagination.

References

1. Dainton, Lord Frederick. (1981) *Knowledge is power. But how can we find what we want?* The British Library Dainton Lectures on Scientific and Technical Information. p.7. London: The British Library

2. Toffler, A. (1970) *Future Shock*. London: Bodley Head

3. Bell, D. (1974) *The coming of the post-industrial society. A Venture into social forecasting*. London: Heinemann Educational Books

    This was a book which sparked off the serious thinking and research into the consequences for society of the computer. Its importance can be judged by the fact that nearly every modern study takes Bell's book as a starting point.

4. House of Lords Select Committee on Science and Technology (1996) *Information Society: Agenda for Action in the UK*. HL Paper 77. London: HMSO

Chapter 6 of the Report contains some 40 recommendations on a very wide range of matters from organizational and funding aspects to educational, health care and environmental ones. Many seem to have been adopted though whether as a result of the Report or whether they would have happened anyway it is impossible to say.

5.   *Ibid.* Paragraph 6.38 of the Report reads: 'Strong, end-to-end encryption must be opened up to business and commercial users as quickly as possible, subject to certain safeguards.' In the body of the report the US embargo on the export of encryption technology is criticised (para 5.92).

CHAPTER 2
The nature of information and knowledge

In the 1960 Warton Lecture [1], John Sparrow, Warden of All Souls, asked, 'What do we mean when we talk – as we so often and so glibly do – about great literature or great art, about a great painter or a great poet?' After many years working in the field of information I am left with a feeling that its denizens face a similar dilemma. Stonier [2] does too, 'The puzzle is this: isn't it strange that with all this information-related activity around us, we still do not know what information is? It is as if mechanical and civil engineers did not understand the concept of energy'.

In practice the problem is not so much that we do not know what information is but rather that we are not agreed. Each of us has his own variant. Badenoch and colleagues [3] introduce their review of a series of definitions that have been proposed in the past with the comment, 'An agreed definition of information is noticeable by its absence from the literature'. One problem is that to a particular individual the meaning of a word is often associated with certain ideas [4]. 'Information' is a fashionable word and, like so many other fashionable words, it keeps getting used in new ways and with new associations. An agreed definition, which Puttnam (1996) in his paper 'Citizens of the Information Society'[5] deems important, depends on separating the term information from the various shades of meaning which associated ideas have given it. Some of those shades can be observed in its use in the following expressions:

- information age;
- information audit;
- information economy;
- information management;
- information repackaging;
- information policy;
- information society;
- information technology;
- information transfer;
- information warehousing.

In each of these expressions the term has a slightly different meaning and the situation is further complicated by differences over when and even whether 'knowledge' can be used as a synonym.

Often the term 'information' is merely the way we start an enquiry. 'Can you give me some information on . . .?' It is an intentionally vague term, almost meaningless, yet the question searches for something specific. If you were to ask someone at work what information he would like, he might reply, 'All I need to know to do this job'. However, on closer enquiry you would probably find that he already knew quite a lot about the job and that what he really wanted was information to fill the gaps in his knowledge. Thus a gardener might have planned a flower bed including the nature, colour and positioning of the flowers. However, to complete the design, he may be seeking a plant which has pink flowers that appear in June, a spread of one foot, a height of two feet, a spiky form and is suitable for the soil and local environment. The information really needed, i.e. which plant should I use?, involves many pieces of information.

To those who claim that 'information is power', usually meaning political power or personal dominance over another, it must be obvious that the word 'information' is being used in a very different sense from that when it is used by students of physiology researching how information is transmitted through the nervous system to control and give commands to our muscles. And surely it is used differently by archaeologists piecing together fragments of information about a dead civilization. To describe archaeological information as power would really be stretching meaning and credibility.

How others perceive information

It would seem appropriate to start by reviewing how others have tried to define the term. Shannon and Weaver [6] were working on the transmission of information as electrical signals when they produced their famous definition of information as that which reduces uncertainty. This much quoted definition does have the great merit of relating information to purpose or value. It certainly could be said to include within its ambit the somewhat startling piece of information on a packet of Sainsbury's peanuts, 'contains nuts', though it is difficult to imagine how much uncertainty there could have been.

Some other researchers, for example Jungclaussen [7] and Kempe [8], consider information as being the meaning imparted by symbols and signs. Mason and colleagues, [9] take a slightly different approach. They define information as 'the symbolic means by which one mind influences another mind'. This gives greater emphasis to the aspect of information as part of the communication process and is a useful supplement to Shannon's definition. However, it seems to exclude the information which we acquire for ourselves by direct observation. Nevertheless, as will be noted later when we discuss knowledge, the realization that information is what is actually being conveyed when one person tries to impart knowledge to another is important.

Davis and Ohlson [10] offer another wide-ranging definition: 'data that has been processed into a form that is meaningful to the recipient and is of real or perceived value in current or prospective actions or decisions'. Bawden [11] also emphasizes the value-addition as one progresses from data to information and on to knowledge. However, perception of value in all information may be rather sweeping. Do we not, all of us, acquire much information each day without any feeling that it may be of any value or use? I notice Mrs. Jones in the butcher's shop but it is of no concern to me. I see that today's paper has a report that a male model claims he is the victim of sexual bias, but so what? Nevertheless, Davis and Ohlson's definition fits the everyday situation well when one is deliberately seeking information or encounters a piece of news of interest.

Vickery and Vickery [12] clearly feel that information is more than processed data. 'Information in the sense we use the term embraces not only worked up data but all the other categories: fact, explanation, theory, law, method, technique, tool, even problem, and more besides: whatever, indeed, that can modify the state of knowledge of the scientist or other recipient' – a phrase similar to but broader than that of Shannon and Weaver. I find this one of the most satisfying and fully embracing definitions provided the word 'modify' is used to mean 'qualify' in the broadest sense. Especially it needs to be understood to include refreshing one's existing knowledge. After all, a shopping list is a piece of information about the things one intends to purchase and contains several items of information each of which modifies the state of knowledge only in the sense of acting as a memory jogger. MacKay [13] echoes both Shannon and the Vickerys in his statement that 'We say we have received information when what we know has changed.'

When we are talking with close colleagues in the same profession as ourselves each of us will normally use the term information in the same way or quickly realise if it is being used in a special sense. However, when talking to people of different backgrounds problems frequently arise. I have listened to confused discussions about STI (strictly, 'Scientific and technical information') in which the participants did not have a common understanding of that term. One such occasion was at an international meeting on STI for developing countries when it became obvious to me that, for political reasons, the term was being used by some participants to cover all information, not just STI. Such malpractices make acquiring information even more difficult.

Some years ago Tom Wilson of Sheffield University made the pertinent comment that, 'the problem seems to lie not so much with the lack of a single definition as with a failure to use a definition appropriate to the level and purpose of the investigation' [14]. This point, that there are several valid meanings, is an important one that I shall pursue later by considering the various categories in which we experience and encounter it.

The physics and physiology of information

A first consideration is how information reaches us. When we perceive some event, then the information is present in whatever impinges on one or more of our senses, e.g. the light waves which connect the scene to our eyes. The same applies to reading text, the translation of the shapes of letters and words into some meaning being a second stage, and, with different waves, it applies to hearing sounds. Those waves are the physical embodiment of the information which we interpret as a scene or as sound and then interpret further into a mental picture or meaningful sounds. Similarly, the electronic pulses which are communicated between one computer and another over a telecommunication link are also information in physical form. However, in the human being the only physical reality of information is a set of electro-chemical reactions in the brain. In the computer the equivalent is the array of bytes on the chip produced by the electromagnetic impulses. Perhaps this is what Stonier was getting at when he wrote [15], 'Information is an intrinsic property of the universe and exists irrespective of whether any human or other forms of intelligence perceive it or utilise it.' Certainly the sun gives out light which reaches the earth even if there is no human being to receive it as information that the sun is shining.

On the other hand, one might, following Plato, question whether such information has any reality if there is no form of life to receive it. It cannot modify knowledge if there is no knowledge to be modified. In that case, one might hypothesise that information was born on the Third Day ('And the earth brought forth grass and herb yielding seed after his kind and the tree yielding fruit', *Genesis* ch.1 v.12). However, if you prefer to believe modern biological theory, information was received when the first form of life came into existence. Information in the physiological sense is older than mankind. All living matter depends on its internal information system: one that makes flowers turn their heads to the sun, that enables seeds to know which direction to send their roots or that enables a newly born mammal to seek nourishment at its mother's teat.

Animal life has a nervous system which serves to register sensations, to convey information about the sensations to the brain, to send messages from the brain to various parts of the body and hence to stimulate responses. Information can arrive through any of the five senses, often through more than one, and usually, when it does, we make some inference by subconsciously comparing it with knowledge in our brain. The knowledge will have been derived from experience or what we have learnt from others. Thus, if you smell the unpleasant odour of hydrogen sulphide and in front of you there is an egg, you will infer that the egg is unfit to eat. You will make this inference, whether or not you know that the unpleasant odour is hydrogen sulphide, because in your experience food which is good to eat smells pleasant.

However, the reaction against unpleasant smell may be prejudice. In the case of hydrogen sulphide and eggs it is not but, to give another example, to many people the smell of Camembert cheese is unpleasant and they may reject it. But the taste is quite different and most who overcome the prejudice find it delicious.

The sense of touch yields an interesting example of our ability to deal with very different sorts of information. One can use touch in the dark to distinguish between metal and cloth. But touch can also distinguish in a different way between a hot and a cold object.

The physics and chemistry of the transmission of senses along our nervous system is now fairly well understood. However, what happens inside the brain is still far from understood though much progress has been made in recent years. Research into consciousness, memory, reasoning etc. continues apace [16] but there is still a long way to go before we have full information about the way the mind works. One aspect that is of interest to me is the way that not only can information as it is received, e.g. touching a hot plate, make the internal information system operate the muscles (one removes one's hand from the plate) but so too can information that has been in the mind for some time. Suddenly one remembers that one has an early appointment and leaps out of bed.

Recent research [17] on how the mind works seems to show that the information which flows along the nerve system into the brain is processed and stored as neuronal assemblies. It now seems fairly clear that conscious processing of information does not involve thinking in words or in pictures as was imagined only a few years ago. Those of literary bent have been known to observe that language is the dress of thought and like a dress it does not describe the thought that underlies it but only hint at it.

Gardner's Theory of Multiple Intelligences [18] indicates the many input/output mechanisms that the mind/information interaction has. He writes, 'we are a species that has evolved to think in language, to conceptualize in spatial terms, to analyse in musical ways, to compute with logical and mathematical tools, to solve problems using our whole body and parts of our body, to understand other individuals and to understand ourselves'. All or any of the seven intelligences can be involved in acquiring and understanding a piece of information even if we do not actually think in words or numbers. One cannot help but marvel at the complexity of the brain, not least at its ability to give the capability of marvelling.

Zeki [19] has described how when we see a moving red object the brain splits the image into at least two parts and stores the colour aspects in one zone and the movement aspects in another quite remote from the first. The new theories make it easier to understand why we find ourselves groping for words to express something that is well formed in the mind. The obvious and trivial example is, 'It's on the tip of my tongue'. The mind knows the message it wishes to convey but cannot recall and match with it a suitable assembly of words. There are many highly intelligent people who find it easier to express their thoughts in certain situations by seizing a pencil and sketching out an illustrative or explanatory diagram. Often this seems to unlock the oral gates, for verbal explanation seems to flow freely as the sketching takes place.

Acquiring pieces of information

As we have seen, we can and do acquire information directly by observing or experiencing scenes or events. This may be through being there ourselves or by seeing it via the medium of television. Information gained first hand in these and similar ways we can designate as 'Primary information'.

The second way we acquire information is second-hand from other people who communicate with us by symbols, most commonly speech or writing, to which we have learnt to giving meaning. In this case what we receive is essentially information which was at one time someone else's observation or experience, or a combination reprocessed in that person's mind. It could even be the product of imagination and might not be real information at all. This second-hand information we may designate as 'Secondary information'.

As a child the first information one experiences is presumably the feel and smell of one's mother. As one grows a little older one starts to take in the sights and sounds of home. How these are taken in and used, whether they go into the memory, which is still in a very undeveloped stage, I do not know and have no recollection of those infant years. Initially what we experience for ourselves and take into our mind through one or more of the five senses is only primary information. What in later life we term 'experience', is essentially knowledge in which primary information has been the principal component.

Later in childhood, as we learn to understand speech and then to read, we take in information in words. But much verbal information is merely a second-hand form of experience. A friend has observed an eclipse of the moon and is using words to try to convey to us his experience. Something similar applies when we obtain information from a diagram or a photograph. Blumenthal [20] got close to this point when he deemed information to be the link between knowledge and observed phenomena.

If information is something that we acquire through our senses, the act of acquiring it is a personal experience. In the case of primary information the experience will be an active one but with secondary information it will be passive. If we enter a very warm room we gather the information that it is hot in there as a result of experiencing the heat. But someone elsewhere, say at the end of a telephone, hearing you say that it is hot will not experience the heat. Even if he has a vivid imagination he will still not experience it as he would if he were present. Secondary information is much less complete than primary information.

The clock reminding us that we are late for an appointment is something that we experience but it is a very private experience. The same event of the clock striking may have no impact whatever on another person who has no appointment to keep. When we receive information which does have an impact on us, are we having a purely individual experience in the same way that seeing the colour green is a private experience? Although we all, except those that are colour blind, may outwardly respond in the same way to what we call a green colour, we have no way of being sure that the colour appears the same to anyone else as it does to us. The impact of much information is personal.

Mackie [21] carries the analysis further. He writes that in addition to phenomenal qualities and perceptions of independently existing things, we also 'have propositional attitudes, beliefs, desires and so on that concern various things other than those mental states themselves in such a way that they cannot be adequately described except by including a description of whatever it is they are about. The desire that it should be fine tomorrow is just that: no way of describing it will do justice to it unless it somehow captures and encapsulates the possible state of affairs of its being fine tomorrow.'

Primary information from observations flows in to our minds all the time that we are awake. Fortunately we are able in some way to discard most of it, otherwise, massive though their capacity is, our brains would soon be clogged. Sometimes, unfortunately, the early discard mechanism causes us to discard information we would wish to keep. We forget we put the kettle on though we did so only a minute or two earlier. It gets worse in old age!

Sometimes information acquired by chance has a significant impact. A photograph of one's mother when young may stir memories of one's own youth. No new information is added but one's store of knowledge is rearranged or refreshed. Similarly, as every creative person has experienced, a piece of information which is totally irrelevant can start the mind thinking along new lines and lead to the solution of a puzzle or to quite new ideas on a specialist topic. This raises the point, which I wish to discuss in more detail later, that the impact of a piece or pieces of information on an individual is very dependent on that person's existing knowledge, intellectual abilities and the readiness of his mind to exploit the information. An instance of readiness to develop information into knowledge is the experience some people have that sleeping on a problem enables the mind to process the information it has and unconsciously generate a solution.

Facts and information

In a discussion of how knowledge is made up of two components, information and judgement, Oakeshott wrote [22], 'The component of information is easily recognized. It is the explicit ingredient of knowledge, where what we want to know may be itemized. Information consists of facts, specific intellectual artefacts (often arranged in sets or bunches). It is impersonal (not a matter of opinion)'.

Information includes facts, but even on the use of that word there seems to be differences. The *Concise OED* defines fact as 'thing certainly known to have occurred or be true, datum of experience'. I have heard it said that the sun is a fact but what must be meant is that the existence of the sun is a fact.

Stonier [23] seems to think that a word possesses information but this I would dispute. It does possess meaning, but that is not the same as information. Frege [24] asserts that a word has meaning only in a sentence. Of course, in some circumstances a single word may be a sufficient utterance, as in the command 'run!', but that is because it is a complete sentence and all the associated information is already present in the mind of the hearer. A word may seem to contain information but only when it stirs meaning already in the human mind.

Secondary information that is transmitted in words is expressed in sentences as are facts. Thus 'roses are red' and 'John is engaged to Sue' are typical of the way information is expressed. In general, each piece of information is expressed in a subject/predicate relation. The sentence may be complex, especially if it contains a number of pieces of information in it, but the underlying expression is simple. Very detailed documents are made up of a great many of these sentences, each – unless repetitive – adding more information. If single words are used it is as a form of shorthand, it being expected that the reader can understand them as if each were a sentence. Thus if a river in Italy comes into view, your companion may say merely, 'the Tiber' but you will register it as if he had said, 'That is the river Tiber'. Tabulations of data are also a shorthand for simple subject/predicate sentences.

Russell examined the nature of facts [25]. He points out that, 'If the railway timetable says there is a train to Edinburgh at 10 am, if the timetable is correct and there is a train and it is on time – that is a fact. The statement in the timetable is itself a fact whether true or false but it only *states* a fact if it is true, i.e. if there really is a train'.

Using Mackie's example (vide supra) of the weather, if in the event we observe that come the day it is fine, we can express the information we have thus gained by the statement, 'It is fine today' and that is a fact unless and until it rains. However, 'it will be fine tomorrow' is neither fact nor information even if in the event it is fine, because at the time of utterance it had not been observed and it was only hope or expectation. But, if we have listened to the weather forecast, the statement, 'If the forecast is correct, it will be fine tomorrow' would be a piece of information, the observation underlying it being in our case listening to the forecast and, underlying that, the observations of the meteorologists.

Facts will include axioms and data, though not all facts are either axioms or data. The statement that the Queen, when in London, lives in Buckingham Palace is an example of a fact that is neither. Elsewhere [26] Russell says, 'a datum is merely a piece of knowledge that is not deduced'. The fact about the Queen could be deduced from multiple observations and is obviously not a datum. But there is much information that is not deduceable which is nevertheless not data.

Data–information–knowledge–enlightenment–wisdom are often expressed in that sequence to emphasise how the facts and experiences we gather are gradually processed or refined into higher and higher levels of sophistication or as distinctions between different categories of mental content. Concepts-ideashypotheses–theories–theorems–equations–laws is a similar sequence on another but related plane.

The novelist, Anthony Powell [27], throws some doubt on the reliability of presentations of facts. 'Facts are after all only on the surface, inevitably selective, prejudiced by subjective presentation.

What is below, hidden, much more likely to be important, is easily omitted'. In this he is close to the post-modernist position. But he is not doubting the validity of facts as such, only deductions drawn from collections of facts, and that because one cannot always get all the facts.

Historians nowadays seem to be having a tremendous argument with the post-modernists on these very grounds [28]. Even when historians rigorously follow von Ranke's principles of sticking to primary sources of information, eyewitness reports and what have been called the purest, most immediate documents which can be shown to have originated at the time under investigation and avoid secondary sources, it is alleged that their conclusions about why events occurred the way they did are flawed because they cannot avoid the bias due to living at another time. Factual descriptions of events are dismissed by both sides as mere chronicles. The historian cannot avoid some measure of selection in the events he chooses to review and hence is open to attack. One can accept as information each of the facts that are presented but one has to be wary of the interpretations. These are not facts but they are pieces of information which may be subject to later amendment.

The concept of information

Developing Mackie's reasoning I think that information is just one of the categories of inputs to our minds that we work with when we are thinking. It takes its place alongside beliefs, interpretations, commands, advice, questions, opinions, theories, forecasts and the products of creative imagination. Recently the term 'content' has come into use to describe what is to be found in information systems. It is useful because it covers all these categories and includes them in verbal (visual or aural), numeric and pictorial form. It also includes such quite different products as music.

It is probably important to remember that there is no such thing as information *per se*. The word usefully describes a category of concepts. There is only information on or about something, some event, some idea. Fundamentally it is the product of observing and perception. Primary information we receive from seeing an event, touching something, hearing a sound. Secondary information is the same, or almost the same, an input conveyed to us or by us by means of symbols, especially words, numbers and diagrams, which we can interpret or translate into the information intended.

However, it is not entirely direct or surrogate observation. There are occasions when information can be generated by a combination of some other form of input acting upon one's memory or knowledge. Thus, hearing a sudden shout of 'Fore!' will provide the information that a golf ball is coming towards you. In all the other inputs listed above there is an element of information though it may prove unreliable.

Nor is everything that is observed registered as information. We possess the power not to treat as information everything we see but to select that which is relevant or of concern. We touch the handles of doors every day but do not treat each touch as information, though if the feel of one is unexpectedly different we do register it. In other words, a sensory perception is information only if it has some impact on us. Obviously this is an arbitrary definition but it is necessary to limit the field to one that has significance and it has the advantage that it will serve, *mutatis mutandis*, for information in electronic systems.

So, information may be defined as a category of concepts which our minds take in, consciously register, to which meaning can be attributed and which normally modify our state of knowledge.

When we receive a piece of information it may:

1.   duplicate or confirm information one already has;
2.   add to one's existing knowledge of a topic;
3.   correct or modify one's existing knowledge of some topic;
4.   open up a completely new field of knowledge.

Those of practical bent may object that it is all very well regarding information as fundamentally merely something in the mind. In reality one is dealing with and using it all day and every day. We meet it as facts and data, as aims, decisions, policies and plans, as laws, standards and claims, and in much else. It exists in a wide range of types of document, it is communicated over various types of network, it is hoarded and it is traded. It has a considerable impact not only on my life but on that of everyone else without necessarily affecting directly my thinking. The reason is, of course, that we have learnt ways of recording and transmitting information about observations so that others may share them almost as if they made the observations themselves. And we can put information into electronic form, e.g. a Smart Card, and let it transfer and process that information in a computer.

Let us, then, before moving on to examine the relation of

information to knowledge, list some of the forms in which we receive information whether through the Internet, on a CD-ROM, on paper or even orally. They include:

1. single items of fact, such as a historical date, the formula of a chemical, an address, the time of a train, a theorem, or an equation;
2. condensed, summarized or otherwise abbreviated statements such as a news headline or the title of a journal article or of a book (though some headlines and titles seem meaningless);
3. cumulations of facts or data as in dictionaries, directories, encyclopaedias, spread sheets, timetables, catalogues and the printed receipt from shop tills;
4. compositions such as Acts of Parliament, technical articles, patent specifications, manuals, textbooks and monographs, reports, market surveys, reviews of progress in a field of research, newspaper articles;
5. pictorial and audio-visual information including photographs, artist's portraits, TV news broadcasts and documentaries.

In those cases, such as a political tract, in which there is an integrated mixture of fact and opinion, the whole is a composite of information about the author's view, together with the items of objective information on which the author's view is founded. Opinion is not information but the fact that someone holds such and such an opinion is information. So in the case of the tract the whole forms a piece of information about the author's position on some political issue.

Information or knowledge

Popular usage often treats knowledge and information as synonymous words. The way the word 'know' is used adds to this. 'What do you know about . . .?' quite often means 'What information can you give me about . . .?' At other times, though, for example when used by a teacher to a pupil, it does mean 'Tell me the extent of your knowledge'. The phrase 'the knowledge society' commonly means no more than 'the information society' but there is a feeling that it sounds better. In fact, the realization that knowledge should be something of a higher level than information does often come through. This is noticeable in the suddenly fashionable 'knowledge management' though on close examination it proves to be mainly a sub-set of information management with special emphases.

Andersson, the Finnish Minister for Culture, sees a clear distinction between the two words. 'Knowledge is information which has been processed through insight into understanding' [29]. If one accepts this one must conclude that knowledge is more than just an accumulation of pieces of information and, consequently, that the two words are not synonyms. Bonaventura [30] states categorically, 'Information is not knowledge. Rather [it] is the potential for knowledge'.

Berlin [31] wrote, 'Knowledge, for the central tradition of western thought, means not just descriptive knowledge of what there is in the universe but, as part and parcel of it, not distinct from it, knowledge of values, or how to live, what to do, which forms of life are the best and worthiest and why'. One feels that there is a mellow richness to knowledge which the possession of a mere miscellany of pieces of information lacks. If nothing else thought has to be added. On this basis Ranganathan's definition of knowledge as the sum total of information conserved by civilization seems inadequate, as though it lacks the human dimension.

In *The Oxford Companion to the Mind* [32] we find, 'Knowledge may be described as representations of facts (including generalizations) and concepts organized for future use, including problem-solving'. The key word would seem to be 'organized' but what does this mean? How are they, facts and concepts, organized for future use? Is it simply that they are stored like with like, contradictions being eliminated? Modern theories of how the mind works imply that considerable deconstruction takes place as each new fact is learnt.

The *Companion* goes on to describe 'facts' as 'useless knowledge' thus making clear its view that the distinction between facts and knowledge is organization for use. One is reminded of Oakeshott's observation [33] that, 'There is no inherently useless information; there are only facts irrelevant to the matter in hand'.

Russell [34] makes the important point that, 'All theory of knowledge must start from 'what do I know?' not from 'what does mankind know?'. For how can I tell what mankind knows?'

A partial answer to Russell's question is, of course, only by inference from what I observe or learn and by personally weighing up the evidence. Once untrustworthy sources, errors and inconsistencies have been weeded out, I then have to trust what is left. This, however, leaves me believing I know what other individuals know. It does not tell me what mankind in total knows.

Russell's point that knowledge is essentially personal to one-self is a crucial one. A very different type of thinker, Drucker, the management expert, agrees [35]: 'Knowledge is always embodied in a person, taught and learned by a person, used or misused by a person'. So they agree that knowledge is essentially personal and private. In contrast, information is public and accessible.

A corollary of this is that knowledge cannot be imparted in its entirety to others and it is changed in the process of trying to do so. When we attempt to share our knowledge of some topic with another person, what is imparted becomes, during the act of communication, information and then on receipt will become part of knowledge again – but knowledge personal to the recipient.

The *Oxford English Dictionary* [36] devotes five columns to Knowledge. Among the definitions offered are:

a.   clear and certain mental apprehension;
b.   the fact, state or condition of understanding; theoretical or practical understanding of an art, science, industry, etc.
c.   information acquired by study; learning; erudition.

The Dictionary also recognises the trivial uses of the word as a synonym for information and collections of information.

Bawden [37] produces one of the best definitions: 'Moving through this spectrum [data–information–knowledge–wisdom] involves various value-adding processes: evaluation, comparison, compilation, classification, etc. Knowledge can then be seen as that form of information characterized by compression, abstraction and categorization, and which is thereby endowed with meaning and significance and transformative power'.

For me, however, the nature of knowledge can be derived even better from an observation of Oakeshott [38]. In a discussion of learning and teaching he concludes that 'Judgement is that which, when united with information, generates knowledge or ability to do, to make, to understand and explain'. Putting this the other way around, one could define knowledge as the combination of information with judgement:

$$Knowledge = Information + Judgement$$

This encapsulates Russell's and Drucker's point that knowledge is personal, Andersson's that it involves understanding, Berlin's that valuing is part of it and our other observation that there is a richness to knowledge which even a massive collection of pieces of information lacks.

It also encompasses the observation of several people, for example Ackoff [39], that knowledge includes practical skills. Oakeshott refers in his discussion to knowing how to ride a bicycle. He claims, it is as much a form of knowledge as historical, philosophical or scientific understanding.

Types of knowledge

The French see a clear distinction between two sorts of knowledge: they use the word 'savoir' when they mean knowing facts and 'connaitre' when they are talking about knowing a person. One feels instinctively that to know, as a result of long study and practice, what makes a balanced diet is a different type of knowledge from that of knowing a close friend. That great scholar Murray wrote [40], 'You may know all the material facts about a man – his income, his hours of work, his debts, and how often his children have had mumps – without any intimacy at all; intimacy will only come, and may then come in a flash, when he really lets himself go on one of the subjects that Plato talks about' (i.e. justice and the State, love, immortality of the soul, etc).

Gardner, as recounted earlier, has concluded that there are seven different intelligences possessed by human beings, each to varying degrees [18]. Each gives rise to a different type of judgement. Handy [41] has expanded the number to eleven and probably more will be added but, in the context of the conversion of a piece of information to knowledge, the intelligence, and hence type of judgement needed, is the one that is appropriate to the information and the sets of knowledge it may affect.

Quite often a single piece of information can modify or increase knowledge of several different topics. The information that Smart Cards may be used for paying taxes adds to my knowledge of their potential value, to my knowledge of ways of paying taxes and to my knowledge of the extent to which the government is exploiting new technologies.

When we acquire a new piece of information, our reaction is to consider how it fits with the knowledge and beliefs we already have on that topic, for it is only very rarely in adulthood that we acquire information on a subject about which we have absolutely no prior information, beliefs or prejudices.

Over the years we build up a huge store of information on a great many topics. On many we just add information as we come across it; on others, fewer in number, we seek information to fill in gaps or to confirm aspects about which we feel uncertain. In all cases we assess the new information, in some fields from the basis of very considerable knowledge and experience, in others from a poorly informed but highly prejudiced standpoint. The utterances of politicians are often treated the latter way because few, other than those directly involved in the political sphere, have the necessary knowledge to be able to understand the full meaning of the utterance. Communicating and understanding information will be discussed in chapters 4 and 5.

The way knowledge develops as it is applied and as new information is added has long been of interest. Bonaventura [30] asserts, 'Knowledge can only be derived from information through the monitoring of use cases'. He goes on, 'The information on which a decision is based is gradually modified over time as the outcome of numerous decisions integrates information points into knowledge. Knowledge, then, can be considered as output(s) from a continuous feedback loop which refines information through the application of that information'. This is a form of judgement at work.

Following Andersson's advice [29] that, 'We should focus our attention on ways in which information can be converted into useful knowledge', let us consider the case of what information the Board of a company considering entering a new field or marketing a new product may want about the competition they will face. Knowing their own product, they will want information on whether it will suit the new market or whether modification will be needed and why. Knowing their existing marketing strengths and skills, they will require information on how they will be likely to cope in the new environment. They will want detailed information about the competition, especially about any firms new to them. They will want much, much more information as well, but putting each piece together with the rest and assessing each in the light of their own prior knowledge will lead them to a position of having the necessary level of knowledge to be able to decide whether to go ahead.

The problem is, of course, that the decision is really a forecast that if the company goes ahead, so and so will happen. It is based on knowledge which implicitly contains an element of uncertainty even though it is only a small one. They do not *know* what the outcome will be. There can always be events which escape one's input of information, such as the unexpected closure of one of the competitors, the impact of which information at an early stage could have had an immense influence on the decision. Of course, nowadays the Board would expect the future market scenario to be modelled on a computer and to have the impact of a variety of possible and even improbable events programmed in. The uncertainty of the future is not reduced but at least one knows what the impact of specifiable future events will be.

Knowledge, whether of a person or a topic, is no more permanent than is any of the pieces of information we have on it. In practice knowledge will change even more than information, for often the addition of a new piece of information will modify one's knowledge of the topic without any of the individual pieces of information that are part of the knowledge changing.

The answer to the classic question, 'Am I today the same person that I was yesterday?' is that I am not. Even if the decrease in the number of neurons in the brain is ignored, since yesterday one's mind has acquired new information (unless one has been asleep all the time) and has been active rearranging the information it contains. Dreaming is one example of this. The inspiration which can arise if one 'sleeps on a problem' is another. Our minds and our state of knowledge are always changing, for some of us mainly through failing memory, and therefore we are always changing.

It is important to bear in mind that, in the progression from data to wisdom, certainty decreases. Data are, within the limits of the means by which they were determined, as certain as anything can be. Facts can be overturned in that what has been believed to be a fact may later be shown to be false. Information can be affected by the next piece of evidence. Knowledge is subject to modification by reconsideration as well as by new information. Russell comments [42] that 'all we count as knowledge is in a greater or less degree uncertain, and there is no way of deciding how much uncertainty makes a belief unworthy to be called knowledge'. Belief, then might be considered a stage between information and knowledge. Belief that since the world seemed round it should be possible to sail round it was eventually verified. On the other hand there have been a great many beliefs which were based on limited information which, on exposure to further data or information proved untenable.

Reverting to the question of uncertainty, if one simply assembles many pieces of information on a topic, each piece has its own degree of uncertainty. One would expect therefore the assembly to have a level of uncertainty which is the product of the individual degrees. However, this would make most knowledge improbable, which is not the case. Apparently the brain works on all the information it has received, comparing, assessing, rejecting etc. to arrive at, usually, knowledge which is more reliable than the arithmetic would suggest. Mason and Culnan [43] reflect this when they observe that 'Knowledge is information that has been authenticated, validated or thought to be true'.

Building up our knowledge is like assembling a jigsaw without any picture of the completed puzzle, and for which we receive the pieces not all at once but in batches. To add to the difficulties, some of the pieces are false ones. So we have to put the pieces together in the right place and in the right orientation. Every so often we fail to spot that a piece is a false one because it fits as expected, or we may put a piece in the wrong place because it seems to fit. Only later do we discover that another piece goes in that place and either reject the false one or move the wrongly placed one to a better location. Sometimes fitting a new piece requires the reorientation of a large block of pieces. Such was the case when Relativity Theory caused a reassessment of the place of Newtonian Theories.

In real life, jigsaws do not contain false pieces nor duplicate pieces. Knowledge building from information is much more complicated than any jigsaw. As one puts the mental components together, the overall picture gradually becomes clearer. One may read in the newspapers the pros and cons of the European Currency but one is not clear, and would certainly not be deemed knowledgeable, about the subject unless one already possessed a considerable amount of information about national and international monetary policy and practice and the consequences of monetary changes. There is obviously a connection between how fully informed one is on a subject and how knowledgeable one is but, whereas one cannot be thoroughly knowledgeable without being fully informed, one can be fully informed without being thoroughly knowledgeable. Thought in the shape of judgement is required to make the transition.

It may be concluded, then, that information and knowledge are not synonymous, though they may often be so used in everyday conversation. Knowledge is essentially personal, and understanding and relation to values are inherent parts. It is formed and increased by thought, by acquiring information and by applying judgement to assess the quality, use and consequences of that new information in the light of one's existing knowledge.

Insight, belief, imagination

Insight has already been referred to as closely associated with knowledge. We do not really know a person unless we have acquired an insight into that person's character, especially the values and beliefs he holds dear. Even so, it is as if something extra has been added to the information and knowledge we have. The most rational explanation is that all the knowledge has been reprocessed, just as seems to happen when inspiration strikes. The way information is conveyed may also be a factor as is shown by the way poetry can heighten insight. The elegance of mathematical solutions can also indicate possession of an insight into the field.

Belief, which we have implied is an inferior or less certain type of knowledge, is quite different. It can arise in more than one way. In the first place it can result from what we have learnt from people, including authors, we trust. We do not check the information or challenge its validity; its acceptance is ingrained. Nowadays it is increasingly the practice to take opportunities to put beliefs arising this way to the test.

In the second place belief can arise from normal expectation. One can have a belief in a colleague's honesty because most people are honest and he has never given any indication that he is otherwise. In this case one would not set about confirming one's belief.

Thirdly, belief arises, often with a great degree of reliability, from extrapolating sequences of past events into the future. We take it as a fact that the sun will rise tomorrow in the east and set in the west. It always has done and always will. But it is really a belief based on the assumption that the sun will continue to exist, and that the world will continue to rotate on its present axis, though there is geological evidence of it toppling in the past. Unfortunately, in many other circumstances extrapolation is an unreliable method of prediction.

A fourth source of belief is inability to conceive any better solution to a problem. Religious belief is based on this though there is an element of acceptance of what we have been told by others. Sometimes unwillingness to accept another, even a proven solution, as in the cases of flat-earthers, creationists and UFO watchers, results in the continuance of an unsound belief. There are still those who believe in horoscopes and phrenology.

An important type of belief is theory. This also arises from an inability to conceive any better solution to a problem. The difference is that a theory is offered with a view to its being criticized and tested. Dalton's theory, that matter was made up of atoms, was advanced as a way of explaining the quantitative basis of chemical reactions. He had never seen an atom nor, until very recently, had anyone else.

Finally, and closely related, is imagination. It can give rise to theories; it can lead to false beliefs; it can even lead to novelty. This can take several forms. The most useful one is the ability to envisage a future situation or the ability to create something new, firstly in the mind and then given expression as an invention or a story or a picture. The situation is fascinatingly discussed by Warnock [44]. As she observes, imagination and memory are closely linked and if we bear in mind a comment of Sartre's, which I jotted down many years ago and have lost the reference, that 'Man is not God: he cannot create, he can only rearrange', we can see that much imagination is the result of the mind processing information, taking what is stored in the memory, stripping it down and bringing together pieces that were certainly not associated at the input stage (see for instance Zeki, [19]).

Know-how

Know-how is, on the whole, a form of knowledge which is gained by experience. 'Practice makes perfect' is one aspect. One planes pieces of wood and the more one does so the better one becomes. One could say that one improves by the advice and information one is given and by the input of information as one sees that the result is better each time but this is surely not a sufficient explanation. Oakeshott uses the example of learning to ride a bicycle but roller-blading or tightrope walking would do equally well. One can be told how to do it. One can be shown. But, the only way one can learn is by trying again and again until it comes. Confidence is an important factor; if one feels one can do it, one generally learns more quickly – though even then some people have an aggressive form of confidence which inhibits learning. With the bicycle when one learns as a child one is often given support by one's father. He runs alongside holding you up. Then after a while, without telling you, he ceases to support you and you carry on cycling in ignorance, until he tells you that you are doing it all by yourself. You know how to cycle.

The other form of know-how is a practice, in trades and professions, that has gone on for ages, often without really knowing why, which may be kept secret or simply not written down because it doesn't seem necessary to do so and certainly is not disclosed to competitors. It is well exemplified by the story of a small electro-plating firm whose foreman retired. The new foreman totally failed to get the electroplating processes to work properly. The vats were cleaned carefully so that contamination was excluded. The propor-tions of ingredients were correct. The electrodes and the current used were all correct but it still would not work properly. Eventually the firm called back the retired foreman. He checked and confirmed that all was as it should be, then took his pipe out of his mouth (he was an inveterate smoker) and spat into the vat. All went well! The bit of know-how, that to make the process work a smoker must spit into the vat, really meant, of course, that a trace of nicotine was needed to catalyse the process.

This sort of thing has been experienced in many craft industries. The know-how is not magic or really mysterious; it is something that can be worked out by rational means even if it proves diffi-cult or tedious to do so. It has proved very valuable to industry. New inventions may be protected by patents but the information has to be published and may be secretly copied by the unscru-pulous. Firms licensing patents can keep control by choosing the conditions under which they disclose the extra information, the know-how, needed for the manufacturing process.

Seeking and generating information: research

Lucky is the person who never needs to seek information, whose existing know-how plus other information already instilled into him and that which arrives each day unbidden is enough for his needs. Yet perhaps not lucky for his must be a very monotonous or pedestrian life, satisfied to do only what he already knows how to do or those things that he is told how to do. For as soon as one starts something new, new information is needed and rarely does the unbidden input prove adequate. In the modern world most of us seem to be in daily need of new information and daily seeking it.

The information we seek falls basically into two categories: that which is known to someone somewhere or has been published – we need to track down a source; and that which is not yet known – we have to do research or create the information in another way.

Usually to satisfy our curiosity we talk to people and we watch, listen to or read news of happenings in our locality, country and abroad. In these and other ways we add to our store of information one might say accidentally. When we deliberately seek information, often with opinion and advice, we may consult family, friends or business colleagues. We may look at leaflets, read instructions on the wrappers of things we buy. We may use the Internet, putting out a query or visiting a Web site. We may look at books, read a road sign or consult a timetable. We choose whichever source is the most likely to yield what we want. Often we need several sources. A patent searcher consults, on average, about 150 documents.

Much has been written on finding existing information and many guides published, such as the Bowker-Saur series 'Guides to Information Sources'. This is not the place to duplicate them. Finding out information that does not exist does, however, merit some attention.

Information that is new can be found in the following ways:

1. working it out or synthesizing it for oneself from existing personal knowledge or published information;
2. going and looking, listening, smelling etc or getting someone else to do it for you. This includes carrying out surveys and polls;
3. by investigative research, modelling situations and setting up experiments.

The new information is what one observes, or what one concludes.

As a general rule, both 1 and 3 require a large input of information in the first place. New information is the product of existing information plus thought and work. With very few exceptions, every piece of scientific research nowadays, and most in the past, start with a search to establish what has already been published on the subject.

Scientific research is one of the most important ways of generating new information. It is not the only way as some non-scientists are at pains to point out. For example, Giddens observes [45] that 'post-modern outlook sees a plurality of heterogeneous claims to knowledge, in which science does not have a privileged place.' The belief that there are several ways of understanding life and increasing our knowledge of it lay at the heart of the 'Two Cultures' debate in the 1950s and 60s. The recent statement that 'nobody [meaning, of course, nobody among the fashionable elite] gets married in Surrey' is a trivial but interesting example of creating new information. It is quite unscientific.

Scientific research, once known as natural philosophy, is concerned with learning more about nature: what does the universe and all that is in it consist of; why is it the way it is; and why do all the things in it behave as they do? It is concerned only with physical reality and with questions to which rational answers are possible.

The deductions which follow from the information revealed by scientific research have indeed been for many people uncomfortable. Concepts, such as the universe's origin in a 'Big Bang', infinite curved space, that the earth is about 4500 million years old, that matter – including ourselves – is made up of atoms which are made up of particles which behave as waves, that we grow from a single cell, that a living cell can be cloned and made to develop into another, identical creature, and that the way we move and think is by complex electro-chemical processes in the brain, are for many people very disturbing, even frightening. Keats felt that science robbed the beauty of nature of its power to charm. However, to others among us knowing that so prosaic an event as sunlight falling on raindrops can produce the splendour of a rainbow adds to rather than subtracts from one's sense of awe. We are no less romantic because we know that the brain not the heart is the seat of the emotions.

Poetry and painting, by presenting information in an imaginative but not strictly accurate way, can heighten our understanding. This then interacts with our knowledge of the actual information and in some way upgrades the knowledge. It is probably another instance of the reprocessing of knowledge, which is constantly going on in the mind and leading, for example, to flashes of inspiration.

A sad feature of life is the antagonism that exists towards science among those of other intellectual cultures. The reasons are several, the overthrowing of comfortable beliefs being only one. Feynman [46] has doubted whether it is feasible to explain science to those of another culture. A consequence is the common confusion between science and technology. Many technologies are the result of scientific discovery being applied to develop new inventions and new ways of doing things. It was applying the information gained about the electrical properties of semiconductors that has led to information technology, or research into what happens when a coil of wire is passed through a magnetic field that has led to street lighting.

However, though related the two are different. Often science is called into play to explain technological practices. Tree grafting and cross pollination of plants were practised long before scientific research had laid bare the basis of genetics. Technology produces information about how can we do so and so, and if we do so and so, will the product be more effective? Science is more concerned with explanation and with envisaging theories and even laws which encompass a range of facts.

Among the charges directed against science nowadays is that it is not value-free but depends on scientists' prejudices and that scientific research is in some way subordinate to prevailing social and cultural values [47]. Since there are a very large number of scientists engaged in research, the work some are doing may well be related to such values. Indeed, it can be that research itself has played a major part in shaping those values. Our changed attitude to the conservation of animal and plant species is one example. Though science started in the Middle East and is still in tune with its values, Western values have largely been shaped by science and hence a continuing methodological relationship is a natural concomitant.

Others, for example Monbiot [48], question whether science is a value-free search for the truth. The influence of those funding it concerns them and the emphasis governments give to the support of 'exploitable areas of science' gives reason for their fears. Of course, much research is funded in the hope that it will yield profit. But much is still done which is purely academic and even the information emanating from research with an applied aim is not necessarily culturally biased.

There is indeed scope for concern if new products, with possible hazards, are marketed before being thoroughly tested. But that is technology, not science. There is also justified concern if the results of only limited testing are published to counter an accusation of hazard. This is misuse of research rather than a condemnation of scientific method.

A principal objective of scientific research is to establish what the laws are which determine the way nature works. One tries to find general patterns in a number of research studies. One postulates a hypothesis which covers them and then considers how widely it applies. Feynman, an eminent physicist, claimed that in general one looked for a new law by first guessing it and then computing the consequences of the guess to see what would be implied if the law that was guessed was right. If it disagreed with experiment, it was wrong. In that simple statement is the key to science. The philosopher Popper put it similarly when he observed that scientific method involves carrying out experiments designed to disprove a theory.

Of course, as Wolpert points out [49], there are occasions when a scientist feels a new theory to be so persuasive that there must be errors in experimental results which seem to contradict it. He quotes the example of Robert Boyle's faith in atmospheric pressure being able to hold two smooth discs tightly together. Many trials failed until Boyle managed to get the surfaces of the discs adequately smooth. I can recall some spectroscopic data published by another scientist ruining a theory which one of my colleagues had propounded. Rather than abandoning his theory, he tried to repeat the experiments which produced the data and failed. After much research he found that the rogue data were the product of stray light and his theory remained intact.

The power of a theory to predict some hitherto unobserved phenomenon is very important as a test of validity. This was the case with Einstein's Special Theory of Relativity. When it correctly predicted that the planet Mercury would be visible near the sun, at a time when Newton's well tried and tested theory predicted it would not, most of the doubters were won over.

One fallacy from which science suffers is that the results of scientific research are often assumed by laymen to be unshakeably right. Yet the most cursory study of the history of science shows that new research not merely adds to existing knowledge, it commonly modifies and often supplants it. Earlier information remains (unless the experiment is shown to be methodologically unsound) but the interpretation or the theory proposed to account for it have to be changed. 'Scientists are concerned not with absolute truth but with theories that provide understanding of the phenomena involved ... [and] must be prepared to change their minds in the face of evidence' [49].

Indeed, much scientific progress has been via errors, through disproving false hypotheses. The theories that space is filled with ether and that on burning matter gives off phlogiston are two classic examples.

Many scientific discoveries are the result of piecing together a very large amount of information, each piece being the result of experimental research. The structure of DNA and the presence and importance of nitric oxide in the brain are two examples [50]. Greenfield [16] gives several examples of the way over the centuries new ideas of how the brain works have followed new observations and then with yet more information have themselves had to be revised.

Another good and easily readable account of the way scientific investigation progresses is to be found in the booklet *Planet Earth; an explorer's guide* [51]. It describes the way that during this century, studies of meteorites, earthquakes, volcanoes, the shape of the ocean floors, the origin of the earth's magnetism and the discovery of parallel bands of magnetic rock, have led to our modern understanding of the earth's structure, plate tectonics and the picture of the continents moving relative to each other, pushing up into mountains where they collide and sliding down into the mantle at the trenches. The studies have brought in large amounts of new information. This has been digested and various hypotheses put forward as each new piece has arrived. Some of these have stood the test of new evidence and become established theory, others have not. Our knowledge of the structure of the earth and of the movements within it has grown but it is still far from complete and there is much yet to be learnt.

Alexander Pope, with his 'The proper study of mankind is man', may have been responsible for a great deal of wasted effort in years past. The problem of trying to conduct research on or with human beings is that very rarely can one set up a rigorous experiment. All human beings are different and thus splitting the batch, a well known method of having two identical samples to compare, does not work with humans. One has to use statistical methods which yield only results with a known probability of certainty. There is also a limit to the things one can do to a human being or to the effects one can cause. One cannot just take a chap's eye out and put it back upside down to see whether the vision is inverted. Trying it with those who have suffered accidents is not quite the same thing, though some remarkable research has been done on those who have suffered severe accidents [52, 53].

However, it is perhaps ironic that some of the most modern research, involving studies in human and animal genetics and behaviour are beginning [54] to give rise to theories of why we behave the way we do, what underlies ethical responses and the value judgements we make. One can even start to speculate that the need to seek knowledge of nature by scientific study is not just a free will response to curiosity but is programmed into some of us as part of a selfish urge for survival. Can an experiment be devised to test that thought?

References

1. Sparrow, J. (1963) *Independant Essays*. p.13. London: Faber

2. Stonier, T. (1991) *Towards a new theory of information. Synopsis of the fifth ISI Lecture*. p.1. London: ISI

3. Badenoch, D. et al. (1994) The value of information. In *The Value and Impact of Information*, ed. M. Feeney and M. Grieves pp.9–78. London: Bowker-Saur

4. Scruton, R. (1996) *Modern Philosophy. An introduction and survey.* p.62. London: Mandarin

5. Puttnam, D. (1996) Citizens of the Information Society. *Journal of Information Science*, **22,** (1), 1

6. Shannon, C.E and Weaver, W. (1948) The mathematical theory of communication. *Bell System Technical Journal*, **27**, 379–423

7. Jungclaussen, H. (1988) Informatik und Physik – Wechselbeziehungen und Wechselwerken. *Wissenschaft Beitreibung Inform – IZ d. Hochschulwesens an der TU Dresden*, **2**(2), 4–13

8. Kempe, V. (1986) Information – Informationstechnik – Informatik. *GI-Mitteilungen*, **1**(1), 8–24

9. Mason, R.O., Mason, F.M. and Culnan, M.J. (1995*) Ethics of Information Management.* p.35. London: Sage

10. Davis G.B. and Olson, M.H. (1985) *Management Information Systems: Conceptual foundations, structure and development.* p.200. New York: McGraw-Hill

11. Bawden, D. (1997) Information policy or knowledge policy? In *Understanding Information Policy*, ed. I. Rowlands, pp.74–79. London: Bowker-Saur

12. Vickery, B.C. and Vickery, A. (1987) *Information Science in Theory and Practice.* London: Butterworth

13. MacKay, D. (1987) Information Theory. In *The Oxford Companion to the Mind.* ed. R.L. Gregory. p.369. Oxford: Oxford University Press

14. Wilson, T. (1981) On user studies and information needs. *Journal of Documentation*, **37**(1), 3–15

15. Stonier, T. (1990) *Information and the Internal Structure of the Universe: an exploration into information physics.* New York: Springer-Verlag

16. Greenfield, S. (1997) *The Human Brain.* London: Weidenfeld and Nicholson

17. Greenfield, S., Sloman, A. and Warwick, K. (1996) Three lectures on Evolution, Consciousness and Conscious Evolution. *RSA Journal*, 5470, 34–51

18. Gardner, H. (1993) *The Unschooled Mind*. pp.11–13. London: Fontana

19. Zeki, S. (1997) Visual art and the visual brain. *Proceedings of the Royal Institution* **68**, 29–64

20. Blumenthal, J. (1969) *Management Information Systems: a framework for planning and development*. London: Prentice-Hall. Quoted by Badenoch et al. (q.v.)

21. Mackie, J.L. (1985) Selected papers. In *Logic and Knowledge*, eds. J.L. MacKie and P. MacKie. Oxford: Clarendon

22. Oakeshott, M. (1989) The voice of liberal learning. In *Michael Oakeshott on education*. ed. T. Fuller p.51. New Haven and London: Yale University Press

23. Stonier, T. (1991) *Towards a new theory of information. Synopsis of the fifth ISI Lecture*. p.1. London: ISI

24. Frege, G. (1987) Quoted in the Section on Meaning. In *The Oxford Companion to the Mind*, ed. R.L. Gregory p.454. Oxford: Oxford University Press

25. Russell, B. (1948) *Human Knowledge: its scope and limits*. pp.159–160. London: George Allen and Unwin

26. Russell, B. (1962) *An Inquiry into Meaning and Truth*. p.118. Harmondsworth: Pelican

27. Powell, A. (1971) *Books do furnish a room*. London: Heinemann

28. Evans, R.J. (1997) *In defence of history*. London: Granta Books

29. Andersson, C. (1996) Editorial. *FID News Bulletin*, **46**(7/8), 233. [Claes Andersson is the Finnish Minister of Culture].

30. Bonaventura, M. (1997) Benefits of a Knowledge Culture. *ASLIB Proceedings*, **49**(4), 82–89

31. Berlin, I. (1990) Decline of Utopian Ideas in the West. In *The Crooked Timber of Humanity*. ed. H. Hardy, p.28. London: John Murray

40   *The Impact of Information on Society*

32. Gregory, R. (1987) (ed.) *The Oxford Companion to the Mind*. p.410. Oxford: Oxford University Press

33. Oakeshott, M. ibid. p.51

34. Russell, B. see ref 26. p.136

35. Drucker, P. (1993) *Post-capitalist society*. p.191. Oxford: Butterworth-Heinemann

36. Murray, J.A.H. (1979) (ed.) *The Oxford English Dictionary, Compact Edition*. pp.1150–51. Oxford: Oxford University Press

37. Bawden, D. ibid. pp. 74–79

38. Oakeshott, M. ibid. p.59

39. Ackoff, R.L. Quoted in R. O. Mason et al. see ref 9.

40. Murray, G. (1946) *Greek Studies*. p.18. Oxford: Oxford University Press

41. Handy, C. (1997) *The Hungry Spirit*. p.211. London: Random House

42. Russell, B. as ref 25. p.113

43. Mason, R.O. et al. ibid. p.50

44. Warnock, M. (1994) *Imagination and Time*. p.7. Oxford: Blackwell

45. Giddens, A. (1995) *The Consequences of Modernity*. Cambridge: Polity Press

46. Feynman, R.P. (1992) *The Character of Physical Law*. p.58. London: Penguin

47. Bowler, P.J. (1992) *The Environmental Sciences*. p.5. London: Fontana

48. Monbiot, G. (1997) Report of lecture. *Oxford Today*, **9**(3), 12

49. Wolpert, L. (1993) *The Unnatural Nature of Science*. London: Faber and Faber

50. *Nature of Discovery*. BBC Third Programme. Broadcast 2 March 1997

51. Jackson, J. (1995) *Planet Earth, an Explorer's Guide*. London: BBC Educational Developments

52. Beaumont, W. (1995) The man with a lid on his stomach. In: *The Faber Book of Science*, ed. J. Carey, pp.67–70. London: Faber and Faber

53. Greenfield, S. ibid (16). pp.17–19. (Describes the change in personality of a man who suffered and survived a bolt through the front part of the brain.)

54. Ridley, M. (1997) *The Origins of Virtue*. London: Penguin. (This book attempts, by pulling together studies of anthropology, animal behaviour, Darwinian theory and modern genetics, to explain why human beings behave as social animals despite the genetic urge to selfish reproduction and survival.)

CHAPTER THREE
The quality and reliability of information

'I have been shown at Kardamyli a ledge of cliff where the local prince used to drink coffee with Menelaus, and a stone on which Lord Byron, who never went there, played draughts with General Kolokotronis, whom he never met'.

Peter Levi, *The Hill of Kronos* [1]

Our knowledge is continually being modified by new information. Time and again we read or hear reports that contradict or disprove previous information. We are so used to information being presented in ways designed to influence us, that we are sceptical of the facts themselves. It would not be too unfair to say that we live in a time when we wonder what can we trust. How much of the information we receive is reliable, in what circumstances and for how long?

The late Professor John Jepson used to give his medical students copies of the technical leaflets which are issued to GPs by the manufacturers of ethical medicines. The leaflets describe the products, their properties and the effects and side effects they may have. The details are supported by references to articles in the scientific and professional medical journals. The students were set the task of getting copies of the references and comparing what was in them with what was quoted in the leaflets. Always, he said, students found that some references had been misquoted and that some references did not exist (presumably wrongly cited references). And these were in leaflets produced by reputable pharmaceutical firms for the information of GPs who would prescribe those medicines! However, these were errors only in quotation and reference; there was no evidence of error in the product or its applicability.

Of course, all scholars know they should always check their references or at least quote the source. Thus if I want to quote the remark of Francis Quick, 'A theory that fits all the facts is bound to be wrong, as some of the facts will be wrong', I must reveal that I came across it in a paper of Wolpert's [2]. However, as Jepson's students found, many authors do not check adequately.

A potentially embarrassing example is given by Ridley [3]. Apparently the speech given in 1854 by the American Indian, Chief Seattle, much quoted in environmental literature, including a book by US Vice-President Gore, is a modern invention. There is no record of the original speech, if it occurred at all.

In business or in official work, one checks rigorously (in so far as one can) any information on which decisions or actions depend. Sound information depends on other information. Whether buying from company A will be more advantageous than buying from company B depends not just on prices but speed and reliability of delivery and so on. In private life, for example when buying a house, we get experts to check many facts, including statements made by the vendor about the condition of it. But much information we take on trust, especially that which is of general interest only, and that which we lack the means, skill or time to check. Unfortunately, some at least of that which is not checked can influence us.

In the academic sector, openly publishing information is accepted, even required, as the approved way of having its reliability examined. As Berlin says [4], 'All statements with claims to truth must be public, communicable, testable – capable of verification or falsification by methods open to and accepted by any rational investigator'. Though this sounds very similar to Popper's principle of refutation in science, it applies to all branches of knowledge and even to any other form of information, even to instructions for do-it-yourself kit assemblies.

A preliminary test of the reliability of technical articles is the reputation of the journal in which they appear. The quality journals submit articles to scrutiny by referees. The reputation of the publisher gives a measure of the quality of a book. With information published on the Internet, the only guarantee that it is accurate is the reputation of its source and the scope given for checking back to its sources. The case of a boy who followed scrupulously a recipe for making fireworks which was given on the Internet and suffered a severe explosion is an illustration that there is unsound information there.

Technical articles, despite refereeing, are not exempt from risk of error. I can recall seeing in the late 1960s and early 70s, in several publications dealing with library planning, the statement that in the UK the quantity of trade literature published amounts to about 18 feet of shelf space per year. The origin of that figure was one of my colleagues who had produced it as an order of magnitude estimate for a particular planning exercise on which we were engaged at the time. It was included in a report which was seen by people not involved in the exercise and from them found its way into the professional literature. At the time it wasn't a bad guess, but it was little more than a guess.

Bias, accidental or deliberate

Without being falsified, information can be biased by the way it is presented. This can happen in any of three ways:

- by being abbreviated and hence incomplete;
- by the need to achieve impact, arouse interest;
- by a desire to influence.

Abbreviating

The news media contribute an enormous amount to our daily intake of general information. So the question of how much reliance we can place on them is important but it is very difficult to arrive at a satisfactory answer. We have all experienced seeing an account of something or somewhere we know well and being shocked by inaccuracies or by incompleteness. We tend to grow cynical and assume that it is as bad in other reports and treat them all as unreliable.

This, however, is unfair. In practice we accept without problem most of what we learn from the media even if we keep our minds sufficiently open to accept further information and even refutation when and if it arrives. (Is the refutation always more reliable than the original story?)

Summarizing news or something one has read is a skilled art but no matter how skilled one is it is rare that nothing is left out. By definition it must be. One cannot expect in the popular media to get the whole story. What is omitted may be insignificant; on other occasions it may be more important than the reporter realized. Accounts in both the popular media and the technical press of the Government's White Paper on freedom of information concentrated on a few aspects only with the result that some wrong impressions were conveyed. On reading the Paper itself one formed a very different impression.

Even TV news presentations direct from the scene of an event can be misleading. Inevitably they depend on how much the camera is able to show and what the presenter chooses to concentrate on.

The extreme example of abbreviating is, of course, the headline. It is common to skim a newspaper and on many pages note only the headlines. Yet how misleading some are, being written primarily to attract us to read the report. If we don't, I suppose it is our own fault if we register wrong information. My favourite headline was, 'Hot stripper starts work'. It referred to the opening of a new steel strip mill.

In one sense the opposite of abbreviation and omission is the inclusion of opinion. The days of aiming to keep it separate from fact have long gone. It therefore behoves the reader or listener to make the distinction. A news item that China has released one of its dissidents as part of its strategy of wooing the West is clearly a combination of fact and opinion. The fact is that the dissident has been released. That it is part of wooing the West is an assumption. Other reasons are possible. Yet it reads as fact.

Aiming for impact

Newspapers have for many years raced to get a story out before their rivals could. Part of competition now is to present it in a dramatic way. A story must have impact to help sell the paper. When one bears in mind the effect of these two pressures on reporters, it is astonishing that the majority of information in news stories is reasonably correct. Bearing in mind also that to report an event often the reporter has to make do with eyewitness accounts from those who were present and reports from officials who were not, and that after a story has been submitted it has to withstand the depredations of the sub-editor, it is amazing how well the reports stand up to later scrutiny. In the case of reports on technical matters, the reporter is commonly nowadays someone with an appropriate technical background or lengthy period of specialization in the field. Nevertheless, he or she too has to select those aspects likely to arouse interest even if sometimes the interest aroused reaches panic level. Nevertheless, if the accuracy of information gained from the media is important in affecting one's plans or actions, as much cross checking as possible is recommended. For example, reports of severe flooding in an area of a country one is about to visit should be confirmed with the tourist office or embassy of the country concerned to find out how serious and how extensive it really is.

Interest can be aroused by giving, often unintentionally, a degree of authority to a report which it does not justify. The BBC's Radio 4 News, normally one of the sounder news sources, reported, 'Scientists say that the sun may be the main source of global warming'. Details, other than that the news came from a scientific meeting of an eminent organization in the USA, were not given. Almost certainly, this report stemmed from a paper given by a small research team, just a few scientists. The phrase 'scientists say' implies widespread acceptance which may not be justified. The absence of any criticism on the floor of a conference does not mean that the other scientists present agree with the report.

Desire to influence

Information from Pressure Groups is always highly suspect. By definition they are not impartial. They are primarily concerned with pushing a particular line and while they may promulgate perfectly accurate information, it is unlikely to be the whole story. Information which is contrary to their interests and the fact that there are serious gaps in the information available are liable to be suppressed.

There are a great many occasions when one realizes that information is being presented with the aim of creating a particular impression: the company report to impress shareholders; the Government announcement to influence public attitudes; the charity to seek sympathy and donations for its cause. One expects the information, once separated from opinion, to be correct (though it isn't always). One needs, however, time and inclination to think through how much relevant information is lacking.

Interviews on TV or radio that skip from one person to another, then to a third and then back again are highly suspect. The coherence of the account each one of those being interviewed is giving is broken up, often only a fraction being broadcast, and the result can be what the interviewer or editor wants rather than the complete story. The result may be entertaining – after all the programme aims to attract an audience, not to be an archive – and it may stimulate one to seek fuller information – a wholly laudable aim – but the product as it stands has to be treated as unreliable in terms of the information given. The danger is that one does not check, one treats it as entertainment, but some time in the future one recalls the information without recalling the circumstances in which it was given. This is an example of David Puttnam's anxiety, to which I referred earlier, about the consequences of the merging of news and entertainment or, in this case, documentary and entertainment.

Conflicting data, preconceptions and beliefs

It is not uncommon to find oneself faced with sets of facts which conflict with each other. The US government claims it has evidence that Iraq has been making materials for chemical warfare. The Iraq government denies it. We assume that one or the other is incorrect.

In a case like 'eggs are good for you'/'eggs contain harmful *Salmonella*' the apparent contradiction does not exist. Eggs are nutritious and are harmless if cooked long enough for any *Salmonella* which may be present to be killed. The on/off argument some years ago about whether cyclamates were harmless sweeteners or not depended on the latest research results. Complete information was lacking; presumably sufficient has been amassed by now.

Human memory and powers of observation are very unreliable except in the case of people who have been trained to observe and notice. It is commonly experienced by those who have to deal with witnesses to a road accident that even if they try to tell the events exactly as they recall them, each witness will tell a different story and the stories can differ substantially. Those with an axe to grind will complicate the issue even further. Beliefs can often be based on wrong conclusions from observation. It has been assumed for centuries that the cause of a hangover after drinking beer, wine or spirits is the amount of alcohol consumed. Some recent research indicates that the cause may be the presence of other organic substances, e.g. acetone, which although not alcohol are consumed only in alcoholic drinks. The fact that the scale of hangovers varies with the type of drink (champagne usually has less impact than a heavy red wine), the total alcohol intake being kept constant, can be explained this way. The cause is still too much to drink, but it is not simply having too much alcohol [5]. Confirming research is needed.

We all have firm ideas about certain facets of life and we share these ideas with friends who agree, hence seeming to confirm them, and use them as if facts. But they can still be wrong. Alastair Cooke, in one of his weekly broadcasts, reported on a survey of Americans, the great majority of whom were convinced that about 25 per cent of the national Budget was spent on foreign aid. Official statistics reveal the figure to be only 2 per cent. The exaggeration probably reflects a built in dislike of giving funds for foreign aid.

Much information transmitted orally is also suspect, as is that recalled from memory, yet we commonly have only that sort of information to work from. No matter how we may decry gossip, most of us enjoy it but the wise treat it as a very suspect source of information. Rather it is best treated as an alerting mechanism and any information of significance should be carefully checked.

On the other hand, information conveyed orally in a lesson or lecture or during a consultation with an expert, e.g. a lawyer or a builder, one assumes to be reliable unless later proved wrong. A major factor in judging whether information is reliable is the source from which it comes. The reputation of a person or organization whence information is obtained is vital. This is one reason – there are several others – why we prefer to consult an acquaintance who is an expert rather than using a reference book.

Of course, if the reliability of the information is crucial, we should still check it, but we don't always. Even distinguished people can be mischievous. Benjamin Franklin wrote to the editor of a London newspaper in 1765, chaffing the English on their ignorance of America. 'The grand leap of the Whale up the falls of Niagara is esteemed, by all who have seen it, as one of the finest spectacles in Nature' he wrote [6]. I trust all other statements by US Presidents are equally correct.

Finally in this section it is worth commenting on the willingness of some people, I have no idea how many, to believe information that has no firm basis. A survey of some 8000 adults [7] led to the conclusion that 'people are displaying greater irrationality in an increasingly rational world'. Certainly more people than in past years are turning to alternative medicine and religions. The examples of the Flat Earthers and the World was created in 4004 BC groups have been commented on earlier. In an article [8], Ferguson, a Fellow of Jesus College Oxford, describes the 1997 publication

The Bible Code as tosh and expresses surprise that it has sold well. He links it with other examples of the ready acceptance as fact of wild speculations for which there is no tangible evidence whatever, and which are in contradiction of the observed facts.

He might, though he didn't, have included the love many people have for the irrational (remember how Von Daniken's *Chariot of the Gods* was a best seller?) and their love of fairy tales. It was not only Keats who disliked the cold logic of science and the rigorous rationality of the Enlightenment. Many people in today's very uncertain world, wherein personal relationships seem no longer stable and jobs all too often temporary, seek something cosy and comfortable rather than grim reality. Astrology, fortune telling and flying saucers retain their hold despite all the evidence of their lack of validity. The irrational is fun and a relief from everyday existence. But it is utterly unreliable as information.

A not uncommon source of error is one to which we are all prone, namely equating association with causation. That two events can occur at the same time does not prove that they are connected by a cause and effect relationship. My feeling unwell today may not be connected with being at a party yesterday. Other causes are possible, yet one would be abnormal not to assume the party was the cause. Berry [9] gives several examples including that of the number of tree sparrows decreasing over time and the number of sparrowhawks increasing over the same period. Putting the graphs of population against time side by side gives the impression that there must be a one-to-one relationship, but in practice if there is any connection at all it must be more complex and a number of other factors such as food supply, loss of habitat and presence or absence of other predators, need to be examined.

Statistical data

Users of statistical data need to look carefully at what exactly the figures stand for, how they were collected and how the results were calculated. One well-known but still often overlooked source of error is that of not ensuring that all the data are measured using the same units. A simple case, now I am glad to say overcome, arose when comparing book collections internationally. Those measuring in the UK counted volumes of books and bibliographic volumes of periodicals and ignored pamphlets. The Russians counted volumes of books, parts of periodicals and included pamphlets. Both methods were right but the results were not comparable.

I earlier commented on the need to put information into context and to give full details. The simple example was the boiling point of water, the temperature varying slightly according to the amount of impurities and the atmospheric pressure. Politically sensitive data should be treated with suspicion unless full details of the method of calculation are known. A report in the *International Herald Tribune* [10] showed sources of discrepancy and misinterpretation in the UK figures: 'unemployment as recorded by the labor force survey fell by just 32 000 – dramatically less than the 114 000 drop seen in claimant unemployment'. Other scope for difficulty of interpretation was said to lie in the number of part-time and temporary jobs.

Handy [11] quotes the following figures for types of employment in the British labour force in 1995:

Part-Time	24%
Self-Employed	13%
Temporary	6%
Permanent	82%

He goes on to say that, 'If you add the unemployment figures (8% in 1995) to the combined total of part-timers, self-employed and temporary, you arrive at a figure of 51% for 1995. In other words more than half the available workforce do not have a proper full- time job inside an organization'. He does not explain how this squares with the figure in the table of 82 per cent of those in employment in permanent jobs. Are all the part-time and self-employed part of the permanent category or do part of them make up the temporary category? Presumably the missing 12 per cent, neither permanent nor temporary, are unemployed, but the data are not clear.

An obvious danger is using data that were collected for one purpose for a different one. It would be unwise, for example, to use figures for the increase in new books published as a measure of the rate of increase in books bought.

A treacherous area is that of sampling. Moroney [12] uses the example of dealing from a pack of cards, which has 16 honours, ace to jack, in a pack of 52 cards, i.e. more than 1 in 4 are honours. As any poker or pontoon player knows, it is not uncommon to be dealt a hand of five cards (a 10 per cent sample) which does not contain any honours. So, even a 10 per cent sample would not be guaranteed to reveal faults in a set of products that had as many as 1 in 4 faulty. In a works testing process one stipulates the confidence limits that one is prepared to accept before deciding on sampling method.

DNA matching is prone to misunderstanding. The whole molecule cannot be matched, only short samples chopped off by restriction enzymes. It is claimed that the chance of the samples matching those from another person is 1:1 000 000. However, there are 58 000 000 people in the UK so that there is a 1 in 58 chance of there being a match of the sample among the UK population. It becomes crucial in a trial in which DNA testing is important that the right question is posed.

Information based on probability is a well known source of error. As everyone knows, the probability of a coin coming down heads is 1 in 2 no matter how many times it has previously been tossed. Yet there is a human belief that if it has come down tails the last ten times, 'on the law of averages' it will come down heads this time. There is no law of averages and it is just as likely to come down tails as heads. On the other hand (the right metaphor?) the probability of a coin landing tails every time in those ten throws is 1 in 2048.

Radford [13] has rightly pointed out that many scientific results have to be expressed in terms of probability. A person's blood group can be determined with certainty and so can the group of a sample of blood. But whether the two blood samples come from the same person involves the probability of someone else, who could have been present, having the same blood group. Even if the group is a rare one, there is still a chance of someone else having the same group.

In health the same sort of problem arises. The relation between smoking tobacco and contracting lung cancer is one such. There is a causal relationship but it does not happen in all cases. There are many people – Winston Churchill was one – who smoke heavily yet do not develop lung cancer. Nevertheless, the probability of it happening is judged sufficiently high to justify discouraging smoking.

Scientific research can lead people to errors of assumption: for example, all people who suffer from a certain disease are found to eat substance A but to have no other discoverable factor in common. The fact is published and the conclusion arises that eating A is the cause. Wiser research would have investigated how many other people also ate A without getting the disease and judged the probability of it being a cause. Even more research might have sought the factor which made some people and not others susceptible.

The Challenger space rocket disaster provides another example of using the wrong data for the problem and in particular the danger of not looking at all the information. It was known that the rubber O-rings on the fuel tanks had been a source of weakness. Those who had to make the decision whether or not to go ahead with the launch, apparently warned by the technical experts not to do so because the weather was cold, looked at the failure data and concluded that the failures did not show a pattern of temperature dependence. They omitted to look at the data for flights when there had been no problem with the rings. Had they done so, they would have seen that on all those occasions the atmospheric temperature at launch was above 60°F; on the day of the Challenger launch it was below 40°F.

Polls and surveys are a very popular method of gathering information and if properly and rigorously conducted have considerable value. However, one is left in considerable doubt about the value of many of them. How carefully was the sample chosen and what is the probability that the results would be the same if the whole population were questioned?

Hoggart [14] expresses a common disquiet about their misuse. 'The popular papers [and now radio and TV phone-ins should be added] conduct polls on this matter and questionnaires on that matter among their readers, and so elevate the counting of heads into a substitute for judgement.' Phone-ins, like the Internet, disseminate to a wide audience the views of individuals without any indication being given about the extent of their knowledge of the subject and the value of their opinions.

Telephone surveys and interviews conducted in the street have to overcome the disadvantage that few people are willing to stop and spend much time answering. Are those who will stop and answer a reasonably representative sample? Some questions require thought, yet the conditions are not conducive to it. 'Do you think that on balance the Government is doing a good job?' is a typical question, a quick answer to which has little value. If all that is wanted is a public relations response, all well and good. But if the survey aims to find a less superficial view, time to think is necessary.

A poll of whether, to take a recent example, there should be an age limit on childbearing is simply a measure of opinion and no more. It may be of value to those, e.g. politicians, to whom public opinion is of importance but it is of no value when individual cases of treatment have to be decided.

Questions are sometimes unanswerable, yet they are asked. A recent telephone survey asked, 'Will you spend next year's holiday at home or abroad?' The answer, 'Both' was not acceptable. It was recorded, I gathered, as 'Abroad'. If that was what was wanted, should not the question have been, 'Will you spend a holiday abroad next year?' or does the either/or question have some merit in not seeming to bias the responder?

Sometimes the choices of answer allowed are quite inadequate. The risks inherent in the either/or type of survey can be illustrated by an extreme question such as, 'Which of the following most nearly represents your views: all children should be shot or all children should be strangled?' 'Neither' and 'Don't know' must not only be allowable responses but should be presented as welcome ones, not as they usually are in most interview surveys as suitable escapes for the weak and feeble.

Graphs can be used to present information very clearly, more clearly than lengthy explanations. At the same time it is common to draw a line through a set of points which do not all lie on it (Figure 3.1). Another misleading simplification is to save space and cut down one of the axes (Figure 3.2).

Averages

It is common to find oneself presented with quantitative data expressed as an average. Cricket averages, average annual rate of inflation and number of persons in a family are typical examples. One does need to treat averages with great care. One example concerned a disease which, though not common, quite a lot of people have caught. The average age of death from it was stated to be 46 years. On closer enquiry it turned out that the disease was so rarely fatal that only two people were known to have died from it, one a baby of 2 years and the other an old man of 90! Thus it would appear that people who contracted the complaint when close to the average age of death were least likely to die from it, though really the data are too scanty for any definite conclusion to be drawn.

In cases where results are reasonably symmetrically distributed about a mean (Figure 3.3), statisticians will calculate a figure called the standard deviation. This is a way of expressing the degree of confidence one has that a new figure corresponds to the existing

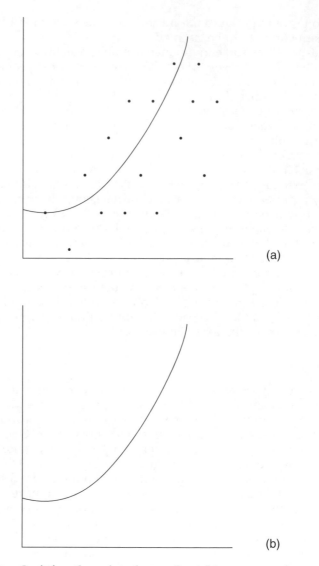

Figure 3.1.   Omitting the points from a 'best fit' curve can give a totally misleading impression.

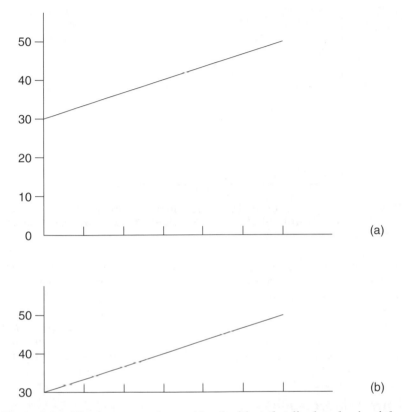

Figure 3.2. These two graphs are identical but the displaced axis of the second makes it look quite different.

pattern. There is little risk of error in assuming that two thirds of the distribution of data lies within one standard deviation of the mean, 95 per cent lies within two standard deviations and 99 per cent within three. Unfortunately, skew distributions of sets of figures are very common (Figure 3.4) and in these cases averages and standard deviations have no meaning, yet averages are still often used.

Averaging averages is very risky. A vehicle travels 40 miles at 40 mph and another 40 miles at 80 mph. The average speed is 60 mph, or is it? If we want the average speed for the journey we note that the first 40 miles took one hour and the second half an

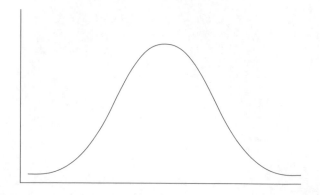

Figure 3.3. Typical example of reasonably symetrical distribution of values. Two thirds of the readings would lie within one standard deviation.

hour. Thus the total 80 miles took one and a half hours, in which case the average speed was 53.3 mph. Information expressed as an average needs to be treated with caution.

Many years ago during a lecture I commented, provocatively, that on average 50 per cent of the information one received had something wrong with it. During question time at the end one person asked me, 'Why did you claim that all the information one receives is wrong?' – a nice way of accepting my point.

Unreal information

Television, with the computer controlled images it presents, can add extra detail to enhance and clarify the information being imparted, or it can distort it. This applies to illustrations in books and magazines as well. In a TV account of the Orsanmichele in Florence, computer manipulation of the picture enabled the viewer to see the building as it probably looked centuries ago when the ground floor was open – the doorways are now closed in. Excellent; it added clarity to the description of the history of the building. Another programme about the life of Julius Caesar used shots of scenes on Roman vases to accompany accounts of events in his life. These were almost certainly not scenes from his life but some people, not familiar with Roman pottery, may well have believed they were. Not long ago a picture was published in a reputable magazine showing the Egyptian pyramids closer

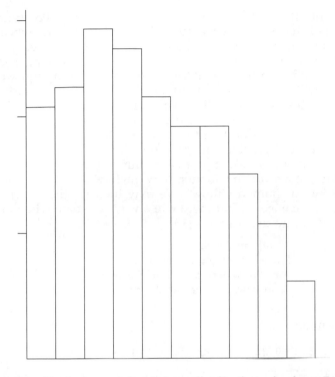

Figure 3.4. Typical example of skew distribution of values. Examples could be batsmans' scores at cricket or numbers of children in a sample of families.

together that they are in reality; it may have been right for its purpose but it could give rise to disappointment to travellers when they saw the pyramids in Egypt. Certainly, the ability that the computer has to manipulate images means that seeing is no longer believing.

There has always been a certain amount of imaginary information being generated and disseminated. It is alleged that the Internet contains a high proportion. Modern technology allows this to be taken to an extreme, namely virtual reality. This is a very exciting tool for instructional work from bringing 'to life' what the age of the dinosaurs was like to teaching pilots to fly aircraft. Properly used it has great potential for raising our levels of knowledge. Misused it could do great harm.

One of the actions to which participating governments committed themselves at the 1996 UN Habitat II Conference was 'promoting equal access to reliable information'. It is easy to be cynical about big objectives and about governments being a source of misleading information but we must have aims to improve life. If we are willing to jog along with no higher ambition than to maintain the status quo, life will be very dreary and uninspired. This particular aim is one that should be strongly supported, provided that it is allied to education to make people better able to distinguish between reliable information, information that merits confirmation and information that is unreliable.

Perhaps, however, no matter how high we aim, we shall be limited by our human failings. We may increase the information literacy of the majority but there will always be some who fall, like Ogden Nash, by the wayside [15].

> 'Gently my eyelids close
> I'd rather be good than clever
> And I'd rather have all my facts wrong
> Than have no facts whatever.'

References

1.   Levi, P. (1980) *The Hill of Kronos*. p. 28. London: Collins

2.   Wolpert, L. (1996) The Unnatural Nature of Science. *Proceedings of the Royal Institution*, **67**, 152–33

3.   Ridley, M. (1997) *The Origins of Virtue*, pp. 213–215. London: Penguin

4.   Berlin, I. (1991) *Against the Current: essays in the history of ideas*, p.163. Oxford: Clarendon

5.   Fletcher, D. (1997) Alcohol not to blame for hangovers. *Daily Telegraph*, December 1997

6.   Webber, R.L. (1973) (ed.) *A random walk in science*. p.9. London: Institute of Physics

     The quotation comes from a lecture given by Professor R.V. Jones which is in the volume.

7.   Uhling, R. (1997) X-file Britain puts faith in the irrational. *Daily Telegraph*, 5 September 1997

8. Ferguson, N. (1997) *Daily Telegraph*

9. Berry, C. (1996) Risks, costs, choice and rationality. *Proceedings of the Royal Institution*, **67,** 126

10. Reuters (1997) UK job data: tinting the picture rosy. *International Herald Tribune*, 8 April 1997

11. Handy, C. (1997) *The Hungry Spirit*, p.69. London: Hutchinson

12. Moroney, M.J. (1956) *Facts from figures*, p.173. Harmondsworth: Penguin

    This is a book I have used all my working life and can strongly recommend to others of no great mathematical bent who nevertheless have to make sure they use quantitative data meaningfully.

13. Radford, T. (1996) Comment. *Chemistry in Britain*, **32**(7), 3

14. Hoggart, R. (1958) *The uses of literacy*, pp.179–180. Harmondsworth: Penguin

15. Nash, O. (1985) *Candy is Dandy: the best of Ogden Nash*, p.225. London: Methuen

CHAPTER FOUR
Comprehending

'The Theory of Relevance has destroyed the belief that communication is simply a matter of encoding and decoding messages; it has revealed people as interpreting what they observe in the light of their own past experience, always being more or less approximate translators, and never wholly certain'.

Theodore Zeldin. *An Intimate History of Humanity* [1]

In this chapter I propose to look at problems of comprehending information, problems which all of us encounter and have to overcome when giving information or when receiving it. Comprehending and communicating are interweaving topics and they will not be kept artificially distinct. This chapter will concentrate on the human aspects of receiving information, the next one on transmitting information and especially the impact of the communication technologies. Although communicating and comprehending is the order in which things happen – after all, until some message is communicated there is nothing to comprehend – for this study the order is better reversed. One reason is that unless the communicator appreciates any limitations there are in the ability of the recipient to understand, his efforts may well be wasted as the information or part of it is lost in a morass of misconceptions or a desert of incomprehension. Even high levels of intelligence do not guarantee understanding if there is a lack of background knowledge of a specialized subject.

However, before considering the problems that arise, it is worth reflecting on just how well we do understand the information we receive. The majority of us, I feel sure, understand quite adequately the majority of what we observe, what we are told and what we read. In respect of most everyday information, the ability to understand improves over the years, at least until old age causes mental deterioration. It is the legacy of lifelong experience, for what we are doing is interpreting the new information in the light of experience, expectations and circumstances. Any difficulty of understanding is commonly overcome by some added explanation which provides the link to existing knowledge. In other words, our ability to comprehend new information is determined by:

1. what we already know about the subject;
2. what the words and phrases mean to us;
3. the way the information is presented;
4. our intellectual aptitude, whether quick or slow on the uptake, what sort of intelligence we have;
5. our built-in prejudices and other emotional reactions to the information or to the giver.

Inevitably, the topic is dependant on the question of how we attach meaning to what we see or hear, to words and phrases and to numbers and other symbols. The subject is well reviewed in *The Oxford Companion to the Mind* [2].

Pinker [3] in his study of how we develop our use of language also emphasises how much the recipient, as well as the communicator, has to contribute to the process of understanding. 'Any particular thought in our head embraces a vast amount of information. But when it comes to communicating a thought to someone else, attention spans are short and mouths are slow. To get information into a listener's head in a reasonable amount of time, a speaker can encode only a fraction of the message into words and must count on the listener to fill in the rest. But inside a single head, the demands are different'. Later he continues [4], 'Understanding requires integrating the fragments gleaned from a sentence into a vast mental database'.

It follows, and fits with experience, that each person's understanding of a new piece of information may be different, even if only very slightly so, from that of another's. Absorbing information is, of course, an act of learning. Gardner [5], as mentioned earlier, has postulated that there are a number of quite distinct modes of learning, which he terms Multiple Intelligences. People differ considerably in the extent to which they use each of these and this will give rise to differences of understanding.

On the whole our ability to convey information is still bounded by language, oral or written, despite the enormous growth in communicating information pictorially. Of course numbers also play an important part and so too does body language but both primarily supplement verbal information. Musical information and other information such as the call of a songbird or the sound of a waterfall can most effectively be conveyed as audible, non-verbal reproduction of the sound, though trained musicians can read music scores and 'hear' the sounds through imagination. But in general, even in the days of multimedia, language remains the primary means of communicating information. So do the limitations of language limit our ability to know and understand?

There is a popular belief that words determine thoughts. However, the growing understanding of the way the brain treats the information it holds suggests that this is not so. Gardner's theories imply as much. Certainly we sometimes find it difficult to find words that express our thoughts properly and it is not uncommon to have something to say and be unable to remember a crucial word. The thought is clear but the words are not. Pinker suggests that we think in a language which he calls 'Mentalese' [6].

There are, no doubt, a great many reasons for failing to understand some piece of information one reads or hears, and even more for only partly understanding it. I will touch on just a few of those that seem important in our context.

Problems in verbal communication

Vocabulary

Words are, I suppose, the most obvious place to start though it may be that the impact of new ways of communicating on style of expression would have been more appropriate. After all, the medium we use – face to face discussion, article in journal, e-mail message – is at the time a fixed constraint. As McLuhan observed, 'the medium is the message'. However, in 1940, Russell [7] had written that words are of four sorts, spoken, heard, written and read. With many words there is a slight difference of meaning in each of these uses. Further, and equally important, the meaning may depend on the context in which a word is used. One's solar plexus is only etymologically related to the solar system.

Ideally, words should be used with the meanings that they are given in the major dictionaries and each of the meanings there should be equally permissible. However, it happens that one use of a word becomes excessively common and makes the use in the other senses impractical. This has happened with the word 'gay' where the homosexual use has virtually made the use as 'happy' or 'carefree' impossible.

Context is crucial especially in cases where words have a variety of meanings. The word 'organic' is a classic case. It means something significantly different to the biologist, the chemist and the food distributor. In this last instance, organic in the context of the production of foodstuffs by entirely natural means, i.e. excluding artificial fertilisers or chemical insecticides, the origin was really a rather sloppy use of the word at a time when a brief term was needed. This is one way in which words change their meaning or add new ones and is what is currently happening to the word 'cool'.

New and imported words usually cause few problems save to those who do not find them in a self-explanatory context and cannot find them in a dictionary. The generation gap is often a source of this problem. The use of English as an international language sometimes leads to the misuse of English words, but there is usually more scope for serious misunderstanding through cultural differences in the way phrases are interpreted. What to an English diplomat is a vague or permissive term may to a German one be an obligatory one and vice versa.

Communication between co-workers in a field nearly always leads to the development of words and phrases whose exact meaning is clear only to those workers. The use of technical terms is crucial to specialists. The words have precise meanings without which, unambiguous, concise communication is not practical.

However, in some fields there develops a tendency to use jargon, as those not specialists in that field call it, to create membership of an 'in group' and to exclude others. Internet user jargon is an example. It is a social phenomenon, not confined to specialists, often indicative of a need to feel superior, especially when used by people to convey some message to each other when in the presence of others not of the group. The phenomenon is well known when people try to mix with a social group different from their own and has been parodied as U and non-U speech as has some of the 'in' body language. The raised eyebrows indicating boredom is an example.

Some authors seem to enjoy including uncommon words. Whether this is done for fun, to show off, or deliberately to try to increase the reader's vocabulary and hence avoid accusations of writing undemandingly one does not know. So much depends on the subject as well as the intended audience. In science, a paper for other scientists will be full of the technical terms of that discipline. History, on the other hand, has few technical terms and they are rarely needed. As the historian Stone said [8], 'one should always try to write plain English, avoiding jargon and obfuscation, and making one's meaning as clear as possible to the reader'.

Nevertheless, it is vital that we should always be building up our vocabulary if the full meaning and significance of information is to be communicated in all circumstances. It is an important part of our lifelong education process. We often need to be able to understand and express complex ideas. There is more to the use of a wide vocabulary than just achieving Quiller-Couch's elegant variation. By choosing the right word from among several one can express subtle shades of meaning. Writing about absorbing information, Zeldin commented [9], 'Picking up perceptions of the right size, in infinitely small detail or in broad panoramas, is an art, the basis of all art and of all achievement'. An extensive vocabulary helps enormously.

People do, of course, differ very considerably in the vocabulary of words they understand and also in those they employ, a number usually much smaller. The British National Corpus in a Press release from 1996 claims that its database contains 100 million words of written and spoken English but that this may include the grammatical variants of each word. A sample survey mentioned during a radio programme estimated approaching one million words excluding grammatical variants. Shakespeare, according to another survey, used about 15000 distinctly different words, i.e. excluding the grammatical variants. The growth of language can be gauged by the claim that the latest edition of the *Concise OED-Rom* contains over 7000 new words and senses.

Shakespeare was not exceptional in the number of words he used. It has been estimated, by sampling in a dictionary words known to a person, that a well-educated person today will know the meaning of over 100 000 words – though not necessarily every meaning of each of them. On the other hand the number commonly used in writing is much less than that, probably about 20 000 and the number in everyday speech fewer still.

In contrast, a poorly educated person will probably use fewer than 1000 words, mainly of what has been termed Basic English plus some names, a few technical terms, a number of expletives and revivals or new coinages in popular use on TV (e.g. 'sleaze').

Therefore the amount of information that can be conveyed is limited when one is restricted to using only the words everyone knows. Those trying to give information to the general public have to bear in mind the limited vocabulary of so many of their audience. It may be a desirable aim to get people used to looking up and learning each new word they encounter but I would guess that less than half the population bothers.

Even between those of similar educational level there can be problems when words, previously used only rarely, start to come into common usage. An example of this was the growth of use in the 1980s of the word 'paradigm'. In use it also moved away from its traditional meaning of 'example or pattern underlying a theory' and was commonly encountered as 'a new paradigm' or a 'paradigm shift' meaning sometimes 'a fundamental change' but at others little more than 'the latest fashion or idea' with a hint of implied mathematical precision. There can be little doubt that it was often not understood by the listener in quite the sense which the speaker intended.

Another cause of confusion can be attempted precision when it is not necessary. Those used to giving orders quickly learn to avoid this mistake. For example when out on army manoeuvres and needing to direct troops' attention quickly in a particular direction one would refer to a prominent tree as 'bushy topped' or 'conifer' as appropriate. Had the sergeant referred to 'beech tree' or to 'Douglas fir' some members of the troop would have been in doubt which tree was meant.

Background knowledge and comprehension skills

It will be obvious that lack of background knowledge makes much information difficult to understand. 'The village of West Wittering is near Chichester' means little to someone who does not know where Chichester is. Yet how often we assume that people to whom we talk have broadly the same knowledge of such matters as our own. It is obvious that a key to comprehension must be a willingness to seek clarification whenever one does not understand some piece of information either by asking questions or by looking up what is needed. It is obvious but there are many people who miss out by not doing so. At the same time it is worth remembering that one can underestimate an acquaintance's knowledge. If we are told something we already know well, our attention may wander and fail to register the important new information when it comes.

Such accidents apart, problems of understanding due to lack of background arise from several causes:

1.   new information may be beyond our comprehension or require a major reassessment of our understanding;
2.   the information may concern a discipline with which we are not familiar;
3.   we may lack a skill or type of intelligence necessary;
4.   the information may be expressed in a way we find confusing.

An extreme case arises when one tries to grasp information which is largely beyond the scope of existing language and certainly beyond one's experience or comprehension. One must use language, with such other aids as may be appropriate, but can one get the information across so that the recipient can make the necessary interpretation and appreciate the real meaning? For example, how does one understand what a temperature less than the absolute zero (it is theoretically possible) or the square root of minus one is?

Such problems arise when the boundaries of knowledge are being extended. The field of cosmology provides well-known examples but similar difficulties occur in explaining new aesthetic advances and in the more abstruse branches of philosophy. One way out is the use of paradox. For example, in his fascinating book *Creation Revisited* Atkins writes [10] 'Once molecules have learnt to compete and create other molecules in their image, elephants, and things resembling elephants, will in due course be found roaming through the countryside'. This, right at the beginning of his book brings home the concept that life and living processes can be mechanistic, and that there is no need to postulate a spirit or life force.

Hawkins faced similar problems in his *Brief History of Time* [11] where he described many obscure events and processes with which few people other than physical scientists are familiar. Indeed, new information may cause problems of comprehension even for those within a profession if, as often happens, their knowledge base is not continually refreshed and kept up-to-date. Even such lucid explanations as those of Feynman on the laws of physics [12] contain difficult passages for those who studied no physics after the mid 1950s.

Lack of sufficient background knowledge is not necessarily due to a low level of education or of a failure to keep up-to-date. It arises because the amount of information is today so great that to be a well informed polymath is now virtually impossible. As a result, a person who works in one field of knowledge may have great difficulty understanding in depth information about another field. The differences in understanding between scientists and humanists were the source of the 'Two Cultures' debate.

Thus, when I, a scientist with a classics background, listened to the Reith Lectures by the sociologist Professor Patricia Williams, I was left with a feeling that I had not properly grasped what she was trying to say, probably because her field of expertise is one in which I have only very superficial background knowledge. One can also find signs of similar lack of comprehension between those working currently in the same field but holding very different opinions about some underlying principle. This seems to be the situation between traditional and post-modern historians.

A quite different type of comprehension problem arises if one's type of intelligence or mental skill differs from that of the person giving information. The most obvious example is that those who are not mathematically minded or who do not appreciate the significance of quantity often have difficulty absorbing information in which number plays an important role. Those of an emotional disposition may have difficulty with objective information about human beings or animals. Those who are entirely realistic or of prosaic disposition might experience problems interpreting artistic or poetic concepts.

One of the most obvious causes of an inability to comprehend is the use of a style of writing or speaking which does not match that of the recipient. It is not only jargon. Consider the following taken from an article on Asia and the Communication Age. 'Learning how to deconstruct information depends on one's access to it. Thus there is a great need for a venue where grassroot and social movements people could get information which will also present the undersides of what it happening to help them come up with their own interpretation of reality'. Even in context it is pretty opaque to me. However, this is the quite normal style of communication between members of the international community for whom it was written.

Sometimes, cumbersome prose which causes difficulty in comprehension is found in publications intended for public con-sumption. Each year the Plain English Campaign awards prizes to outstanding examples. It has done much good but occasionally it misfires by not recognizing that the publication of some statement does not mean that it is intended to be read by everyone. Thus the DTI's description of a pram: 'A wheeled vehicle designed for the transport in a seated or semi-recumbent position of one or two babies or infants who are placed inside a body of boat- or box-like shape, but does not include any carry-cot or transport therefore' was written to be read by a specific group of people who need a very precise definition to prevent them classifying as a pram some other vehicle which could be used for carrying babies.

Comprehensibility has to be judged from the standpoint of whether the intended information is conveyed effectively to the intended recipients. The fact that it is publicly available does not mean it has to be comprehensible to everyone any more than the fact that haggis is publicly available means that it has to be palatable to everyone.

Unfortunately, we cannot just leave it at that. It is necessary to communicate across the comprehension gulf. The British Asso-ciation for the Advancement of Science, the Royal Society's Committee on the Public Understanding of Science, The Royal Institution and several other bodies are working to bridge the gap between science and nonscientists in general. Whether there are similar bodies trying to make the discoveries of other specialized disciplines – sociology and economics for example – equally comprehensible I do not know but I hope there are.

It is not just to achieve broader awareness that one needs to study ways in which those without the necessary background knowledge, skills and even education can understand information that is normally outside their range. Juries can be faced with cases in which quite technical problems have to be grasped. They may have to understand what degree of confidence should be placed in evidence based on sampling methods.

Memory and imagination

I must admit that it is reading Warnock's book [13] that leads me to put these two topics together. The impact of memory, or lack of it, on one's ability to comprehend information will be fairly obvious. Lack of memory will result in lack of background knowledge. It may be a cause of failing to relate two matters and result in imperfect understanding.

But it is more complex than that. A good memory does not always lead to good understanding. There are many cases of people with exceptional memories who appear unable to appreciate the significance of a piece of information. They can memorise it; they can churn it out again unaltered; but they do not use it in any way. They can pass exams when the only requirement is to reproduce information. They fail when originality is called for. One must conclude that memory is not the most important factor in comprehending information and building up knowledge. Rather, it is the ability to interpret information, to relate it to what one already knows and to rearrange one's ideas.

Zeldin [14] comments, 'Memory has traditionally been lazy, preferring to remember the same things: some memories have established a supremacy like tyrants, and most information has been used to reinforce them, confirming old beliefs, instead of being dissected to reveal new facts, which are not easily recognisable'. The point was made earlier that the mind is not able to record a large part of what we see around us all the time, and there is no doubt that we also possess the power to fail to note, or memorize, information which does not at the time interest us.

On the other hand, for those who have it, the power of imagination helps understanding. This is especially true in the field of poetry where words are used with a greater depth of meaning than in everyday speech, a depth which requires the reader or listener to exert the imagination. Similarly, if we have experienced the pain of gout, when we hear of someone else suffering we can imagine more clearly what that other person is feeling than can those who have not experienced it.

Russell [15] makes a similar point. 'Sentences heard in narrative are, of course, not necessarily understood in this purely verbal manner; indeed a purely verbal understanding is essentially incomplete. A child reading an exciting adventure story will 'live through' the adventures of the hero. If the hero leaps a chasm, the child's muscles will go taut; if the hero sees a lion about to spring, the child will hold his breath. In adult life, the same result can be produced by good writing'.

Imagination, that bedfellow of memory, also helps understanding by putting right ill-expressed information or something heard imperfectly. It makes mistakes, of course, but it is generally beneficial. Thus when we read the UNESCO statement on 'the elimination of all forms of discrimination' we interpret it to cover only the achievement of equal opportunities for men and women and for people of different races and religions. At least, that is what I hope it means and that it is not intended to ban discriminating between Château Latour and Plonk du Pays. The ability to discriminate between things of quality and those that are trash is one that improves the quality of life and which every good education system seeks to inculcate.

Other examples of our power, through imagination, to correct matters are less serious. Some of my favourites are:

> 'The Department of Agriculture is conducting a sample census of pigs. Persons selected for inclusion have been issued with the appropriate form which. . . .' *Daily Telegraph*.
> 'Police hunt handbag snatcher in stolen car'. *Reigate and Banstead Independent*;
> 'One witness told the commissioners that she had seen sexual intercourse taking place between two parked cars in front of her house'. [16].

Carelessness

Misreading sometimes helps comprehension. We overlook the typos that the patient proofreader has failed to spot. Many will read the following without seeing the error:

I
think
it is quite
possible to find that the
the answer is less than fifty miles

There are dangers of course. Quite often, reading what we expect to see rather than what is actually written, we gain the wrong information. I have seen a notice saying, 'Please walk on the grass', which was painstakingly ignored although it was alongside a path which was under repair.

On the other hand mis-hearing, because the speaker articulates poorly or in a strong accent, or because the listener suffers partial deafness or because his attention is distracted, is an obvious cause of failing to understand information. Even radio has to be careful to avoid announcements being mis-heard. A few years ago the announcement on a regular weekly programme that, 'Now Alfredo Campoli will play . . .' had to be changed to, 'Now Campoli will play . . .' because some listeners thought the announcer had said, 'Now I'm afraid old Campoli will play'.

Pace of communication

Correct pace is a most important aspect in achieving comprehension. We have all, I am sure, suffered from people who speak so quickly that it is difficult to grasp more than a part of what they are saying. On the other hand there are those who speak so slowly and ponderously that one's mind races on to other thoughts. A normal steady rate of speech utters about 140 words per minute. A person of similar level of intelligence, background knowledge and vocabulary to the speaker would have no difficulty in absorbing information at this speed for five minutes or so. However, if the speaker continued at this rate for much longer, the listener would start inserting his own breaks, albeit brief ones, perhaps switching off for a moment to ponder a point made. A good lecturer, speaking for 40 minutes or more, inserts breaks – an anecdote, a picture, a recording etc – to allow the listeners to recharge their attention batteries.

Pace is not just a matter of the number of words per minute. Also important is the number of pieces of information per minute. Many people when speaking insert breaks in every sentence. "Y'know" is a common one, a few years ago 'actually' was fashionable. In some circles, the meaningless insertion of swear words serves a similar purpose. They enable the speaker to keep up mentally with his speed of uttering ideas. They also enable his listeners to keep pace though excessive use can result in loss of attention. A better way of slowing the rate of giving information is to repeat it in different words. As used to be said about the parson's sermon: first he tells you what he's going to say, then he says it, then he tells you what it was he said. A similar practice is followed in News Bulletins: the announcer, then a recording of the original speaker, then a commentator all make exactly the same statement.

Even in writing the pace of giving information has to be judged and ways introduced to ensure, as far as is feasible, that the rate is appropriate for the anticipated readership. Writing which lacks sufficient breaks is described as dense. Varying the length of sentences and of paragraphs has to be supplemented by the insertion of relaxing phrases, judicious repetition and explanations which serve merely to reassure the reader that he has got it right.

The need to break up information and present it in quantities that the recipient can cope with has been well expressed by Zeldin [17]. 'Information has never arrived in convenient chunks, let alone with all its implications spelled out or its contents clearly labelled; so the lorries full of facts driving round our minds have seldom been properly unloaded; only if they break up their cargoes into little packets can they deliver them to a destination where attention will be paid to them'.

First, perhaps, comes assessing how much the client can absorb and remember. The physician ensures that, if failure of memory could be serious, his patient has written instructions for the medicines to be taken. He is fully aware that by the time he gets home a worried patient will have forgotten or garbled part of what he heard. The solicitor carefully translates legal documents and the provisions of Acts of Parliament into terms his client can understand. In Court, counsel will speak in lay terms to the jury but to the judge in the legal language of their profession.

When we watch a child learning to read aloud, going very slowly and struggling with enunciating some of the words, it is obvious that what he is reading means very little to him. On the other hand some people have to enunciate what they are reading in order to understand it. Slow readers may have difficulty understanding fully what they read, often because they are so painstaking that they do not retain much of what they read a few minutes ago. Research [18] suggests that, as far as written information is concerned, the comprehension limit of a substantial minority may well be the snippets, or bite sized packages, one finds in the less demanding popular press, display adverts and short announcements.

Degree of interest

Understanding is much influenced by the degree of interest we have in the topic. This is obvious. If we are interested we will have a determination to grasp the meaning of the information we are being given; if not, the slightest barrier to easy comprehension will result in our 'switching off'. One listens to a boring person telling us all about his holiday without mentally registering a word he says.

The differences in ability to absorb written information will depend not only on verbal intelligence but also the extent to which the recipient is willing to use it. If one is interested in philosophy one will wrestle with difficult sentences; if not, one makes no effort. Even when the subject is interesting initially, a speaker or writer has to work at retaining interest unless the topic is one of vital concern to the recipient. Dialogue is one of the best ways. Discussion has the added advantage that it can reveal lack of understanding and enable the giver of information a chance to clarify what he is saying.

En passant, I cannot help wondering how many readers have read the above section and commented that its author is guilty of most if not all the sins listed.

Information rejection

A different cause of lack of understanding is sheer refusal to accept information, even when it is correct and given in good faith. The cases of those whose beliefs do not admit that the earth is round or that it was created millions of years ago have already been mentioned. More worrying are cases like the following:

• A golfer used to lick his ball to improve its flight. He became ill and was told that it was due to weedkiller used on the golf course and that he must stop licking the ball. However he doubted the diagnosis and on recovery returned to his former practice. He promptly fell ill again.

• Years ago, during a management course I was attending, a case was described of an employee who was summoned into the manager's office and severely reprimanded for the very poor quality of her work. On leaving the office she told colleagues proudly how she had been praised by the manager! He came to hear of this and asked a psychiatrist friend to investigate. It turned out to be not, as one would expect, covering up to avoid her colleagues' scorn but a genuine belief that she had been praised. She firmly believed that her work was good and, therefore, that any comments, no matter how strangely worded must be praise. This is an extreme instance but mental blockage and hearing only what one wants to hear is not uncommon.

The problem arises more often than is realized when communicating with someone of a different culture. A friend told me of an instance when a Chinese visitor, who spoke perfect English, invited him to pay a return visit to the visitor's organization. My friend explained carefully and courteously why he could not accept.

When he finished the visitor said, 'Good, then you will come!' It is possible to speculate on several reasons, among them the possibility of unwillingness to lose face, for the failure to understand that the invitation was being declined, but language difficulty was not one of them.

Other reasons for not accepting new information include doubts about the credibility of the informant. It is sadly commonplace nowadays, to treat any information given by a politician with a large measure of scepticism. The reasons are many: unwillingness to reveal all the facts and factors involved, consequent sudden major change of policy, in a few instances dishonesty to cover up a mistake, political expediency, and so on. An undue emphasis is given because the media need dramatic stories to keep readers interested and this has made matters worse. The result is that though politicians' statements are still heeded, explanations are treated with suspicion and the information, even though added to our mental store, seems to be held as if in a reserve store where it is not allowed to affect our knowledge. The views of some businessmen, who have just given themselves a huge pay rise or sharply reduced the workforce, on matters of business ethics get similar scant attention.

Disbelief can take other forms. Puttnam told [19] the delightful story of a little girl undergoing a test in school.

> 'The pupils had each been given a list of different countries and asked to tick those in which they thought an elephant would be found. Instead of just ticking a couple of names, the little girl wrote firmly at the bottom of her paper, 'This is a silly question. Elephants are much too big and much too clever to get lost in the first place'.

Targetted information

Francis of Sales is reported to have observed that the practice of devotion must differ for the gentleman and the artisan, the servant and the prince, for the widow, young girl or wife. In our context we might equally well feel that the practice of acquiring information has to differ for the teacher, the undergraduate and the 16 year old school-leaver, for those of high IQ and those of lesser mental ability, for those of open mind and those that are prejudiced, for those that are knowledgeable in the topic of discussion and those largely ignorant of it.

Background knowledge or prior preparation can be used to ensure information reaches only the intended audience. Codes are used for this purpose to hide information from an enemy or to avoid the attention of the censor. Parents who break into French to avoid their child understanding are an example. Those who draft patent specifications are another. A patent for an invention is granted in exchange for the disclosure of details of the invention such that others could make it once the monopoly lapsed. In the cases of some complex products, skilled drafting leaves out background know-how and prevents the invention being copied save by a narrow range of other experts.

A well known example in writing is that of job references where a past employer needs to protect himself against claims for damages. He will write a reference in which the text appears to recommend the applicant to a future employer but uses phrases which contain a coded warning. For example, 'Mr. X can be relied on to carry out his instructions to the letter' sounds good but contains a strong hint that Mr. X. does not think or stubbornly resists variations.

Pinker seems to consider the conveying of hidden meaning quite normal [20]. 'It is natural that people exploit the expectations necessary for successful conversation as a way of slipping their real intentions into covert layers of meaning. Human communication is not just a transfer of information like two fax machines connected with a wire; it is a series of alternating displays of behaviour by sensitive, scheming, second-guessing, social animals. When we put words into people's ears we are impinging on them and revealing our own intentions, honorable or not, just as surely as if we were touching them'.

References

1. Zeldin, T. (1994) *An Intimate History of Humanity.* p.252. London: Sinclair-Stevenson

2. Gregory, R.L. (1987) (ed.) *The Oxford Companion to the Mind.* pp.450–454 and other sections. Oxford: Oxford University Press

3. Pinker, S. (1995) *The Language Instinct.* p.81. London: Penguin Books

4. Idem. Ibid. p.227.

5. Gardner, H. (1993) *The Unschooled Mind. How children think and how schools should teach.* pp.11–12. London: Fontana Press

6. Pinker, S. Ibid. [The subject of Mentalese occupies his chapter 3, pp.55–82]

7. Russell, B. (1962) *An Inquiry into Meaning and Truth.* p.21. Harmondsworth: Pelican Books

8. Stone, L. (1992) *History and Post-Modernism II. Past and Present,* **135** (May), 189. Quoted by R.J. Evans (1997) *In Defence of History.* London: Granta Books

9. Zeldin, T. Ibid. p.440.

10. Atkins, P. (1994) *Creation Revisited: the origin of space, time and the universe.* p.3. London: Penguin

11. Hawkins, S. (1988) *A Brief History of Time.* London: Guild Publishing

    [This book is a very lucid account, though most non-scientists may find one or two short passages difficult]

12. Feynman, R.P. (1992) *The Character of Physical Law.* London: Penguin

    [Feynman is a very clear lecturer but even so most new-comers to physics will find parts of chapter 3, for example, hard going]

13. Warnock, M. (1994) *Imagination and Time.* p.170. Oxford: Blackwell

14. Zeldin, T. ibid. pp.440–441.

15. Russell, B. (1948) *Human Knowledge – Its scope and limits.* p.112. London: George Allen & Unwin

16. Pinker, S. ibid. p.109.

17. Zeldin, T. ibid. p.440.

18. HMSO (1996) *Social Trends 1995*. London: HMSO

19. Puttnam, D. (1996) Information in the living society. *RSA Journal*, 5472, 37

20. Pinker, S. ibid. p.229–230.

CHAPTER FIVE
Communicating

Our incredible capacity to communicate is one of, perhaps the, most important features of human beings. Social life depends on it; huge industries have been built to further it; at work greater and greater importance is being attached to communication skills. Over the centuries we have found more and more effective ways to communicate, especially over long distances and across time barriers. At the same time we have been refining our skills and revising and increasing the codes (words and sentences) we use in order to cope with new and increasing demands. There is much more to communicate and time pressures have had their effect.

A major source of interest is, of course, the impact of the new ICTs. However, we should firstly consider some of the factors which underlie any communication process, whether face to face speech or remote high-tech.

The five basic factors are:

- what is to be communicated?
- for what purpose?
- from whom and to whom?
- by what medium?
- in what circumstances?

Those that get involved when there is an element of social interaction have been usefully categorized by the Vickerys [1].

Obviously the nature of the information to be communicated affects the way it is transmitted. The announcement of a person's death is not dealt with in the somewhat jokey way one describes one's efforts on the golf course. The Tax Office request for information about your income last year is very different from a friend's request for information about growing cucumbers.

Its purpose also affects the way the information is communicated. Danger to shipping may be communicated by the presence of a lighthouse, an entertainment to which the public are to be attracted by an announcement in a newspaper. Information is communicated very differently in an educational textbook from that in an advertisement.

The impact of comprehensibility, or lack of it, on communication was highlighted in the last chapter but there are other personal aspects. In the case of person-to-person transfer the style of speech used will depend on whether those involved are strangers, regular colleagues or close friends. Much too will depend on the roles of those participating: are they transmitter, channel or recipient; is the flow one way only or are they exchanging information? What is the age, sex, nationality, native language, intellectual type and level, educational standard, occupation, status in workplace and position in society of each? The act of communication will differ very much according to whether the participants have characteristics in common or whether they differ. Parents talk differently to their children from the way they do to each other. Children talk differently to each other from the way they do to a teacher.

A high proportion of the information one receives comes from those one knows well, members of the family, friends and neighbours, local traders and those one works with. A relaxed informal style will normally be adopted, quite different from the more formal style used when negotiating with strangers. Different again is the style adopted when talking with those to whose views one is opposed.

It is not only the words used that are important but also the way in which they are spoken. Obviously meaning is affected by the stress or emphasis given but also by less obvious factors. One's social group is revealed by the inclusion or exclusion of fashionable or unfashionable words as well as by the manner of pronunciation. Body language adds much to the information one is giving. The classic example is the depth of the Japanese bow. Another is whether enthusiasm or indifference is displayed. Most body language is much subtler than these examples but is very informative to those who are receptive to the signs. There are, however, dangers in deliberately using body signs to foreigners [2]. A nod means 'yes' in Western Europe but not in the Balkans or parts of the Middle East.

Although the flow of information is from the haves to the have-nots, this does not mean that it is always from someone of higher status to one of lower. The junior employee has to inform the managing director, the child a parent, the Civil Service Principal the Minister. The way information is presented in these situations will differ markedly from how it would be if the flow were in the opposite direction.

An important aspect is whether the information transfer is being made directly person-to-person or via some impersonal medium such as the Internet, book, newspaper, broadcast etc. Communicating to a large audience or to a readership one never sees, and which will include a variety of people of different backgrounds, tastes, education and knowledge, calls for a very different style of speaking or writing from that used when one is giving information to a person one knows. One's style of writing depends on whether one is writing a textbook or the answer to an examination question, putting a message on the Internet or drafting a paper for publication in a learned journal.

The occasion for the communication influences the transfer. Owning up to some peccadillo calls for a different style from giving a helpful briefing. Is the information required to help further some project? Is it needed urgently, so that even partial information supplied quickly is of more value than complete information in a week's time, or is speed of response of less importance than thoroughness?

What are the physical circumstances? Is communication taking place in a private office, in a meeting room with several participants or in a lecture theatre or at a public gathering? It is well known that some people can express themselves more effectively in a large public gathering than they can in an office; others are quite the reverse. Some of those who can communicate well on paper experience great difficulty putting across information at a *viva voce* examination. Communication between people by e-mail, by letter, or orally by telephone is so different that the way the information is expressed and the fluency of the transmission differ markedly between the three media. Quality can also be affected. Someone who is pedantic when writing may express himself quite sloppily when speaking on the telephone.

The physical medium and the nature and purpose of the communication affect the way information is expressed. The way we write and the way we speak differ enormously, even allowing for the fact that each differs according to circumstance. In the case of writing – letters, office minutes, reports, legal documents, briefings for a decision, entries in a diary – each calls for a different style of expression. So too does broadcasting by radio as compared with television or encouraging mail order by Web site as contrasted with printed catalogue.

The impact of communication technologies on information

There are many who feel that this is the Communication Age rather than an Information Age. They could be right. We have nowadays so many technologies at our disposal to enable us to communicate information, each of which has its merits for particular situations and drawbacks in others. Has the information any value to posterity or is it merely of significance only to the immediate recipient? Can it just be sent or is a quick response required? The new technologies have expanded the extent to which we communicate information in terms both of the frequency and of the distances over which we can do so. In general the technologies have been more enabling than compelling but there are now exceptions to this. There is a growing reluctance in some circles to accept letters other than by fax or e-mail. Manufacturing companies which have set up automatic (just-in-time) ordering systems will deal only with suppliers who have compatible systems. Organizations with intranet systems are reluctant to allow staff to send paper copy memoranda.

An ad-hoc survey at an Institute of Information Scientists meeting in February 1998 revealed that 60 members had booked a place by e-mail, four or five had used fax, two had phoned, but none had used the post. It seems from this and other enquiries, that, where it is possible, e-mail is often the preferred channel for communication.

Although at present it is the Internet which is the centre of public attention, among international and multi-site organizations just as much attention, sometimes more, is being given to in-house networks or intranets.

There is no doubt that each new technology has altered the frequency, extent and way we communicate, including the way we express ourselves. It is probably most pronounced in its impact on social communication but business communication has changed too, becoming very much more terse. The presence of a telephone in the homes of each of our friends has resulted in its use for expressing one's appreciation for a party or a present. Before the spread of the telephone, a 'thank you' letter was *de rigeur*.

The telegram service provided scope for the quick communication of brief messages for which the telephone was not really appropriate or not available. Without it, would Noel Coward have sent such a stream of witty messages across the Atlantic to Gertrude Lawrence or we have known of them? A by-product of the method of charging for a telegram was the development of a very abbreviated style of writing known as telegraphese. Typing one's own e-mail rather than dictating to a secretary may have a similar effect, particularly as abbreviating where possible, e.g. using acronyms, is quite standard already.

It could be argued that the first significant communication technologies were the instruments for writing, first the stone chisel and then, more usefully, pen and ink and crayon. It is difficult to imagine what the world would be like had writing not been invented. The only transmission of information would have been by speech, by picture, by artefact or by scent and touch. The transmission of ideas and information from one generation to the next or between distant countries would have been seriously impeded. The teachings of the Bible and the Koran, and the works of Plato and Aristotle, would have come down by oral tradition but probably in considerably degraded form (though Homer's verses seem to have been transmitted more or less intact). Galileo might still have gazed through his telescope and Newton have propounded the laws of gravity but would we have known? Only when recording machines were invented would we have had a permanent record of verbal information. However, since accurate information, which is essential for progress in the natural sciences and technologies, would not have been disseminated widely by oral means, progress would have been very, very much slower. Our standard of living would probably still have been about that of the Middle Ages. It is fortunate that writing was invented and the many improvements in the means of disseminating written texts, from printing to computer network, have been focal to progress.

Increases in the pace of life, or rather in the amount of activity we try to cram into the time available, have led to a decrease in the fullness of information which we send by personal letter. Technology, in the form of the telephone, has reduced the need to write letters although the fax machine and now e-mail will lead to a new balance being established between writing and tele-phoning. In many cases the telephone has an advantage for information transfer in that it permits instantaneous dialogue.

Curiously there seems to be little enthusiasm for a video-phone although the technology exists and might become reasonably cheap if the demand were to increase. The potential advantage of the video-phone is, of course, that body language can be brought into play just as it is in face-to-face conversations. The video-conference has gained adherents in some large institutions and a few smaller ones, particularly those wishing to reduce their travel budgets. British Telecom has reported that the demand is growing. At the time of writing a query has arisen [3] over whether a Board meeting held by videoconferencing is legally quorate if all the participants are in different places. It is going to be very interesting to see how these two technologies develop in the future. One problem with both is the self-consciousness that many people feel when faced (literally in these cases) with a new technical gadget. It was a long time for many people before they became sufficiently at ease with the telephone to be able to talk naturally. Many still find it difficult to talk naturally to a computerized answering service.

Although magnetic tape was invented in 1942, it was the 1970s before, thanks to aggressive Japanese marketing, personal tape recorders and portable tape players became commonplace house-hold accessories. However, their main use was recording and playing music, and their use for communication was largely confined to business, especially sending dictation back to one's secretary or to a typing pool. Nevertheless, for a while tapes of oral messages were sent by some people to relatives or for other specialized purposes. In these it was noticeable that the sender took care to speak with a greater degree of grammatical accuracy than was the case in his normal speech.

The typewriter, a technology long used purely for business which made letters easier to read and which produced a copy or two simultaneously, had little impact on letters other than, perhaps, to increase the number of them. It did improve information storage, leading to the huge filing systems which used to be a feature of many businesses and were the beginning of information management. Computerized storage of records came just in time

to prevent many organizations facing the choice of being over-
whelmed by paper and microfilm copies of paper or having huge
bonfires. For a long time a typewritten letter was socially unacceptable though this was relaxed in the 1960s provided that the
'Dear John' and 'Yours sincerely' were hand written. However, it
is only with the widespread possession of personal computers with
word-processing capacity that typewritten personal letters have
become acceptable. This has been due also to the fact that owners
of a PC have usually acquired keyboard skills so that they themselves not a secretary actually produce the letter.

The telecommunication age can be said to have started with
the electric telegraph, invented in 1833 by Gauss and Weber and
developed into a very effective system of communication by Morse
who, with Bain, devised the Morse code to enable verbal communication to take place by a code of long and short sounds. This
code remained in use until quite recently, especially in circumstances where the quality of radio transmissions was poor, as for
example from ships at sea. The crucial need for unambiguous
transmission in times of distress was met by the well-known
SOS signal $\cdots--\cdots$.

Allied, as it has been with a keyboard for input and a printer
for output, the telegraph system remains in use as a means of
conveying information from news agencies to a wide range of organizations. A short-lived development was the Telex system. In
all these telegraph systems, because of their tedious slowness,
messages tend to be as short as possible, though rarely, if ever,
reduced to the same extent as in telegrams. Modern high speed
networks have killed the Telex system. E-mail is really the modern
equivalent.

The telephone, which eventually removed most of the need for
the telegraph, was invented by Graham Bell in 1876. The next great
invention, as far as communicating is concerned, was the Wireless
Telegraph, invented by Marconi in 1895, and which soon developed
into what we now know as radio.

Radio had a remarkable impact on the way information was
communicated. Like the telegraph and telephone it transmitted its
message virtually instantaneously. Thus, as ownership of radio sets
(receivers) became common and the technique of outside broadcasts established, people for the first time experienced receiving an
account of an event as it was happening. They also heard the voices
of the people, politicians and other celebrities, who were actually
making the news and heard their opinions direct.

Standards and variants

At the same time, radio had an impact on speech itself. For many years in the UK at least, the BBC was the arbiter of correctly spoken English. Announcers were trained to enunciate in a standard way. Except for individuals, such as J.B. Priestley, who had achieved sufficient eminence to be allowed to broadcast as themselves, dialects and accents were heard only in plays or among comedians. Only in the 1940s did this change when the popular Wilfrid Pickles was allowed to make announcements in his natural Yorkshire accent. Even today, the BBC is still looked upon as giving an acceptable standard way of pronouncing words and complaints arise when there is too frequent departure from what purists regard as the correct way. For the pronunciation of personal names, which the BBC usually checks with the owner of the name, the announcers are taken as models of correctness.

Printing established the written English of the East Midlands as a standard. The BBC built on this and established an Oxbridge speech, shorn of its occasional eccentricities, as the oral equivalent. The merit of both was an improvement in the clarity of communication. If there is to be unambiguous communication of information, there should be as nearly as possible a language, written and spoken, which means the same thing to speaker and listener, writer and reader. As we have seen earlier, this is often not achieved but that is no reason for not trying.

Other standards are also necessary to facilitate communication. Computers must have compatible software. For producing printed material in electronic form the Standard Generalized Mark-up Language (SGML), or similar standard, is needed. To correct proofs for printers there is a standard set of correction marks, and so on. There are two drawbacks to standards. The first is that rigid adherence to them can inhibit development. One almost humorous consequence of the incompatibility of standards and progress has been the fact that by the time international bodies have agreed standards in the ICT sector, new developments have rendered them obsolete. Market dominance has often been more effective. It used to be said of computers 'the standard is IBM'.

The other drawback is that standards can drive out long existing beneficial variants. Language is the obvious example. The universal use of English as a standard for communication is resulting in the demise of some minor languages. If, taking a global view, one believes that the purpose of language is to be able communicate with everyone else, then such a change may be no bad thing. After all, those who find themselves having difficulty expressing what they want to say in English will not live for ever and their children will grow up fluent in the universal language. Research has found [4] that Vietnamese orphans brought up in England talk English, not Vietnamese, without so much as a hint of Vietnamese in their English.

On the other hand, language is intimately linked to culture and the loss of a language will result in a reduction in cultural diversity which organizations like UNESCO are devoted to preserving. As is well known, exact translation from one language to another is not possible. There are the subtle differences of meaning which become lost in translation. However, the language differences between the various English speaking countries, the persistence of local accents and dialects, and the speed with which new words and expressions are coined, suggest that even if more languages do die out, the influence of the Tower of Babel is still with us and new languages will eventually take their place.

Nevertheless, a common language links people into a community which has considerable information sharing powers. At the moment the pressures of communication technologies are all directed towards uniformity, especially within communicating groups. Airline pilots and air traffic controllers must have a single language. The ability to establish discussion groups on the Internet increases the need for a single language within each group.

Most information products and services are in English, the majority of them in American English. The dominance of Hollywood in the film industry started some years ago to change the content of English as used in England. Pressure to conform to American practice continues with the result that generally, when they differ, most English people can understand American expressions; many Americans cannot understand the equivalent English ones.

Naturally, this one way pressure is meeting resistance. Few people like being obliged to learn another language for everyday life. But if it is necessary, as it is, to communicate globally without having to learn a large number of languages, a universal *lingua franca* as a second language is essential.

Channels and Networks

Another ubiquitous communication technology which increases the pressure towards a single language of communication is Television.

Nowadays, TV programmes can be beamed directly via satellite to other countries; the only barrier is not having a set tuned to receive each available channel. In the UK, for example, most people still have sets which will accept only the five terrestrial channels though increasing numbers are gaining access to satellite and cable channels.

Radio has long provided not only news broadcasts but many other types of informative programme (5). Currently in the UK the BBC Radio 4 provides a wide range of such programmes, a day chosen at random containing some on history, politics, geography, medical research, a discussion on interpreting music, science, information for 'visually-impaired people' and arts news. On television, channels 2 and 4 provide a wide range of informative programmes as well as those which are purely entertainment.

Cable and satellite TV contain channels which are devoted exclusively to one type of information or another. Thus there are National Geographic, Discovery and History channels. On both radio and satellite TV there are channels which broadcast news all day long. Commercial broadcasting, for so long forbidden in the UK, also carries advertisements, indeed depends on them for revenue, and thus also carries information about products from corn cures to motor cars, though, as with virtually all advertisements, the information component is usually scanty.

With most broadcasting, radio or TV, there is the drawback, from the point of view of seeking information, that one can acquire it only when it is broadcast. We learn from broadcasts rather than use them to supply us with information when we want it. However, the tape-recorder and the video-recorder have gone some way to meeting the problem, though not the whole way. By recording a programme one can keep the tape of it and play it when one wishes. However, it is not yet common to build up an information store this way.

The ability to record has, however, led to overnight broadcasting of instructional programmes such as those of the Open University. One can build up from them, and by buying tapes and CD-ROMs of an instructional character, a collection of audio-visual textbooks. There are dictionaries and encyclopaedias on CD-ROM which are likely to be referred to frequently as and when information is required. Their impact is to enable us to search information much more readily and extensively than we could using printed dictionaries and encyclopaedias.

The TV set has enabled a Videotex information service to be developed, well-known forms being CEEFAX and ORACLE in the UK and MINITEL in France. In these services one can choose from a menu of information services, which range from weather forecasts and the latest news to information about a large number of events and even items for sale including houses and motor cars. Though one obtains only current information, one can access it when one wishes rather than having to tune in at a particular time. So far Videotex has not proved as popular as was hoped. It must be probable that as more and more homes and offices gain access to the World Wide Web the use of it will decrease.

The photocopying machine, that took the world by storm in the 1950s and 60s, is a technology that has been invaluable for information transfer. No need to copy out a text or to paraphrase it, the whole original can be copied – subject only to legal and size limitations – and filed or used to send to someone needing the information it contains. It has been misused, of course, by those wishing to avoid buying a publication and it has also resulted in a measure of laziness, a copy being sent to a client rather than a carefully drafted report tailored to the client's needs. At least, though, the client receives the original verbatim without unintentional misinterpretation while the addition of photocopies of original documents as appendices to a report is normally wholly commendable, provided copyright requirements are observed.

Fax has been around longer than many realize. Newspapers were using it to send copies of pages to and from provincial offices in the 1960s. By the end of that decade CIRIA, the Construction Industry Research and Information Association, had set up a network via the telephone system for moving messages and photocopies to several centres. But the technology was slow catching on. As with so many new technologies there has to be agreement between manufacturers of the equipment to conform to a standard so that the machines of different makes can talk to each other. Then sales have to reach a critical mass. Unless there are enough organizations with whom you wish to communicate with the equipment there is no point your having a machine. Now that most organizations and many private individuals have fax machines, its use is commonplace.

The advantage of fax is that not only a complete letter but also diagrams and pictures can be transmitted. Over voice quality telephone lines using Group 4 fax machines, the quality of pictures is poor but adequate for many purposes. Good quality transmission can be obtained by using Group 3 machines over wideband cable where this possibility exists. Fax drove out telex and itself faces competition from e-mail. But the ability to send a hasty handwritten note, a photocopy or a diagram with an explanatory comment is a factor which favours a continuing role for fax as does the fact that so many places can receive it. It has certainly improved our ability to communicate information in detail very quickly to any part of the world. As with e-mail, one does not have to worry about time zones; the fax can arrive during the night and be answered next morning. Central libraries, like the British Library Document Supply Centre, can supply photocopies of articles by fax to meet urgent demands from business.

Communicating with remote computers over the telephone system has been happening since the 1960s. Online searching of computer held databases really took off in the USA, replacing batch searches of databases. In Europe online systems arrived a little later, Britain being in the vanguard. Important factors were that the big abstracting journals, like *Chemical Abstracts* and *Medlars*, were being computer typeset, that they were becoming too expensive for all but big libraries to hold, that they were uncomfortably bulky for extensive searching, and that suitable software became available for preparing a search programme.

So familiar had searchers become with the techniques of online searching that, when the Internet became available, a large body of potential users already existed. Another group was familiar with using personal computers and merely needed to obtain a modem to link into the networks. All that and the immense sense of freedom to be able to communicate anything one wanted to anyone else who was 'on the Net' and took the trouble to view or download it resulted in the number of users growing at an astronomical rate.

Access is still via a keyboard but that has proved no problem, for most people quickly acquire typing skill and many think on to a screen. Probably the greatest impact on the way information is communicated on the Internet has been brought about by computer graphics. There has been an enormous growth in graphic and pictorial material thereby increasing the range and clarity of information which can be transmitted.

In principle, personal communication over the Internet is putting an open letter and/or pictures into a network where it can be read by anyone who knows the sender's address or happens to find its site. Of course, messages can be specifically targetted to particular addresses via e-mail or access can be restricted to specific viewers. Otherwise, one can search to find sites likely to contain needed information by using keywords which define the subject. However, there is now so much material on the Internet that the number of hits is likely to be enormous for all but the most recondite words or combination of words.

Group discussion has been greatly aided by the World Wide Web. Those likely to be able to make a worthwhile contribution to a topic are sent the address of the Web site so that they can read what is there and then add their own information or opinions. It is a development of the Bulletin Board where one posts news and requests for information allied with the old concept of the Invisible College.

Nevertheless, some groups of scientists are establishing electronic archives of shortened versions of papers that they have submitted for publication in the usual way. These archives can be accessed ('visited' in the Web jargon) even before the paper is published, thus reducing delay, and also even after publication without the labour of getting a copy from a library. Indeed, The World Wide Web had its origin in the needs of nuclear and high-energy physicists for these archives. It has become a set of sites, owned by identifiable organizations and a few individuals, on which also can be found promotional material, publications and news type information. Some of the information provided by these sources is available only to subscribers who, after payment, are provided with IDs and passwords or 'keys' to the encryption used to prevent unauthorized access and/or downloading.

Newspapers and magazines, directories, data compilations such as lists of share prices, government publications and much else is available through the Internet from Web and other sites. It is far too early to do more than guess what the eventual effect on print-on-paper publishing will be. One suspects that in due course the type of reference information which needs to be kept up-to-date will be available only via electronic channels but possibly of more than one type, i.e. not just the Internet but perhaps some modern version of videotex on the TV as well. Some compilations of information are available only through the Internet. An example is the directory of insurance law referred to elsewhere. It would not have been published and kept up-to-date, as is crucial, were it not for the existence of the Internet.

The Web is also being used for trading despite anxieties about the security and integrity of information. The well publicized activities of hackers, though illegal, have created an atmosphere of distrust. There is also the risk that with only a Web site address one may find one is dealing, especially in the financial sector, with a fly-by-night company. In this respect as in many others, the Internet is highly suspect as an information source and the only guide to quality is probably the reputation of the institution which has posted the information. There is no refereeing of most that is there.

Many large organizations have established intranet systems, i.e. networks that are accessible only to members of the organization. This principle has been extended to establishing such closed networks to groups of organizations like banks which need a high degree of security in their transactions.

Although the Internet has generated among its adherents a jargon of their own, and it has become a major channel of communication among those who have ready access to it, it does not so far seem to have had a wider influence on communicating. The growing use of pictures and graphics to convey information simply continues the trend that TV and optical discs had started. It is, however, for most people still very new. We can expect that it will change generally the way most people communicate and will cause a revision to the extent to which the other channels are used.

We can summarize by saying that we are arriving at the situation that all of us (except the very poor) in the industrialized countries can communicate with other individuals irrespective of place and irrespective of time. We have a range of technologies at our disposal and can choose the one that best suits the persons, the information and the circumstances. Domestic use of new technology is growing. Interactive communication is growing – soon TV sets will have this facility added – but, according to reports, communication orally within the home over the dinner table is decreasing. There are other signs, referred to elsewhere in this book, that many of us prefer to communicate via a technological medium rather than talking face-to-face.

The balance of ways of expressing ourselves, especially between written, audible and visual means, is changing. The context in which information is placed is changing. Puttnam, for example, has drawn attention [6] to the way news and entertainment are becoming indistinguishable. News is being presented in a manner more and more akin to entertainment.

Government can now communicate decisions and information to the people very quickly. Businessmen can use the ICTs to have up-to-the-minute data and information on which to make decisions. They can make contact with employees wherever they are. Those working at home can feed information into and draw from databases at their offices. In the education sector teachers can draw illustrative material and even ready-made lessons from remote databases and pupils can learn databases at home.

Overall, the principal impact of advances in communication has been to increase the pace of life. No longer can one relax and wait for a reply. The pressure to get on with work is greatly increased by the capabilities we now have for communicating.

One last thought. In the past the development and adoption of new technologies has been fastest in time of war, when cost considerations have been ignored. Even now this still happens. Pale *et al* [7] recounts how Croatia installed modern high-speed communications to facilitate winning the war with Serbia and Bosnia. Generally, though, new technologies evolve in times of peace, when the principal requirement is that they shall 'pay their way'. Probably it is the immense amount of risk capital that multinational companies have and an acceptance that new products are essential to keep up with or ahead of their competitors, that have led to the development of new ICTs being as fast now as it was in time of war.

References

1.   Vickery, B.C. and Vickery, A. (1987) *Information Science in Theory and Practice.* p.44. London: Butterworths

2.   Axtell, R.E. (1998) *Gestures: the Dos and Taboos of Body Language around the World.* Chichester: Wiley

3.   Report in the *Daily Telegraph*, 9 September 1997

4.   Pateman, T. (1987) *Language in mind and language in society. Studies in linguistic reproduction,* p.46. Oxford: Clarendon Press

5.   Briggs, A. (1995) *History of Broadcasting in the United Kingdom,* Vols. I–V. Oxford: Oxford University Press.

6.   Puttnam, D. (1996) Citizens of the Information Society. *Journal of Information Science*, **22**(1), 2

7.   Pale, P. et al (1998) From nothing to the leading edge information infrastructure: the Croatian model. In *International Federation for Information and Documentation. Globalization of Information*. The Hague: FID pp.183–189.

CHAPTER SIX

Some aspects of information, knowledge and document management

Information management

For several years now the crucial importance of managing one's information and knowledge resources and services has been accepted as part of business life by many advanced companies and other organizations and institutions. In the UK, this is due in no small measure to ASLIB, the Association for Information Management, which has been successfully promoting the benefits of more effective management and exploitation of information since the 1960s. It has been emphasizing that just having a special library is only a first step and that progressive organizations need to go much further to provide for all their information needs and activities and to see them as a whole. The KPMG Impact Study [1], published in 1995 under the guidance of the Hawley Committee, has brought home to most companies that the Board needs to have an articulated policy towards the use and management of its information resources.This includes both those resources it has and those it needs to acquire, those it will use internally and those it will disseminate to outside stakeholders – suppliers, customers, shareholders, officials and the public. Organizations as complex as the NHS are finding this a very substantial activity but, even in the preparative stages, a very rewarding one [2].

Until about 1960, commercial and industrial companies regarded having a library as all that was necessary by way of managing information. The handling of in-house paperwork was the job of filing clerks usually with each department keeping its own files. Gradually the libraries (categorized as Special Libraries to distinguish them from National, Public and Academic ones) began to acquire more complex information tasks such as preparing reports based on information acquired from a range of in-house and external sources. Since then, as a result of the great importance given to maximizing the exploitation of information from all suitable sources, not just books and journals, the situation has changed. Though a few firms still have only a library, in most instances the library if it still exists at all, is a part, often only a small part, of the information management (IM) unit.

Like information, IM means different things to different people and institutions. It is, of course, quite different from people management which Drucker [3] has described as 'passing information up and orders down'. Martin's simple definition [4] 'management of the information resources of an organization in pursuit of its aims and objectives' is as good as any other but leaves it to us to spell out the details of what is involved.

Best [5] distinguishes two situations. The first arises 'when information is the raw material and subject of the process, for example social security or credit card activity, investment activity or research grant funding'. The second arises when 'information facilitates the process by way of allowing control, monitoring or oversight as occurs in accounting systems or manufacturing operations'. He regards the distinction as crucial for IM because in the second case 'the underlying process could be carried out without the information, albeit at a much reduced level of efficiency, economy and performance'. Marchand [6] makes much the same distinction. He calls the two categories 'management of information' and 'management with information'.

Certainly what is done in the name of IM varies enormously from one institution to another. For example, managing information in a public library [7] is very different from managing the information resources in an international solicitor's company [8] even though in both there is still a substantial emphasis on printed material. In a large store such as a supermarket where stock control and financial records are crucial, in a social service like the Citizens' Advice Bureaux [9] in which the aim is to match information to an individual with problems or in a high-tech firm like Advanced Risk Machines [10] where virtually all work is on computers, IM is different in each case.

Marchand [6] distinguishes between IT (information technology), meaning the technology infrastructure of an institution from desktops and servers to networks, IS (information services), meaning applications and database software which perform business functions and support key processes and IM, which is concerned with the information necessary for running the business, including supporting key processes, functions and decisions. For the purposes of his paper, which were to identify the ways in which information could be used to create business value, the separation was useful. However, in practice IM should integrate all these aspects in order to maximize the organization's intelligence system.

Enser [11], looking at IM from the point of view of the Head of a School of Information Management, emphasizes the importance of the linkage between IS, IT and IM. 'The digital integration of audio, visual, textual and communications resources links technical, creative and conceptual issues. The first of these involves the design and implementation of human–computer interfaces, and databases hospitable to a wide range of data type and interactive processing environments, whilst the second is engaged by the generation of original material in a variety of media, including electronic formulations employing computer graphics and animation. The last component is concerned with the organization and exploitation of information records in the generation of multimedia products, and the creation of dynamic information structures as the result of user interaction with such products'. (To avoid conflict with the earlier conclusion that knowledge is personal, I have changed the word knowledge to information).

In offices and laboratories documents are created on terminals connected to the computer network. In shops and warehouses stock and sales data are fed to the computer system. Representatives abroad produce their reports on laptops linked back via telecommunications line to the company network. All this information and that derived from other sources, both electronic and paper, have to be co-ordinated so that information can be put to use for Executive Decision Support Systems, for activating just-in-time ordering, for activating currency transactions or merely for generating letters. The degree to which integration can be achieved or even attempted varies from one organization to another and depends on the nature and form of the information to be handled as well as the purposes to which it is to be put.

IM involves the following core responsibilities and tasks:

1. ensuring that each member of the organization has access to the information he needs when he needs it;
2. setting up systems for storing, organizing and retrieving internally generated documents and reports;
3. selecting, acquiring and storing appropriate published material in all or any of the formats described earlier;
4. arranging access to online sources and Web sites and to conventional sources of documents especially the British Library's Document Supply Centre;
5. storing in-house information such as technical and intelligence reports. Some storage may be in paper copy but more and more will be on the computer system. Storage involves preparing means of retrieval when required, either by the enquirer at a terminal or by traditional supply of paper copy. It also involves organizing different levels of access so that confidential information, e.g. staff records, is accessible only by those authorised to have access;
6. disseminating new information to those needing to be aware;
7. ensuring that members of the organization can communicate easily with each other, e.g. by establishing an intranet, and subject to appropriate security, the Internet;
8. including in the communications systems access to the company system by staff out in the field or working from home;
9. managing computer-to-computer communication with outside suppliers and customers such as just-in-time ordering systems;
10. providing a source of expertise on limitations, restrictions and requirements regarding the use of information such as data protection legislation, copyright law, etc. and having such expertise for all countries in which the organization operates;
11. discarding no longer needed information or up-dating existing material; ensuring quality control of the company's information resources and systems.

The way all this is undertaken will vary considerably from one organization to another. It may be co-ordinated in one department, or it may be carefully divided between two or three. Often the hardware and software aspects are handled separately from the information content aspects. This can cause serious problems unless there is good co-ordination somewhere below Board level. The development of the policies and strategies to be pursued and the relations of the IM operation with such normally separate activities such as dealing with the media and dissemination of information to shareholders, officials and the public should all be determined at Board level [1].

Knowledge management

Knowledge management has suddenly become very fashionable. Courses on it are being run. Responsible authorities refer to its importance. Sometimes, however, it seems that the term is simply being used as a synonym for information management to make it sound more posh. A definition quoted by Kalseth [12] describes it as 'a discipline that promotes an integrated approach to identifying, managing and sharing all of an enterprise's information assets'. He himself says 'it is about being capable of using the information resources available within and outside the organization'.

Nevertheless, I think that there is an emphasis within knowledge management that makes it worthy of its title – that of being aware of the level of expertise and know-how which resides in members of staff and outside contacts and trying to make best use of it [13]. Knowledge, as illustrated earlier, resides in a person's mind. Any attempt to record it can never encompass the whole richness of it, only those pieces of information that are considered crucial blended together with theories, suppositions, informed guesses and proposals.

Many enterprises that have down-sized in order to cut costs, especially those that have shed middle-level staff, have found that they have lost a great deal of information which was stored in the individual. Executives often know a great deal about how customers need to be treated, what they think about products and services and even how they are using the products. Customers become used to dealing with a particular company representative who knows what they need without lots of time-consuming explanation. When the representative leaves, so may the customer. Ideas for new products and services spring from the executives' experience, not from the computer systems which have replaced them. Within the firm, the efficiency of operations is often greatly improved by the usually unrecognised help of the 'gatekeeper', a term coined many years ago by Tom Allen for the people who give of their knowledge, especially experience, to help workmates resolve their difficulties.

Knowledge management

- tries to ensure that a company retains as much as possible of every employee's knowledge when he or she leaves;
- tries to encourage employees to share their knowledge;
- tries to encourage staff to increase their knowledge.

In the event the enterprise will require more detailed reporting. It will set up a directory of staff, supplier and customer expertise and personal quirks. It will encourage staff to communicate within and without the company and to keep notes of discussions: in old-fashioned terms to establish invisible colleges.

All this should, of course, be linked in with the information management system, otherwise the expertise and knowledge of those who run it may be lost. In addition to keeping the company's information base at a high level, it is anticipated that knowledge management will help increase, or at least retain, customer loyalty.

Records of information

Preserving as much as is feasible of the knowledge and know-how of staff who leave is not the only reason for recording information. Nor is it only that memories are fallible; there are a great many reasons.

Recording information has the obvious advantage that it can be made available to people distant in space and/or time from the original record. An advantage of using recorded information rather than consulting a colleague is that we can choose how much we use and avoid any superfluous material. If we ask a friend for some specific information, we may also have to listen to an account of how he successfully played the third hole yesterday at his golf club. However, we may lose some additional useful information or the opportunity to clarify matters by asking questions.

The invention of writing was as important, if not more so, than that of the wheel. A goodly proportion of the information we receive is from written sources of which the range of physical forms is very considerable. These include the handwritten letter sent by post or the typed e-mail message; the printed monograph or the CD-ROM; the journal article or a Web site. However, writing is not the only way of recording information. The tracker going through the jungle blazes his trail in order to leave information about his route. The layout of an area is recorded as a map. The results of experiments are often expressed as graphs. Engineers often describe their inventions with drawings. Spoken information can be recorded on audiotape.

Originally, permanent records of information could be made only on cave walls or cliffs, on stone, wood or papyrus. Paper came later. When deciphered much of the writing found on ancient stone tablets from Assyrian or Egyptian times turned out to be information including laws and business records. That writing on stone, laborious though carving hieroglyphics and letters must have been, was important in the life of those times is illustrated not only by the amount that has survived but also by the nature of some of it.

Writing as a medium for communication grew when papyrus came into use. Surviving material includes letters, religious texts, precepts for good secular behaviour and literary compositions. In colder climates vellum was used, though this was mainly for religious texts because writing skills were largely confined to scribes who worked in the great monasteries. Nevertheless, some domestic records of those monasteries were kept and there is some information too of farming practices and the way people lived.

Two inventions dramatically changed the ability to record and disseminate information: paper and printing. Even before the advent in the West of printing, technical treatises such as Pliny's Natural History and Ptolemy's Geography were well known and studied by scholars – most people could not read – but, since each copy had to be hand-made only a few copies existed, especially of secular books. Lord Dainton [14] relates how it took four and a half centuries for an Arabic manuscript on optics to come to the attention of a European artist and bring the concept of perspective into Italian art.

Widespread study was possible only after the invention of printing in 1450 (earlier in the Far East) enabled multiple copies to be produced. Although at first the majority of books were still either religious or classical texts, the number which were primarily informative in content gradually increased until nowadays there is an enormous number of such books: monographs, textbooks, dictionaries, directories, encyclopaedias etc. Nor are only books produced: magazines and maps, reports and sheet music, patents and posters are exemplars of the range of other printed material.

It is not too sweeping to claim that books have done more than anything else to advance human culture. The eminent American scholar, Daniel Boorstin, regarded information as of short-term interest only, but scholarship, as expressed in books, he deemed to be of permanent value. Even he would agree, I am sure, that many books are of short-term interest only, though he would not go as far as Hutchinson and Adler [15] who claimed that 'knowledge in its entirety consists of a few great books'.

The ability to publish many copies of books led to the spread of learning. This increased the amount of new information being discovered which in turn led to more pressure to publish more books and, since printing by metal type and mechanical presses was slow, to the introduction of new forms of publication. Scientists led the way in developing journals and magazines with the *Journal des Scavants* and *Philosophical Transactions*, both first published in 1664 and quickly replacing private letters as the main medium of communication on scientific matters. They were, however, preceded by newspapers which, as news-sheets had started in the first quarter of the 17th century.

Over the years, due to the demands of the enormously increased numbers of authors and readers, pressures have built up which could be resolved only by quite new forms of publication and methods of publishing, disseminating and storing. The pressures were:

- the enormous quantities being printed of all types of publications and having to be stored. The new British Library building has storage for 12 million books yet many will still be outhoused. In the UK alone, 23 000 books were published in 1995. Worldwide some 50 000 scientific and technical periodicals are published;
- the problems of finding required information in such a mass;
- the need to cut costs, which for conventional printing were rising very rapidly;
- the demand for greater speed in publishing, a consequence of competition not only among publishers but also among authors;
- demand for rapid worldwide dissemination;
- the need to update many publications;
- buyer resistance when only one or two articles in a journal are of interest.

Over the years a number of ways of alleviating the problems and meeting new demands have been tried. Of them microforms in various degrees of reduction and form, letter journals and loose leaf publications still find some use. But it was the advent of the computer as an aid to publishing, of its link to greatly improved telecommunications and of the electronic disc that has opened up the range of options we now have for recording and storing information in ways which answer some of the above problems.

Computer databases can store not only text but also pictures and sound. A single disc can hold the equivalent of many thousands of pages of print. The store is searched automatically to find passages of information that correspond with the search terms used (provided, of course, that the database has been suitably structured). One prints out what one wants for oneself, assuming that reading on the screen is not adequate. One can view the information as soon as the author has put it into the database, and provided the computer is linked to a suitable network, one can access the information from a terminal anywhere on the network.

Updating these databases can be undertaken as soon as is convenient after the revised information is available. However, with large-scale operations, such as putting in updated information at a clearing bank, it is normal to carry out an updating run at weekly intervals. If the amount of data is very large the run can take a long time, e.g. a day, but even that is much quicker than producing an updated printed volume.

Originally online databases were limited to company financial and production data and to abstracting and indexing services, but now all manner of information can be found. The World Wide Web (WWW), whose sites are really online databases, has found particular favour for publicizing the services and products of commercial and official bodies, though it was originally designed as a means of rapid publication of brief notes of new scientific research, especially those concerned with the structure of matter.

A good example of commercial use is the publication by a Canadian insurance broker of a directory of the insurance laws of over 100 countries. The need to keep such a directory up to date is obvious. Another interesting use is a virtual reality display of the contents of museums, thus making frequent visits a simple matter. Newspapers and journals are now being published on Web sites though still continuing to be published in their printed versions. Indeed the amount of whole text material available through the Internet is increasing rapidly as is pictorial and graphic material.

Optical discs, especially CD-ROMs, are another means that have been developed for recording and storing multimedia information electronically. It is common for directories issued as CD-ROMs to be updated annually, half-yearly or even quarterly by simply issuing purchasers with a revised disc at the agreed intervals.

Storing information for four or five years on optical or computer hard discs raises no problems. The storage life of the discs is good. However, attempts to store for longer periods can run into difficulties. The problem that arises when archiving is that in this age of rapid technological development, the discs may become incompatible with future computers or their software. Machines and software to play the discs have to be kept or the contents transferred to an upgraded format.

Microchips can store information on a very small space. The information can be read or modified on suitable computers. The first result was the personal credit card. It provided the computer with details of the number of your bank account and allowed instructions to be given for payments to be debited to that account.

A Smart Card stores even more information. Personal identification can be programmed in, fingerprint or iris pattern for example, to make them more secure than credit cards. They can be credited with sums of money which can then be used to pay accounts, important personal information, e.g. medical records, and the means to unlock the door of one's residence or to borrow a book from a library etc. Exeter University was an early test-bed for a Smart Card which included such value-loaded features as access control, student voting, product discount and identity and library cards [16].

In addition to all this, we must not forget that sound can be recorded and stored on tape and on optical disc, and visual material can be recorded by camera on film and on disc. Minute broadcasting devices, telephoto lenses and keyhole cameras linked to videorecorders have greatly increased our ability to record and store events without the participants being aware they are being observed. One interesting use has been by manufacturers recording the way their customers, or more usually their customers' staff, actually use the equipment they have bought. A knowledge of user practice enables the manufacturer to see ways of redesigning and improving the user-friendliness.

A problem with the new ICTs is that we usually have to adapt to their logic rather than they to ours. We can compare the text of three books by laying them side by side; we can't do that readily with computer stored text, we have to print it out. On the other hand searching can be much easier – provided we can specify precisely what we want and know how to limit the responses to manageable quantities.

Full or abbreviated?

It has to be admitted that monographs, magazines and newspapers with their blend of information, analysis and comment make more sustainably interesting reading than abbreviated compilations of information no matter how well the information is arranged and presented. Even such excellent compilations as the *Oxford Companion to . . .* series or the *Dictionary of National Biography* pall after reading a few entries. Patent specifications, which are one of the best organized and produced pieces of entirely informative text make very dull reading save perhaps to one or two enthusiasts.

However, the size of books and volumes of technical journals is such that few people have time to read all they want. Even single articles and reports take time which today is precious. Government ministers and company directors cannot afford the time to grapple with the lengthy complications of a technical report. For them abbreviated versions are necessary.

Writing brief condensed packages of information is a highly skilled art. Each package needs to be directed towards a particular audience. Précis writing is a very important part of schooling and one that needs regular practice throughout life.

Consider how widely encyclopaedias differ. The one or two volume version is generally directed at those who just want minimal details to get them into the right ball-park. Even in these, though, accounts differ considerably in length and detail. Information given in the lengthy articles of the multi-volume *Encyclopaedia Britannica* is very full, especially when compared with the brief entries in the *Hutchinson Softback Encyclopedia*. They each serve a different purpose. The Britannica is giving a thorough introduction to each subject, the Hutchinson a brief definition. One advantage of electronic encyclopaedias is that on any subject one can gradually increase the level of information presented until one has reached the amount one needs.

Short accounts, called abstracts, are written to enable a person to decide whether he wishes to find and read the full account. Journal articles often are prefaced by an abstract. These fall into two categories – indicative and informative. The first category simply explains, more fully than the title, what the full article is about; the second category gives in brief the results or conclusions of the article.

Reports are often prefaced by a synopsis of the main conclusions and recommendations. Frequently this proves sufficient for action to be taken. It is common for the authors of such reports to be disappointed that the "top brass" have not read their full report but only the summary. Yet it should be taken as a mark of trust in their abilities. It is when company directors doubt the conclusions that they look at the report as a whole.

Another type of short account, a brief for a government minister, has to be written with a very clear idea of its purpose, the extent of the minister's existing knowledge and how much extra needs to be known.

Information records as sources

Information recorded on the electronic media, whether in–house computer discs, external online databases or CD-ROMs, tends to resemble conventional publications, though the ability to manipulate the text, pictures and sound is reducing the resemblance. Many sources of information via the World Wide Web, e.g. some newspapers and magazines, are merely electronic versions of printed products.

The nature of the information received through the Internet or any other electronic network is, in principle, no different from that one receives by letter or any of the printed media. That the Internet has taken on something of the quality of an international Speakers' Corner merely means that individuals can publish on it material that a commercial publisher would not handle, and that they can send a single letter to a large number of recipients. A discussion group on the Internet is really only a modern, and much more effective (but probably read by a smaller audience), version of the letters column of newspapers or the invisible college of senior academics. There are, of course, other benefits but their significance is secondary. The real difference from a paper message lies in its lack of permanence. It can be changed, updated by the originator or even modified by a third party.

In the case of information packages which one wants as up-to-date as possible, this is a good feature. However, there are many situations in which permanence of the information is crucial. In these, information gained through the Internet will be suspect. Institutions who wish to maintain a reputation for reliability will take suitable precautions such as encrypting and ought to be meticulous about stating the date of the latest update. Control of the ability to modify electronically stored data is crucial, hence the care being taken to make Smart Cards unique to their owners.

Despite the huge amount of information now available via the various electronic systems, the traditional sources of information are still fully in use. Even tablets of stone are still used in appropriate situations, e.g. memorials, but, of course, it is paper that predominates. For permanent record, electronic information is printed out for the reasons stated earlier.

The range of material that forms an information resource is considerable. It includes collections of letters (shall we in future store collections of the e-mails of eminent people?), monographs, reports, pamphlets, broadsheets, newspapers, periodicals, patent specifications, standards, trade literature including both product descriptions and service specifications, user manuals, laws, by-laws and regulations. Then there is material that contains information in other than alphanumeric form: maps, diagrams, graphs, photographs, moving pictures, music scores, sound recordings and, of course, artefacts.

To make it easier to find the information one requires in this vast mass, other publications have been produced. The condensed versions and compilations, data books, encyclopaedias and reviews have already been referred to. So too have finding tools: directories, abstracting and indexing services, catalogues and so on. There are so many directories that there has to be a directory of directories.

Those in large organizations and increasingly those in small ones and private individuals are starting searches for information at the computer terminal. There are cases where even asking a question of a colleague in the same room is carried out terminal-to-terminal. It is not silly. It avoids breaking the concentration of someone also working at a terminal, for the message waits until the recipient chooses to open his/her mailbox.

Libraries as a source

Ever since books were invented, and until the arrival of the Internet, libraries have been one of the three most important information resources, the other two being personal research and people one knows. Nowadays things have begun to change and those who have access to a terminal and a network may make that their primary resource. For those without one, PCs are now being made available in libraries both for reading optical discs and for access to the Internet.

Nevertheless there is still so much information published in print that libraries will be needed as the principal means of access for many years yet. So, if the network cannot supply the answer, or only part of it, then access to a library's more traditional materials is the next step. A sizeable organization may have a library of its own or have in place arrangements to borrow any necessary publications from a library, most probably from the British Library's Document Supply Centre. Otherwise an information seeker can go in person to one of the many public, academic and professional libraries.

The future for libraries, which are traditionally the place to find organized collections of printed publications, is a popular topic for debate. The public debate, not surprisingly, is usually limited to public libraries but there are other types of libraries serving different clienteles.

The public library could be said to have the role of providing for recreation, education or information a wide range of printed publications and other appropriate material such as recorded music and videotapes. A sizeable portion of the book stock is always fiction, both literary classics and more ephemeral novels, but it is rare for this to be the larger part. The greater part is usually nonfiction. There is always a reference collection of dictionaries, encyclopaedias, directories and material of local interest. Whether or not one deems the books held to be the best for any particular subject (and for specialist topics they rarely are), a public library does contain a huge amount of valuable information. For certain publications which one prefers to look at in printed form they can be invaluable. My local library has a good collection of parliamentary and EU Commission papers, thus saving me a journey to the Westminster Official Publications Library or staring at the documents on the Web Site. In practice I would download after making sure that the document was the one that contained what I wanted.

Academic institutions, including most schools, have their own libraries, those of the major universities having huge collections of major books and journals. A great many commercial companies, professional organizations and official bodies and other institutions of various types have their own private libraries which contain a wide variety of publications and unpublished documents appropriate to their specialized needs. However, it is the company library which has changed most dramatically as access to electronic publications has advanced. In the 1960s the company information unit was, if it existed at all, usually housed in a corner of the library as a sub-department. By the 1980s the library was a unit of the information department. By the 1990s many company libraries have disappeared as distinct entities, most of the information that used to be stored in the library as books, journals and reports etc now being stored and accessed electronically. Those that continue tend to specialize even more than before on publications, often ephemeral, which are not available electronically and are not worth converting into electronic format.

Traditonal libraries, of course, do not usually store information, they store packages, i.e. books and journals, which contain information. The great virtue of the library is that it stores the packages in a way, and with additional search tools, that makes finding what one wants reasonably easy. Catalogues lead from a title, an author or an index term to the volume on the shelf. The shelf arrangement may make browsing through books on related topics or the volumes of a journal feasible. Other material may not lend itself to browsing but direct access to the shelf can save time. Each library has its own way of arranging material ostensibly to suit its clientele though it may be that some of the visitors have chosen the library because of the way it manages the information packages.

Information audit

Finally in this chapter on managing and storing information, it is worth mentioning the new practice which has grown up of conducting an information audit. The logic is that if information is deemed to be a valuable resource and one that needs to be managed and exploited, then every so often a check should be carried out to determine that this is being done properly.

It makes sense. An independent expert will check that the information held or accessible within the enterprise is appropriate for its stated mission. The auditor will also note any significant gaps that should be filled. The check will also look at how information is managed within the organization, whether it can be readily communicated or accessed and that the necessary security bars are in place. The check should also examine whether the resource is being properly and fully exploited or whether its potential is being wasted.

Audit of the information and knowledge management sector of an organization is important because, with rare exceptions, the directors are not experts in it themselves.

References

1. The Hawley Committee (1995) *Information as an asset: the Board agenda*. The KPMG IMPACT programme. London: KPMG

2. Haines, M. (1997) Library and information policy development in the NHS. In *Understanding Information Policy*, ed. I. Rowlands pp.168–177. London: Bowker-Saur

3. Drucker, P. (1993) *Post-capitalist society* pp.96–97. Oxford: Butterworth-Heinemann

4. Martin, W.J. (1995) *The global information society*, p.171. London: Aslib-Gower

   [Martin spells out what his definition of information management includes and also brings in Burk and Horton's definition of information resources management.]

5. Best, D.P. (1996) *The fourth resource: information and its management*. Aldershot: Aslib-Gower

6. Marchand, D.A. (1997) *Managing the I in IT: creating business value with information and technology*. Lecture to the Royal Society of Arts, London, 19 February 1997.

7. Dieckmann, H. (1997) Managing information at Sutton Public Library. *Managing Information*, 4(3), 18–20

8. Tooms, E. (1996) From Bleak House to the Rainmaker. Aslib Conference, *The future of the information professional*, London

9. Myers, J. and McClean, J. (1997) *Knowledge management for citizens' advice in the 21st century; an innovative strategy*. London: Solon Consultants

10. Pye, D. (1997) Changing the Corporate Culture. In *Understanding information policies*, ed. I. Rowlands pp.191–205. London: Bowker-Saur

11. Enser, P. (1997) Information management for an information profession. *Managing Information*, 4(4), 40–41

12. Kalseth, K. (1997) Knowledge management: putting information and people's competence to work together. *FID News Bulletin*, **47**(7/8) 191–2

    [The issue of the Bulletin contains four other articles on the topic of knowledge management.]

13. I put together some of these thoughts after attending a lecture by David Skyrme, *Knowledge management – a passing fad or ticket to ride?* given to the IIS Southern Branch on 10 Feb 1998.

14. Dainton, F. (1987) *Knowledge is power. But how can we find what we need?* p.10. London: The British Library

15. Hutchinson and Adler. The remark is quoted in Drucker, *Ibid.*, p.192.

16. Anon. (1997) Smart move at Exeter University. *Library Technology*, **2**(2), 42

CHAPTER SEVEN

Information ethics: expectations and rights

Ethics has exercised the minds of thoughtful people for at least 3000 years, probably ever since human beings started to live together in communities. The proper balance between the rights and freedoms of the individual and the advancement of the greater good is a vital aim. Even animals of the same species have an instinctive code of behaviour towards each other which contributes to the continuation of the species. For human society, frequent review of ethical principles is important. As Williams [1] comments, 'The obvious fact is that the repertory of substantive ethical concepts differs between cultures, changes over time and is open to criticism'.

Reassessment now is even more important than ever. We live in a new social order and are adjusting to a multi-ethnic community. The new ICTs enable each one of us to communicate worldwide yet they also enable the owners of information to restrict access to it. Information about each of us can be easily gathered and exploited for commercial benefit and laws are being passed to establish our rights over such information. Increasingly, the ability to access and use information, to which previously freedom of access was taken for granted, is becoming dependant on ability to pay.

Information and its use are not only important subjects for ethical consideration in their own right, they also play a major part in ethical considerations of other aspects of life. A wide range of rights and responsibilities, economic and social issues are involved as the following list shows:

right to seek information;
freedom to study and do research;
right to know; freedom of information; and freedom of the media;
right to receive information; and limits of censorship;
right to communicate information;
duties and responsibilities; professional ethics;
right of equality; information rich – information poor gap;
right to withhold information;
right to privacy; and data protection;
ownership rights; and copyright.

The first five of these will be considered in this chapter, the last five in chapters 8 and 9.

In each of these issues one is looking, among other aspects, at the balance of interests of individuals, of social communities of individuals, of private sector institutions, and of official bodies and government.

To start with, the information sector embraces such important ethical principles that they have been incorporated into major declarations by representatives of the people of most of the world's countries, by representatives of groups of countries and by the governments of individual countries. All these, be they Article 19 of the United Nations' Universal Declaration of Human Rights, the European Convention on Human Rights (now being adopted into UK law), Amendments to the United States Constitution, or President Roosevelt's Four Freedoms, all say in slightly different words that human beings have a right of freedom to seek, receive and impart information.

Unfortunately, such a broad degree of freedom would be subject to abuse and accidental misuse, so a number of qualifications have had to be added. Thus Clause 10(2) of the European Convention on Human Rights says, 'The exercise of this freedom [of expression], since it carries with it duties and responsibilities, may be subject to such formalities, conditions, restrictions and penalties as are prescribed by law and are necessary in a democratic society in the interests of national security, territorial integrity or public safety, for the prevention of disorder or crime, for the protection of health or morals, for the protection of the reputation and rights of others, for preventing the disclosure of information received in confidence, and for maintaining the authority and impartiality of the judiciary'. One might be forgiven for wondering after such a long list if any worthwhile portion of the freedom is left.

Nowadays discussion has turned to defining our rights as individuals, probably because of the complications which arise from the considerable social changes of recent times and because we are living in larger and larger cities. The consequence has been that more and more rules and regulations are prescribing our actions and limiting our freedom. The same is happening in the professions where codes of ethics and of conduct are multiplying or, where they already exist, are expanded as each new problem arises. Such codes are imposed by the ruling council and are often dictatorial in tone. Scope for the individual to think and act morally and autonomously then lessens.

One realises that in a society in which increasing levels of anti-social and self-seeking behaviour are the norm, preventative action is necessary. But, if we are to try to restore an acceptable level of personal responsibility, we should limit rules to the inescapable minimum and instead promulgate guidelines which ensure that important factors are not overlooked when we try to think and act morally. Oakeshott is severe in his view of the value of applying codes of ethics to judging the morality of any particular behaviour: 'When society attempts to make itself perfect, a few impose their interpretation of perfection upon the rest and chaos, absurdity and repression reigns' [2].

Rights are very difficult to define in unexceptionable terms, as we have seen with the Convention Clause above. Though there are many who are quick to claim rights, there are few who attempt before claiming them seriously to think through the justice and consequences of rigorous observance of those rights. After all, if I have rights, then so have you and our interests may conflict. My right to seek, receive and impart information may well conflict with your right to privacy. My right to privacy has to give way to the State's right to know. Does Government or a commercial enterprise have the same rights as an individual? If I can demand to see what a commercial firm has on its computer files about me, should that firm be able to demand to see what I have on my computer about it?

A right to seek information is not synonymous with a right to know information, nor can rights always be combined. What one learns through one's right to know cannot always be used when exercising one's right to communicate. Property rights may come into the equation, for information is a property some of which has financial value. Nevertheless, we will examine each right separately, indicating the links and overlaps as necessary.

A right to seek information

It can be argued that, since it would be quite impossible to live in modern society without a continual intake of a large, undefinable, amount of information, there must be a right to seek and receive essential information (defining 'essential' as that without which life today would be impossible or intolerable), just as there is a right to a supply of air to breathe, water to drink and food to eat. At the very least there is a right not to be deliberately deprived unless one has offended against some law or other. If there is a right not to be deprived, then any information that is genuinely essential must either be supplied or, if it cannot be supplied, one must have a consequential right to seek it where one can.

That does not necessarily mean one has a right to even basic information free of charge, but it would be unreasonable if the cost were beyond one's means or capabilities. That would be tantamount to deliberate deprivation. By saying that the acquisition must be within our capabilities, I mean that the source must be one that we can reach and that using it must be within our mental and technical capacity.

Moving beyond rights to basic information, the right to seek information generally does not always mean we can get it even if we know where to look and the owners of the information are willing for us to have it. Weisberg [3] somewhat ironically draws attention to the difficulties one can experience extracting information from the UN Centre for Human Rights. More commonly, provided we have all our faculties and can read and count, we are flooded with information, but even then it does not amount to all that we feel we need. If, as is the case with most adults, we have a duty to vote in local and national elections or in referenda then we quite reasonably feel that we should have the full information about the issues on which the vote depends.

There are two strands to seeking information: one may be seeking information which one knows exists or one may be seeking some which does not yet exist, i.e. carrying out research. This will be discussed later. If the information that one wants has been published, surely one has a right to be able to seek it? One may have to pay for access or agree not to republish it, but one must be free to seek it. The fact that it may be information which affects a case in law, invalidates a government policy or disproves religious dogma should not be allowed as grounds for forbidding someone to seek it if it has been published.

The freedom or right to seek information must mean that one should also be able to seek unpublished information without suffering any penalty. One should be free to ask a Government Minister to explain why he decided on such and such a policy. One should be able to ask the police how people might get hold of drugs like cocaine or ecstasy. One can ask a manufacturer what his product is made of. One should be able to ask an army commander how many soldiers he has and where they are deployed. Similarly, an institution, whether in the public or private sector, should be free to seek information either from another institution or from a private individual.

Asking questions, even like these, should be entirely permissible and without penalty. However, two corollaries must be accepted. The first is that a freedom or right to seek information does not of itself include a right to receive an answer. The right to know is another issue and I will deal with it shortly. There can be perfectly valid reasons why the person asked will decline to answer. In the case of the army commander it could be security; the manufacturer may not be willing to give information that would benefit a competitor.

A second corollary is that the person asked also has a right to seek information and may wish to be assured that the information will not be misused before he releases it. The policeman might fear he would be deemed to be acting irresponsibly if he gave you information about how to get drugs without first ensuring that your need to know was for a lawful purpose.

A number of circumstances under which information could be withheld were given in the European Convention on Human Rights, quoted above, though the clause was concerned with rights of expression. Most are obvious but two raise questions concerning expressing or seeking information. They are 'the protection of morals' and the 'protection of the rights of others'.

There are certain people who are vulnerable and there is a case for arguing not that they should be penalized for asking questions but that they should be prevented from asking those questions of a potentially harmful source. An example is whether children should be allowed to seek sexual information over the Internet where they would be likely to be 'answered' by unsavoury pornographic material. There is no question that they should be allowed to seek information about sexual matters and that they should be given answers but, as with so many information needs, the request will be poorly formulated and needs to be answered by someone who understands what lies behind it and knows how to express the answer so that it will be properly understood.

Much information that we receive is incomplete, inaccurate and sometimes misleading. Well educated people have learnt to cope, their extensive background knowledge providing, as has been discussed, a sounding board. Those less well educated are possibly more at risk of being misled. With the majority of adults one has to leave them to manage as best they can, the result being, as is often obvious, a very poorly informed body of people. Nevertheless, except in the case of children, and even that is questionable, the right to seek information must not be restricted, especially since the right to seek does not imply an automatic right to receive. Whether it is right to use any available means of seeking is another matter.

Certainly we should be mindful of the rights of others when seeking information. For example, wantonly digging in an archaeological site merely to satisfy one's own curiosity could in no way be condoned. Nor should we monopolize access to any documents we are using for longer than is necessary.

Freedom to use new technologies

If we have a right or freedom to seek information, presumably we have a right to use any legally available means to do so. Thus there is freedom to use the public library and to use the telephone. The European Commission introduced a Directive in 1992 giving all citizens of the European Community the right to subscribe to telephone services. Very important now and being vigorously defended against attempts to restrict use is the right to use the Internet. Leaving to one side for the moment that the requirement to pay a fee to use a service may in practice restrict its use, surely any public service should be open to any member of the public to use as of right. The use should be limited only if it is abused and then restrictions should be applied only to those who perpetrate the abuse.

On the other hand, an important question is whether we have a right to seek information by any means available to us. If the answer were to be 'yes' it would be tantamount to saying that a right to seek is equivalent to a right to be able to find out. If we accept that human beings have a right to some measure of privacy or that Governments have a duty, in the interests of the safety of the population as a whole, to keep some information secret, or that industrial espionage is illegal, then there must be limitations on how one seeks. One's right must be only openly to seek information; to seek by underhand means cannot be acceptable.

That this is accepted is already evidenced by the law against hacking (*Computer Misuse Act*, 1990) and the very strict rules governing when the police may use bugging and surveillance devices in the detection of criminal activity. As is well-known, governments can use satellite mounted cameras to reveal activity of a potentially hostile nature in other countries, or to monitor farms where rules about the permitted use of land are being ignored. The ability to intercept telephone calls and the use of cameras with telephoto lenses to gain information about a person's private life is generally deemed improper unless there are circumstances surrounding the individual which make such information seeking behaviour arguably permissible. The recent suggestion that those who leave children in the care of an au pair should instal a spy camera linked to a video recorder is to my mind unacceptable unless the au pair knows about it and accepts the covert supervision. If misbehaviour is suspected, then the device may be needed to gather enough evidence to dismiss the offender. But the au pair also has rights and these should include freedom from covert supervision as long as there are no grounds for suspicion of malpractice. Surely, too, if the parents are so mistrustful as to instal a spy camera, then they should not leave the child in the au pair's care.

The use of helicopters and long range cameras to obtain information about the way celebrities relax in private is an information seeking practice which is generally deemed unacceptable. In general, a right to seek information does not give a right to seek by whatever means one wishes. Hi-tech equipment may be sometimes appropriate, as in technical enquiries such as, 'Is that painting you are trying to sell me genuine or a fake?' but it should be used only with the responder's knowledge and agreement. It can be invaluable as a time saver, for recording the observations and for calculating the results, but the same ethical principles should be followed as if ICTs were not being used. A right to seek information can survive only if the seeker is entirely open about what he seeks and how he is doing it.

Freedom to study and to do research

Freedom to study and to carry out research is a part of one's right to seek information. The student is gathering information that is already somewhere in the public domain; the researcher seeks information that is as yet unknown to anyone.

Study may be undertaken simply to increase one's own knowledge of a topic, e.g. as part of one's education, or it may be to increase understanding for a wider audience. In both cases it is, of course, much more than just seeking information to help with a task. Personal study is, or should be, much more than merely learning texts or memorising lecure notes. One correlates information from a variety of sources, examines the quality and reliability of each piece, considers whether together they reveal inconsistencies or gaps, and seeks additional information to complete the picture. If gaps or inconsistencies remain, then one chooses whether or not research should be undertaken. Study, like research, sometimes reveals that what has been assumed to be correct is not. Therein lies a reason why the right to seek information must extend to a right to study. Study must not be stifled, as it has been in some totalitarian countries, because someone's cherished beliefs or some institution's dogmas may be found to be in error or in need of revision.

At the same time, if one has freedom to undertake research, one has a duty to do it thoroughly and responsibly and not to leap too soon to conclusions nor to suppress unpalatable facts. It is very regrettable that in the race to be first with a new piece of information, there are occasions when results are published before they have been properly verified. The result is often excitement in the press which then has to be corrected, but not everyone who saw the first announcement sees the retraction. A recent unfortunate case concerned a theory of the cause of cot deaths. One can, however, see the dilemma. Should one really wait for verification if, during the time that would take, more babies would die? The solution to the dilemma must lie in the way and to whom such results are reported.

On the other hand, the fact that press reporters monitor science journals to see if there is material for a story must not be allowed to deter researchers working on topics of potential public interest from publishing their results in the appropriate journals. Only in that way can other researchers have the opportunity to verify or contradict the findings and make use of them for their own work.

In some research projects, the information needed exists but is not in the public domain. This situation can arise when doing historical or biographical research and one needs to see family papers. It is generally accepted that the personal papers of a famous person, like any other of his goods and chattels, are the property of his heirs unless they have been bequeathed to the State, a library or a museum. If they are the property of the heirs, the claim of 'public interest' is not deemed sufficiently great to over-ride the rights of possession in the case of a deceased person. Thus there can be freedom to research a chosen topic but there may not be a right of access to all the information resources.

There are other limits to freedom to do research. It is generally agreed that the way research is conducted where experiments on human beings and animals are involved should be controlled. Very rigorous controls exist on the use of animals for testing drugs but it is widely accepted, that if the knowledge of disease and its treatment is to advance, tests have to be carried out on animals before trials are undertaken on humans. For the latter, too, rules now exist which require human beings who are taking part in research testing of new drugs to be given full information about the anticipated effects and any known risks. They may not know, though, whether they have actually received the drug or only the comparative placebo. Surely the right to undertake research to advance knowledge cannot be accepted if it is known that the consequent harm to the subject will outweigh any potential benefit?

Human beings are also required to participate in other types of research including that into patterns of behaviour. Following the recommendations in the 1979 Belmont Report on the protection of human subjects of research in the USA, care has to be taken that ensure people's susceptibilities are not affronted. Questioning people about their political opinions or studying the way they move around a department store is quite acceptable, but a study of how different categories of people react to particular sexual advances would have to be very carefully managed.

One question that keeps arising is whether there are topics on which the right to do research should be withdrawn. Research in the natural sciences has, in the past, revealed information which has greatly disturbed people. The theory of evolution is just one among many examples. Now genetics research is under scrutiny.

This field is one which raises several interesting questions, some of them highly pertinent to the impact of information. The immediate response to the cloning of a sheep, that no more work on cloning should be allowed, seemed to arise not merely from a fear that the information gained would eventually be used to clone human beings but also from a vaguer fear that it would exploited in some undesirable way by commercial organizations and lead to a reduction of biodiversity. In other words, there was fear raised about the ways in which the information would be used.

The same applies to work being undertaken to elucidate our genetic code and to establish the extent to which our health and behaviour is predetermined by our genetic make up. If it can be shown that an individual's likelihood of developing some disease can be foretold from his genetic make up, will the situation arise that insurance companies will demand to know this information before they will grant any life insurance or medical insurance policy? So far the insurance companies seem to have agreed not to demand such information, but the likelihood that before many years are out we shall all be able to know the chance we have of developing certain genetic ailments will bring a need to clarify where National Health protection ends and insurance begins.

Those are the fears. Potential benefits can easily be hypothesized. Cloning of healthy cows, were it already commercially practicable, could be used to eliminate the disease BSE completely in each breed of cattle. Knowledge of the hereditability of genetic defects could eliminate the risk of giving birth to babies with those defects.

One feels that research and development which could only yield harmful products should not take place, but it is difficult to envisage many such cases where this is likely to happen. Research which simply increases knowledge and development which yields products that have some benefit despite possible negative effects should surely be allowed. Better to do it oneself and have control than let others without any scruples take charge.

At the same time, it has to be said that previous attempts to restrict human enquiry have all failed eventually. It is difficult to believe that any ban on this work would be effective for long. Far better is to ensure that it is done and reported openly, like any other research, and that commercial exploitation etc. can be regulated. It is human nature to be inquisitive about what gives rise to life and how life controls itself. We have eaten the fruit of the Tree of Knowledge and must put up with its after effects.

Right to know

One may be led to conclude that it is right to continue research until we are quite clear what the risks are of defects being carried in our genes. We may also conclude that each of us has a right to know what our genetic make-up is and whether we carry a particular complaint in our genes. However, we may at the same time conclude that only we ourselves and no-one else has a right to know that information. Attitudes to a right to know tend to be highly subjective. Ridley, author of *The Origins of Virtue*, reacted strongly [4] to reports that there might be DNA testing of everyone from birth. 'Government', he wrote, 'has no right to know details of my genome, however beneficent its intentions'. Parents, he felt, should be able to have details of their baby's genome and especially what it revealed by way of its future disposition to ailments etc. so that they could, if they wished, take action to have that disposition corrected, assuming that it were possible to do so.

Discussions of the topic of right to know are usually limited to the question of to what extent has a member of the public a right of access to official information. One of two extreme attitudes is usually taken that either:

1. each person has a right to know everything except those things that for reasons acceptable to the majority of people must be kept confidential or;
2. everything is confidential except those things which are deemed safe to make public.

We may ask for information about a new fighter aircraft and will be told much but some details will be withheld, not because there is anything morally wrong in our knowing them but because the only safe way to keep these details from a potential enemy is to keep them secret from everyone except those with a need to know. Likewise, we do not expect the police to reveal full details of how they detect certain types of crime or how an investigation is progressing because we realize that to do so may hamper the investigation and even lead to criminals escaping justice.

On the other hand, we do believe we have a right to know enough to be sure that the police are not acting improperly. When it is not feasible for us to know sufficient or to know in time to prevent them acting wrongly, we delegate the right to know to reliable representatives; in the case of using hidden surveillance devices we delegate our right to magistrates and judges, whose prior approval the police must seek before installing one. A remarkable feature of social change since 1980 has been the growth in the numbers of supervisory bodies and regulators, watching over official and privatized bodies to ensure they behave in accordance with public requirements and expectations. It should not be forgotten that these officials must be able to access all the information they need.

In a free country like the UK or the USA, we generally believe that we have a right to know what Government is up to. In the USA this has been enshrined in its *Freedom of Information Act* of 1966. So far there is no equivalent in the UK but the publication late in 1997 of a White Paper [5] on the Government's proposals for a Freedom of Information Act makes it likely that one will soon be enshrined in UK law.

Obviously openness involves risk. It used to be joked that the US Act decimated the Soviet intelligence service because Moscow could simply ring up the White House for whatever it wanted to know. Discussing a National Academy of Sciences Report on communication and security, Chalk [6] observes that there are essentially two options: the first is to decide what risks should be accepted to maintain an open society; the second is to decide what controls should be introduced to avoid running certain risks. The second option, she points out, implies that someone has a right to introduce controls.

In 1993 the then UK Government published a White Paper, *Open Government*, which stated that, 'Open government is part of an effective democracy. Citizens must have adequate access to the information and analysis on which government business is based. Ministers and public servants have a duty to explain their policies, decisions and actions to the public. Governments need, however, to keep some secrets, and have a duty to protect the proper privacy of those with whom they deal'.

Appendices to the White Paper indicated the complexity of the situation. Some 280 Statutes were listed which had clauses prohibiting the disclosure of information but only 100 which had clauses granting discretion to disclose or enforce disclosure.

Despite that statement about open government, the pressure that has arisen for a Freedom of Information Act owes much to cases where information that should have been made available, and was not, and, it must be admitted, to a measure of distrust in both Ministers and public servants. Worlock [7] has pointed out how the Government policy of encouraging tradeable information through partnership with the private sector was repeatedly frustrated by the actions of civil servants. Incidentally it is interesting to note that the French version of a freedom of information act, 1978, gives individuals wide rights of access but specifically excludes any right of exploitation.

'The right to know is linked inextricably to accountability. Informed judgement and appraisal by public, press and Parliament alike is a difficult, even fruitless, task if government activities and the decision-making process are obscured from public scrutiny' [8]. On these grounds one supports freedom of access to official information. But it is desirable to bear in mind that, as always happens, the freedom will be exploited for personal benefit just as, some years ago, the granting of freedom to make a photocopy of a patent abridgment led to an enormous demand for copies, many times in excess of the demand for printed copies. The consequence was inconvenience for other searchers since the volumes containing the abridgments spent more time at the photocopy machines than on the library shelves.

The proposals for a Freedom of Information (FoI) Act [5] envisage that all official records and information will be made available except any whose release would cause 'substantial harm'. If information is withheld, there will be a right of appeal to yet another regulator, an Information Commissioner. The test of substantial harm will be made against the requirements of national security, defence, international relations, criminal investigation, commercial confidentiality, public safety, personal privacy and information supplied in confidence. There will also be a 'simple harm' proviso in the case of high level decision-making and policy advice in government.

The *Official Secrets Act* was amended in 1988 to limit the categories of information which civil servants must not release without prior permission, a necessary first step. Nevertheless, if it and the FoI Act are to be compatible, further amendments will be needed to clarify which categories of information should be released.

One suspects that there will be difficulty encountered in relating the openness of FoI with the restrictive rules of Data Protection (government files hold an immense amount of information about individuals, most of which individuals would not want made publicly accessible or used for commercial purposes) and the provisions, particularly those of right to personal privacy, of the *European*

Convention on Human Rights. There is the difficult task here of defining what information may and may not be released. The limitations given in the Convention (see p. 112) are too broad for day-to-day decisions. It is entirely proper to want to know what the government is up to but not to use access to official files to find out what individuals and institutions are doing. Civil servants are not being deliberately obstructive when they decline to make files available. They are being cautious, about possible unintended consequences. The White Paper implies that personal privacy will be respected unless there is over-riding public interest. One hopes this will remain so in the Bill and that 'public interest' is properly interpreted as 'legal concern' and not as 'public curiosity'.

It will be interesting to see, assuming the Act is passed, just how much difference it will make in practice. If there is still a requirement that Ministerial statements must be made in the first place to Parliament, as the Speaker has been insisting, there will still be a strong temptation to arrange a leak. Apparently, the 30 year rule on the release of official documents will still apply to those which are withheld under the 'substantial harm' test.

It is intended that the Act will apply not only to Government departments but also to official Quangos, local authorities, schools and universities, privatised industries and other private bodies that carry out statutory functions. In these two latter cases one foresees problems of 'commercial in confidence', because they are likely to be in competition. Part of the policy of privatizing state industries was to introduce competition in order to raise efficiency. Surely they should not have to make even more information available than do their rivals?

Employees' and stakeholders' rights

These days, private sector companies which have been registered at Companies House and not-for-profit institutions including charities have to publish to all their stakeholders a considerable amount of information about the organization's performance. By various means, including internal newsletters and reports from trade union representatives, employees also get much more information. Managers are expected to keep their staff well informed about relevant matters. Internal networks make communication and access to information much easier, though some confidentiality barriers are built in.

In the past, we have generally surrendered with good grace any right to know information which would be deemed 'commercial in confidence'. Most did not even imagine there might be a right to know. This has changed dramatically in the last fifty years as the pressures of a need-to-know have taken effect. The following examples will illustrate this.

Firstly, the employees of an organization now have a right to see what is recorded about them in the employer's staff files and to request correction of any errors. Second, as our knowledge of the causes of ailments has increased, so employers and manufacturers have had to give more attention to ensuring that the conditions of employment are not harmful to health; they have also had to give much more detailed information about the materials used in factories and the nature of materials sold. The reasons are that ailments, previously regarded as 'one of those misfortunes of life' have been traced to long-term exposure to contaminants in working environments. We have become increasingly aware of the possible adverse effects on health of a wide range of substances. There is now public insistence on knowing what chemicals factories use and whether they are emitted deliberately or accidentally into the air or into rivers. There is insistence on knowing what additives are put into our food. No longer are people content to rely on factory inspectors or on health and safety officials; people feel they have a right to know what there is in the environment or in food and drink which may affect health.

Employer–employee relations have changed considerably since the first half of this century. Then it was regarded as the 'proper' thing to be loyal to one's employer to the extent of keeping secret his processes and materials, even if one suspected they might be harmful. That was the ethic of the time. I worked at one time for a company in which only half a dozen senior staff knew the details and specifications of the raw materials and processes being used. It would have been deemed quite unethical by any of us who knew what the materials were to release that information to anyone else, inside or outside the company, without the permission of the Directors.

Companies seeking to attract investment or to increase their share price realize that they must publish enough information to convince investors not only that they have exciting plans for the future, but also that they are financially sound and being prudently managed. As a result of a few very serious cases of the misuse of funds this is enshrined in laws which require considerable financial detail to be published each year and distributed to shareholders. Indeed, though the need to keep details of specific dealings confidential is still officially recognized, companies nowadays make a virtue of disseminating an enormous amount of information about their activities to all the stakeholders and the public at large. One sometimes feels that a right to know has been turned into an inescapable duty to receive a torrent of information.

Right to receive information; the limits of censorship

As a general rule, those of us in so-called democratic countries are free to receive any information in the sense that there is no crime in receiving unsolicited information whatever its content. Even if the information compromises national security, personal privacy or religious or secular morals, there is no crime in passively receiving it. Although information is a property, as will be discussed further later, there is no crime of receiving stolen information as there is of receiving other forms of stolen property, though there could be if it were in physical form as a photocopy or a computer disc. Of course, if one sets out deliberately to seek such information and one entices sources which should not do so to give it to you, then you are committing an offence. Similarly if one instals a listening device to eavesdrop on private conversations, that is not passively receiving information, it is seeking it by an unethical method.

In some countries it is an offence to listen to information broadcasts by foreign radios. This was the case in the Soviet Union for many years. But in the UK even during the 1939–45 war, listening to broadcasts from Germany was not an offence, though it might be frowned upon. Similarly, although the UK is officially a Christian country with a State Church, it is many years since it was deemed an offence to listen to someone preaching another faith. It is imparting the information, broadcasting sedition, brainwashing with weird beliefs that may be treated as illegal or immoral. Even then, attempts to ban those who preach socially unacceptable faiths have generally failed on the grounds of freedom of belief and expression. Attempts to censor even the most undesirable faiths are usually deemed contrary to the UN Declaration of Human Rights.

Nevertheless, one feels fundamentally that there must be a limit somewhere. Leaving aside that the offence of brainwashing, if offence it is, is treated by preventing its imposition rather than making suffering it an offence, one feels that there are those who are vulnerable to persuasive messages and need to be protected. Whether information or not, the ability of children using the Internet accidentally to receive pornographic information has given rise to anxiety. In America, the Communications Decency Act has been swept away by a ruling of the Supreme Court that it infringed the right to free speech [9].

Libraries are very sensitive to attempts to limit their choice of books on political or religious grounds and resist firmly unless the law requires such action. The American Library Association has a very clear code of ethics which states, 'Librarians must resist all efforts by groups or individuals to censor library materials' [10]. The US Library Bill of Rights goes even further stating not only that censorship must be 'challenged' but that libraries must provide material representing all points of view and that none must be excluded on the grounds of the origins or social, political or religious views of the author [11].

Unfortunately, provision by libraries in the USA of access to the Internet is causing difficulties because it contains material deemed unsuitable for children, i.e. pornography. Some libraries are using software which restricts access not only to this but also to sexual health information and controversial political material [12]. Libraries that are not restricting access are under siege from anti-access pressure groups; those that have restrictions are under siege from the American Library Association and civil liberties groups. The most obvious solution is to allow access, but only on request, to children under a certain age only if accompanied by a responsible adult. However, where firm principles are involved, anything that smacks of compromise is unlikely to be acceptable.

Censorship may be necessary in the interests of national and personal security. Soldiers writing home from the battlefield have their mail censored to avoid risk of disclosing strategic military information. News of a kidnapping may be withheld from the Press in order to avoid risking the victim's life. These are, however, extreme or rare cases. Censorship by the Government of news is deemed by most people to be unacceptable. Similarly, so too is any attempt by a state religion to suppress access to information about other faiths.

One form of censorship is telling lies. Finnis makes the point [13] that human beings have a right not to be positively lied to in any situation. Any right to information is a right to correct information. As children we are taught (or should be) that telling lies is wrong and as adults we feel that to tell the truth is a moral obligation. In a Court of Law, witnesses are put on oath to tell the truth, the whole truth and nothing but the truth, though the second of those requirements can be met only by telling as much as we know. Few people ever know the whole truth about any event.

The phrase, 'not to be positively lied to' expresses a moral right but one to which there can be exceptions. Surely those little white lies so necessary to preserve good social relations ('How do I look, dear?' 'Absolutely charming') should not be condemned as immoral. But such minor fibs apart, the right should be there. Whether it should include the whole truth is less certain. Medical people dealing with a patient of hysterical disposition or one whose chances of recovery may be impaired by the news of, say, the death of a spouse, may quite properly be sparing of the truth in the interests of the patient – to whom is their first duty. It is very common for ethical principles to conflict with each other. If one accepts (not everyone does, which is another problem in establishing ethical rules) that one's first duty is to one's family, then taking a stand at work on an ethical principle with the result that one loses one's job could be very difficult if one was unlikely to get another job and, in consequence, be unable any longer to support one's family.

Freedom to communicate information

This is another of the rights listed in the various declarations of human rights. For many years it was associated in the minds of people in the UK with the freedom of people to mount a soapbox at Speakers' Corner, Hyde Park, London and say just what they liked about Government, religion and any other topic. While we are still free to say, in public, what we like on a great many subjects, there are now some which are forbidden by law. We can no longer say anything that could lead to interracial strife nor preach any form of sexual discrimination. We may agree that it is morally indefensible to stir up racial tension but we have then to accept that freedom to impart information is not an absolute right. It is a consequence of the fact that even if information, a fact for instance, is impartial, the manner or circumstances in which it is presented removes that impartiality. As was discussed earlier, information, when it is transformed into knowledge, is judged against knowledge already in the mind.

Disseminating immoral or libellous information is contrary to the law in the UK and many other countries. That networks which enable it to be distributed from a site in another country where it is not illegal is a problem yet to be solved. Were there to be a universal law, as is being attempted for copyright, it could be exploited to prevent democratic groups in exile broadcasting opposition to a totalitarian regime.

An interesting situation occurs in Germany where denial of the Holocaust is a crime. Is uttering a denial of the existence of a fact really immoral? If so, what about the rights of the Flat-earthers to promulgate their views? Obviously it can be argued that denying that the Holocaust took place is a form of racial harrassment or incitement to racial hatred. But, if that is the argument, then the problem should surely be dealt with via that route rather than by introducing a restriction on freedom of communication which may later be used as a precedent for further restrictions. In the USA the First Amendment to the Constitution, which guarantees the right of free speech, would not allow such a restriction, nor, I hope, would any British law.

A new impediment to our freedom to impart information is social pressure. At the moment one sees the pressures of the Political Correctness lobby creating a need for everyone to take great care in the way they express information. Certain words have become taboo and circumlocutions have to be used. Similarly, the postmodernist anti-judgemental attitude can impede the expression of fair criticism.

One feels that the right to be able to impart information should be accompanied by a duty to ensure that one does so correctly, in a way which the receiver will understand correctly. If the use of politically correct terms improves understanding, even if only by avoiding arousing antagonism which would distract from understanding, then they should be used. If, however, the politically correct circumlocutions reduce the clarity of the message, perhaps they should be avoided. An example of political correctness improving the quality of information is the following: in the *Hutchinson Softback Encyclopedia* [14] it says, 'J. H. Speke became the first European to see Lake Victoria'. In the old days one would have written, 'the first person to discover Lake Victoria', totally ignoring all the local inhabitants who saw it every day long before Mr. Speke arrived.

There has been in recent years a significant rebalancing of freedoms and restrictions on the right to communicate information and the process is continuing. The restrictions of the Official Secrets Act have been relaxed. The provisions of Data Protection have been extended. 'Whistle blowing', at one time socially taboo, is now encouraged officially (support is promised for a Private Member's

Bill on Public Interest Disclosure) as a way of bringing to light those that are misusing welfare funds or manufacturers that are not observing safety laws correctly. Guy Dehn, Director of Public Concern at Work, believes [15] it actually strengthens the duties of trust and confidence at work. In terms of benefitting the community, the aims may be entirely laudable but it is giving official backing to breaking the old code of honour that one does not sneak on one's friends. It seems that just as we now lack the moral fibre to tackle our neighbours directly if they do something which offends us – we get the police or the Council to do something – so we lack the courage to set about persuading colleagues to be honest.

Imparting information with the deliberate aim of harming someone or making that person unhappy cannot be morally right and rightly, one's freedom to impart information in that way is restricted. Laws that cover these cases are those of libel and slander. However, even safeguards can be misused. One remembers that it was alleged that at least one company director used threats of suing for slander, which if proved would have led to huge damages being awarded, to discourage people disclosing information about his misuse of company funds. Nevertheless, the ability to sue if one is libelled or slandered is an important right, for incorrect information maliciously used can seriously harm one's life and personal relations as well as causing financial damage.

Harming the nation as a whole is covered by national security and treason laws. There have been attempts to restrict freedom to disseminate technological information on the grounds that it could be of help to an enemy country but it is difficult to substantiate this case if one's country is not at war with any other. There were understandable efforts to do the same thing on the grounds that the results of US expenditure on research, which is considerable, could be used free of charge by other countries. One sympathizes but, experience shows that big disseminators are also big importers of information. Barriers would be in no one's interests.

If there is freedom to impart information, does this mean that it can be imparted in any way and to any extent that we like? Is there, for example, freedom to flood with information?

Cases have been reported of the owners of e-mail terminals finding that they have received so many messages from one person that the system was for all normal uses blocked. One's knee-jerk reaction is to claim this is unethical use of a right to communicate. But is it? Most likely the reason is to express annoyance or to make a point about some aspect of the facility. We must surely have a right to complain and protest if we have a grievance. If blocking an individual's e-mail system is the appropriate way to do it and no innocent parties are harmed, then it may be ethical behaviour. Each case has to be judged on its merits: there should be no general rule.

Most of us object to receiving junk mail by fax and e-mail but that does not make its distribution unethical. The proper answer, as is done, is to set up an equally proper means of restricting what one receives. There is, I think, a general acceptance that the right to impart information applies not only to individuals but to all manner of institutions as well. Advertising and public relations work are the outcome. Some restrictions are imposed on the way it is done, such as it must not offend normal cannons of decency, but in principle the same rules apply to all forms of communicating and to individuals as much as to institutions. If we cannot see the trees for the billboards, it is not freedom to advertise that we must attack but the ways in which it is done.

References

1. Williams, B. (1993) *Ethics and the Limits of Philosophy*. p.96. London: Fontana

2. Annan, N. (1991) *Our Age*. p.525. London: Fontana [Chapter 24. The Deviants – Michael Oakeshott]

3. Weisberg, L.S. (1996) Access to UN human rights documentation. *Focus* **17**(3), 174–183

4. Ridley, M. (1996) Tell-tale. DNA readings that are no business of government. *Daily Telegraph*, 29 July 1996

5. Chancellor of the Duchy of Lancaster (1997) *Your right to know. The Government's proposals for a Freedom of Information Act*. Cm3818. London: HMSO

6. Chalk, R. (1987) Commentary on the National Academy of Sciences Report. In *Contemporary Moral Controversies in Technology* ed. A. P. Iannone. Oxford: Oxford University Press

7. Worlock, D. (1997) Real policy or virtual policy? A case study of tradeable information policy. In *Understanding Information Policy*, ed. I. Rowlands, pp.146–158. London: Bowker-Saur

8. Page, J. (1996?) (ed.) *Information and Public Awareness. Transparency International Source Book*. p.93. Berlin: National Integrity Systems

9. Free speech victory fires filtering row (1997) *Library Association Record*, **99**(8), 408

10. American Library Association (1981) *Librarians' Code of Ethics*. New York: American Library Association

11. American Library Association (1987?) *Library Bill of Rights*. New York: American Library Association

12. Filtering controversy grows (1998) *Library Association Record*, **100**(1), 16

13. Finnis, J. (1994) Absolute human rights. In *Ethics* ed. P. Singer, pp.257–8 Oxford: Oxford University Press

14. *Hutchinson Softback Encyclopaedia* (1996) p.818. Stockley Park: Helicon Publishing

15. Dehn, G. (1997) Whistleblowing. *RSA Journal*, 5483, 26–27

    Also worth reading is R.O. Mason, F.M. Mason and M.J. Culnan, (1995) *Ethics of Information Management*. London: Sage

    From a preview I have had of the contents, so will be: M.M. Smith, (1999) *Information Ethics*. London: Bowker-Saur

CHAPTER EIGHT

Information ethics: duties and responsibilities

Fredom to communicate leads naturally on to the duties and responsibilities of those who have privileged access to sensitive information. Prominent among such are members of the professions, doctors, lawyers, auditors and, especially in our context, those members of the information professions who work on behalf of clients. Of course, much that applies to these applies to many others in public service, industry and commerce. Indeed, it forms an important aspect of the current interest in improving business ethics, one campaign to do which is being pursued by the Institute of Business Ethics and the Royal Society of Arts, Manufacturers and Commerce (RSA). Professionals have always maintained a tradition of pursuing high ethical standards, and handling information responsibly has always been at the heart of their work. Thus they make an important group on which to focus.

That rights bring in their train duties and responsibilities is an old truism. It is certainly so where handling sensitive information is concerned. The Biblical Commandment of 'Love thy neighbour' sums up concisely the basic principle underlying how we should use any such information we hold, 'neighbour' being understood to mean all other human beings. Obviously it should, in general terms, be exploited only for people's benefit and without causing any harm. Unfortunately, things are not always that simple.

In 1997 a UK Government committee, the Committee on Standards in Public Life (the Nolan Committee) listed seven principles that MPs and other public figures should be expected to follow:

1. selflessness (decisions should be taken on the basis of public interest only)
2. integrity (not to be in a position to be subject to improper influences)
3. objectivity (choices to be decided on merit)
4. accountability (decisions must stand up to scrutiny)
5. openness (reasons must be given for decisions)
6. honesty (no lies to cover up mistakes, no economy with the truth)
7. leadership (should set an example for others to follow).

While these principles require very little amendment to apply to professionals generally, there are pitfalls of which to be wary. Selflessness is taking decisions on the basis of client's interests but these can be agonizing for them should they conflict with public interests. Openness is giving the client all the information one can; it is not giving that same information or part of it to all and sundry. Personal privacy and commercial in-confidence information should be respected save in exceptional circumstances.

As was said before, there is a realization nowadays that there are no absolute rules of behaviour, which is one reason why judges object strenuously to laws which specify mandatory sentences for specific offences. One has rules or principles to guide, but in real situations one is balancing them against each other and also against a great many other relevant factors. For example, the simple question when someone is found guilty of falsifying expense accounts, 'Is greed the motive?' is inadequate and has to be replaced by, 'To what extent is greed the motive and what other motives are in play?' One cannot always be open about one's sources of information as others may be compromised. One's client's interests cannot always override other interests. A copyright owner refuses you access to certain information you need for your client: you know a way of acquiring it but doing so would breach the copyright – what do you do?

We should have the courage to be open and honest about our own mistakes, but what about other people's? For example, we know a colleague has made a howler and is incommunicado busily trying to put it right. Should we, if questioned about it, be honest and open? If we do not tell the questioner what he wants to know are we denying him his right to know?

This may be an easy example but in general balancing all the factors to come to a fair conclusion requires a high level of reasoning and makes greater demands on reasoning ability than some people can achieve. It is all very well requiring people to 'think and act in a good way rather than learning rules' but to put it into practice requires the capability to acquire all the necessary information, to assess the weight to be given to each item, to think through the consequences of each possible decision and so on. It is much more practicable to have rules or principles which to apply with the recognition that in some cases there may be ethically sound reasons for departing from them.

Rules and principles

Duty to client

For professional people there has always been a tradition that their first duty is to their client. The contract is with the client and the contract must be honoured unless a clash of interests arises such that the honourable action is to withdraw from the contract. One should not have two clients whose interests would be in competition.

This is clear for the professional who is self-employed. Unfortunately for clarity most are not. Many physicians are employed by the National Health Service, many solicitors belong to law firms, public librarians are employed by local authorities and so on. In these instances the client's contract is with the organization providing the service. The professional provides a service direct to the client at the behest of his employer. The balance of responsibility between the professional and his employer for the quality of the service has been a major factor in a number of court cases.

Divided loyalties or responsibilities are nothing new and opinion differs on the interpretation in this case. The General Medical Council clearly states [1] that, 'as a doctor you must make the care of your patient your first concern'. There is no ambiguity in this. Similarly the UK Library Association (LA) says in its *Code of Professional Conduct* [2], 'Members' primary duty when acting in the capacity of librarian is to their clients, i.e. the persons or groups of persons for whose requirements and use are intended the resources and services which the members are engaged to provide.' There would appear to be no ambiguity here either. However, later in the same rule the LA recognizes that there will be variations in the applicability of this rule according to the nature of the employment. A company librarian will surely regard his main duty as being to the company rather than to the other employees who are 'the persons for whose requirements and use his services are engaged to provide'. The British Computer Society prefers to leave matters open [3] and contents itself with, 'Members shall carry out work . . . in accordance with the requirements of the employer or client . . .' though one notes that the employer is put first.

In providing an information service, as one would when working in an information consultancy, there is a presumption that the professional's first duty is to the client wanting the service and that in doing this he is serving his employer. The sort of situation in which conflict of interest can arise is when the employer sets a time limit on the amount of work to be done for the client and the professional finds that significantly more time is needed to meet the client's needs. With forethought the situation can be avoided but when it does arise fine judgement is needed and the professional may have to sacrifice his own time if that the only way to a satisfactory solution to the impasse.

One of the greatest dangers in making judgements when a conflict of principles arises is that of being sure one possesses sufficient facts about the situation to be able to make a sound judgement. Froehlich [4] cites the problem of whether one should help the authorities introduce computerized information management systems into a country where labour is cheap and plentiful. One's immediate reaction is that computerized systems will result in a reduction in the number of jobs and increase the number of people with no work. However, taking a broader view, may it not be that not to computerize would eventually mean even more job losses because the growing global marketplace is computerized? May not computerizing lead to better quality jobs and by improving the economy make other jobs safer? Surely one should depart from the guiding principle of first duty to your client or employer only if one is certain one is in possession of all the facts.

Trust

Subject only to any contrary requirements imposed by law or contract, one treats all dealings with a client in confidence. Where information is concerned, trust between a client and those whose services he has engaged is vital. The client has to reveal information so that the professional can do the best job possible. An information search or the installation of an information system can only be successfully undertaken if there is full co-operation in the exchange of information between the parties. Each trusts the other to provide information that is truthful, relevant and clear. The professional will, in the course of these exchanges, learn much about the client, whether a person or an organization.

The General Medical Council again expresses this very cogently [1]. 'The doctor/patient relationship is founded on mutual trust, which can be fostered only when information is freely exchanged between doctor and patient on the basis of honesty, openness and understanding.' The same applies to all other professions, including the information professions, and should apply to dealings with those in public life. The solicitor cannot help his client if the client withholds part of the story because it might incriminate him. One has to be able to trust any professional to keep confidential information to himself, though it may be necessary to point out that it is being given in confidence.

The difficulty for the professional arises if he learns information which concerns the safety or well-being of third parties. In the medical field there is a long tradition, encompassed by law, of notifying a central record if a patient is suffering from a highly infectious disease (a notifiable disease) so that transmission of the disease can be monitored. HIV has posed another problem in that some patients try to hide the complaint from their spouse or partner. The GMC advises that if the patient does not consent to informing their partner 'the doctor may consider it a duty to seek to ensure that any sexual partner is informed, in order to safeguard such person from infection.' It is emphasized strongly that this advice is for guidance only and is not in any sense a code. This is certainly an example of utilitarian principles being adopted. That a law is now proposed to make wilfully passing on a life-threatening disease a serious offence, would seem to justify the GMC recommending a departure from the normal client confidentiality principle.

An information professional may, in the course of work for a client, learn something that seems to be contrary to public interest. Perhaps a company is already conducting extensive trials of a potentially dangerous substance to see if the benefits outweigh known disadvantages. It would be perfectly proper for the professional to discuss this with his employer and leave it to the latter to decide whether disclosure is merited. Otherwise, he should not break the customer/professional trust unless absolutely certain that he has all the facts and that a breach of the law is taking place. But it would be entirely appropriate, as in the case of auditing, to refuse to endorse the publication of information which one knows to be inaccurate.

Another aspect of trust and confidentiality arises in the field of commercial information when a second client asks the same question as a previous one. Does one reveal that the question has been asked before? For information professionals, including librarians, the answer should be, No! Is one justified in giving the second client exactly the same answer as one gave the first? Probably one is if the question is identical. Probably also, to avoid giving one client an advantage over the other, the same fee should be charged even though no extra work has been done. If one's conscience is troubled, the extra fee can be given to charity.

A more serious worry comes if both enquirers are from the same company. While the sensible thing then is to point out the duplication one may wish to explore the situation a little to try to avoid causing internal company wrangles.

A guiding principle here is that one endeavours to treat all clients equally and fairly but that should apply in all walks of life.

Use of sources

A professional should seek information only from sources which he will not be embarrassed by having to admit using. It would be quite improper, whatever the client's interests, to indulge in bribery, unauthorized searching of private files, hacking or breaking confidences. Published information poses no problem but if information is sought from an individual or institution, should one do so if one is not freely able to reveal why and for whom it is sought? If one uses the Bulletin Board to put out a request for information, the answers one receives should be regarded as freely available for use; no-one would post confidential information there in response to an open request. However, if seeking the information from members of a discussion group, should one not reveal one's intention to pass on the information?

An important role that information professionals, among whom one must number most consultants, play is that of spreading information. Problems in one organization may, in part, best be resolved

by applying what the consultant has learnt during an assign-
ment in another. Obviously great discretion is needed to ensure
that confidences are not passed on, only information that can be
regarded as open.

Acknowledge one's sources

A feature of the huge amount amount of information available is
that much of it is wrong, of poor quality, or not appropriate for
the study in hand. For this reason, as well as for reasons of courtesy, one should always cite one's sources. One should also, as far
as it is feasible, validate and verify any information one commu-
nicates to a client or indicate its degree of reliability. To do so is
a measure of one's professionalism. When appropriate one should
not be afraid to include even rumour and hearsay – they can be
very valuable, as long as their nature is made clear. Many
salesmen's reports include this sort of information and those in a
company who know the field well can infer much from such items.

Validating information one has gleaned from the Internet may
be very difficult and should also be treated as hearsay unless the
source is known as a reputable one. Web sites can usually be treated
as sound but in all cases it must not be forgotten that after one has
visited the site, the information can be corrected or just changed
without any indication being given. It is sensible to download the
information and include the date in the citation.

Use all the sources one can

One exploits all the relevant information one can find provided
that it is of requisite quality. It follows that one does not deliberately omit any for political, religious, philosophical or racial reasons
unless required to do so by the law of the country in which one
is working. When one is carrying out an information search
one must not omit some work because it disproves the theory one
has carefully constructed. However, one can argue that the balance
of evidence is in favour of one's theory, if that is the case.

Nor, even in this competitive world does one hide a key source
so that others cannot find it. Of course such things happen. We are
not all angels. I can recall in the Patent Office Library cards being
torn out of an index so that subsequent searchers from other
companies would not come across a particular patent. Computerized indexes make such stratagems impracticable – and probably

unnecessary – though it would perhaps be feasible to hack into and change one that, like the British Library Catalogue, is on the Internet.

Maintain integrity in one's own records

One should always keep a record of any alteration that one makes to a piece of information, especially to records held on a computer and especially if ignorance of the change could have serious reper-cussions. The mutability of records in electronic format has long been a reason why they are not accepted in courts of law. Some discs cannot easily be altered and their content may be acceptable, CD-ROMs of patent specifications for example, but in general one is chary of relying on electronic records in a critical situation. The alterations made by hackers to the Web pages of the UK Labour Party at the time of the 1997 election may have been very funny (to some) but they did serve to undermine confidence in what one reads on the Internet. A practice of adding something such as 'revised 22.12.97' would go some way to gaining confidence.

Integrity

Obviously any information put into a database or supplied to a client should be as complete, accurate, unambiguous and fairly presented as we can make it. Quality and reliability should be para-mount. Nevertheless, one has to recognize that in the real world we cut corners, especially if there are deadlines to be met. Also, since information is valuable and has an impact on our lives, the unscrupulous find it to their advantage to pollute the resources of information with material which is unproven, unreliable and even totally misleading. The same caution is as necessary as it always was when dealing with cowboy builders, high pressure salesmen and other sources of possible cons. The information society is different only in that there is even more scope for wrong infor-mation, both unintentional and deliberate.

Honesty in dealings

It is very easy to take advantage, for personal benefit or for that of friends and relations, of information that has come to light in the course of one's work. It is quite proper to use much of this oneself or to pass it on but for some it is not. The law against insider trading is one that has been introduced to restrict this practice. Unless it is that no disadvantage to others would accrue, it is just as unethical to exploit for personal gain information which one learns in confidence when one is undertaking a project for a client as it is for a company director to use information learnt in the Board Room or for a Government Minister to use information learnt in Cabinet.

Disclosure, accidental or deliberate

The Internet has greatly increased the ease with which information can be disclosed to a wide, indeed world-wide, audience. It may be done deliberately but even more worrying for companies is that it can happen accidentally. Pye in a paper *Changing the corporate culture* [5] described how in a small high-tech company the whizz-kids had a habit of communicating with each other, even if in the same room, via the Internet, developing bulletin boards and discussion groups. It was easy for a competitor to access such information and hardly unethical to make use of it since it was open to the whole world on that system. This sort of practice gives added incentive to companies to install intranets because it is astonishing how more and more young people find it easier to communicate via keyboard and the Internet than they do by speech. It is not entirely surprising. The capacity to think better on to a typewriter than on to paper is one that has long been known among writers.

If accidental disclosure on the Internet has to be watched, what about deliberate disclosure? It is not disclosure of information that properly belongs to other people but one's own information that could be a problem in some cases. A recent example was that of an academic research worker who published the numeric data which formed the basis for many of the encryption systems in use. According to one newspaper account, he claimed that publishing the data which for him had not been difficult to derive would make others revise, and hence make more secure, the encryption systems they were using.

Anyone who believes in freedom of access to information needs to think very hard before agreeing to install firewalls. Nevertheless, they are necessary for any business that uses the public networks. Commercial confidence is an essential part of business life and it should be possible to use networks just as one used the mail without risking accidental disclosure. Only if the firewall is intended to prevent information that should be in the public domain from being so, should the information professional decline to install it.

Information-rich – information-poor

It is all very well to talk about right to know and right to access information but not everyone can. Not everyone has access to the new ICTs; not everyone has the degree of literacy or level of education to take advantage of available information; not everyone regards a need to be well informed or to have information-seeking abilities as particularly important.

In the distant past, people's need for information was quite limited. The need has increased as the world has become more technologically advanced, as trade has become more important, as the population as a whole has become richer and as life in general has become more sophisticated. For those in industrialized countries the economy has become increasingly information dependent. Despite that, there are those who miss out on much information that would benefit them and there are quite a significant number who find learning or keeping up with the latest information technology daunting.

In the Middle Ages in Europe farming and craftsmanship did not call for very much by way of information skills. Techniques were learnt from one's parents; all the produce was consumed by the local Lord of the Manor, one's own family and other local people. It was only much later, when farming changed from communal self-sufficiency to large factory scale production, so that much of the produce was sold to distant, even foreign, markets, that it became necessary to learn about new practices that would increase yields and what was happening in distant parts that might affect prices. Similar considerations applied to people's private lives: they did not need to learn much about what was happening outside the village (except how to avoid getting caught up in some war or feud) until governments began to establish programmes and initiatives that impinged on them.

For some people, particularly those in the poorer parts of Africa, it must seem still as it was for us in those Middle Ages. But whereas in the Middle Ages there was virtually nowhere else significantly more advanced, today there are huge discrepancies between countries, glaringly exposed by trade being undertaken on a global basis.

At first sight it would make sense for advanced nations to help those in developing ones increase their information abilities, and much has been done by many organizations. But there are anxieties about how the situation may develop.

One worry is that the advanced countries themselves have a large number of information-poor people who lack adequate education or information skills, many of whom are unemployed. Present programmes will eventually solve this as all schoolchildren are given IT training and as the number of homes having a computer and interactive links to the networks grows. Current media enthusiasm for the Internet will help.

Ensuring a high level of information literacy may call for a national strategy and for expenditure of national funds on ICT equipment for schools and other educational institutions, but in the end it is a matter of ensuring that individuals are motivated and take the opportunities offered.

The second worry for advanced nations is that people in poorer countries could easily be trained to become computer literate and take on work that could be done remotely. International firms already have offices in countries remote from their main centre of activity and satellites make world-wide interactive communicating possible. A loss of jobs from high wage countries is feared.

The topic of the information-rich – information-poor divide has been explored by Haywood [6]. I shall not attempt to cover the subject in the depth and breadth that he has done but there are some issues that do need to be included here.

The issues which are important can be considered under four broad headings:

1. Personal: level of background knowledge, education, keeping up-to-date; language skills;
2. Facilities for accessing sources: telecommunications infrastructure, availability of IT equipment, libraries;
3. Financial aspects: sufficient funds to acquire equipment, charges for using information sources and services;
4. Restrictions on access to information: ownership by a few.

Personal aspects

It is very easy to get the idea that everyone needs to be constantly using the latest ICTs and to be searching for or communicating information. It is not so. At the individual level, IT-poor does not yet mean information-poor. There are, in the industrialized countries many very knowledgeable, well educated and well informed people who do not use the Internet or e-mail or fax machines or computers. They use the telephone and have radio and TV sets. There are many educated people who get more from reading a book or a journal than from a computer screen; many of them write a fair amount too. They do not feel deprived because they do not participate in 'discussion groups' on the Internet. They discuss a great deal on a very wide range of topics with friends, with acquaintances and with other knowledgeable colleagues. This may change if they become isolated, if the supply of suitable reading material dries up to be replaced by electronic publishing and if public service radio and TV cease to provide news and infor-mation. Until that happens they may choose to leave the latest IT to others, though using plastic credit cards and any other clearly useful gadgets that become widely accepted, for they are not anti-technology or anti-progress.

However, these people apart, the use of computers at school, at university, in offices, laboratories and factories is now common-place. Therefore serious problems have already arisen for those who lack the skills and education which are needed by the majority, but not all, of those who have to earn a living in modern industry and commerce where ICTs abound.

The basic need is for an extensive fund of general knowledge and of background information, and for a good level of literacy and numeracy. Worries have been expressed about the level of literacy and numeracy of many members of the population of the UK. Though there are various official and charitable information assistance services to help with problems of private life, the majority of jobs require an ability to read fluently and to under-stand and apply what is read. Jobs like copy typing, which could be done even if one did not understand a word, are virtually a thing of the past. Manual jobs which require no ability to read and understand instructions are getting fewer and fewer. As the materials used in construction, for example, become more diverse and more sophisticated, labourers need increasingly to be literate and numerate. Those who operate precision machinery have to be highly skilled and, of course, using IT equipment means being able to read what is on the screen and to use a keyboard. At the same time, it must not be forgotten that many employers point out that, for the young job seeker, IT skills are a bonus, not an essential requirement. Given literacy and numeracy, ICT skills can be taught.

While one may have scant sympathy for some of those who have recently squandered their chances for education despite knowing the type of skills and qualifications that employers require, there are many in their thirties or older who have been caught by the suddenness of change. The state has accepted that there is an obligation on society to retrain these people but it must involve more than just work experience in another job. A major effort will be required to retrain people who never were good learners of other than manual skills.

The other problem is that posed by the speed with which new information is emerging, often changing old ideas almost overnight, and by the rate at which equipment becomes obsolete. Keeping one's skills and knowledge up to date is a task that cannot be shirked if one is to be confident of being able to remain in employment. Many of the larger companies are conscious of this and help their employees to find time for 'lifelong learning'. For many others it is a case of evening courses or self tuition. Professional people expect to have to keep up to date with their subject and acquire new skills: for others this is a new experience.

Facilities for accessing sources

For an individual, to access information on the Internet one needs a computer terminal, a means of linking it to the telephone or cable system and a subscription to one of the network providers. To move large files and quantities of data around requires access to a broadband system if the process is not to be unbearably slow. Technology improvements often bring a need for consequential improvements in associated systems. Thus the development in the 1980s of Group III fax machines, much faster than the old Group IV ones, meant that broadband cables had to be laid specially.

Were the acquisition of these facilities a one-off activity with any need for replacement determined only by the equipment wearing out, many individuals and small companies would cope. Unfortunately, modern ICTs evolve so quickly that replacement, or up-grading, has to be undertaken every three or four years. It is a serious deterrent, especially for the private individual who can almost overnight change from being 'with-it' to 'past-it'.

The ICT rich–poor gap is to be found in institutions too. Big firms put in the latest, fastest system in order to keep up with competitors. Gradually a gulf builds up between those organizations that have the latest gadgets and systems at their disposal, and are inclined to deal only with those organizations that are similarly equipped, and those other organizations that are trailing along with what they can afford. Already if one has neither fax nor e-mail one is noticeably limited in one's ability to send, to a growing number of organizations, messages of which notice will be taken. Fashion and status symbols also play a part, as with the mobile telephone.

Despite all that multinational companies and the international agencies like the World Bank are doing, for many people in developing countries, too poor to have even a conventional telephone and lacking, too, a reliable electricity supply, facilities like fax and e-mail and telephone banking are beyond imagination. The recent invention of a clockwork radio for those where there is no electricity supply is a marvellous step forward: at last these people can, if they wish, learn what is happening in the world outside their immediate area. But the welcome for it emphasizes how information-poor communities that need a clockwork radio must be.

There are worries about the future of even those traditional sources of information – libraries, books and journals. Not only are costs rising but electronic publishing is increasing. Although at present most journals that are published in electronic format are also still published in print, there are publications appearing only on the Internet or only on CD-ROM and only in multimedia. Even in advanced countries not all public libraries will make these available. In some areas of some countries doubts surround the future scale of public library provision. In some poorer countries, public libraries, if they exist at all, have very scant stocks of anything other than shoddy fiction and donations from rich countries, often not in the local language. What hope is there for even those that are literate to improve their lifestyle?

Financial aspects

Obviously for those that are poor financially, the scope for entering the modern world of information technology is minuscule. For most of us in the industrialized countries, expenditure on information and ICT is rising. The cost of a telephone call may be falling (postal charges keep rising) but most of us make more calls as we become increasingly reliant on telecommunications. New services, such as automatic redialling when a number is engaged, save us a great deal of trouble and time so we use them and pay. Mobile phones are invaluable for some people but the cost of using them is higher than that of using a conventional telephone. Connecting to the Internet costs money and so does regular access to send and receive e-mails.

We buy more gadgetry and find it is soon obsolete and has to be replaced by a new model. TV sets may soon require additional equipment to receive digital broadcasts. In addition to borrowing books from a library we also borrow tapes and CD-ROMs, for which we must pay. Instead of searching the bound volumes of an abstracting journal, now a very time-consuming task, we carry out an online search for which a fee is charged (though for our employer this may save money).

Despite the way the cost of equipment gradually falls, and rises again for the latest gadget, overall the cost of keeping up with the ICT revolution is increasing. Partly this is because one uses it more, partly it is because equipment has to be replaced ever more often, partly it is because new systems are designed and partly it is because more inhouse training is required. Services which used to be free, such as Telephone Directory Enquiries, now charge a fee. It may be significant that organizations which want to attract callers often now bear themselves the cost of the telephone call. Different charging practices in different countries are a source of much displeasure.

Information searching and transmission, unless we could do it using only our own personal skills and resources, never was free. It was paid for by state funds or those of our university, by our firm or other institution. For the sort of information that can be found in books, the public library has provided a resource that everyone can use without paying a fee. It is not really free except to those who pay no taxes, either state or local. The rest of us pay for it through taxes and therefore subsidize the poor. Those who never use the library subsidise those who do and that is sometimes a cause for argument, though it is heard most strongly when subsidy for the arts is being reviewed.

The free service of the public library is being eroded. Though Ministers in the UK repeatedly say that no charge will be made for the core library service, by which it is assumed they mean use of reference collections of books and the borrowing of books, charges are made for borrowing other items and for an increasing number of other library services. True, many are leisure directed, such as the loan of music tapes, CDs and videos of films, but more and more have information content.

Public libraries are now providing facilities for access to the Internet and World Wide Web and are charging for them. In the case of at least one library, that at the London Borough of Sutton, the facilities are provided by a separate organization which is housed within the library. It charges by the hour for Internet access (£5 in 1997) and also provides training and a range of other do-it-yourself computer services. The Internet fee is obviously well within the means of most UK citizens likely to want to use the service but it must not be forgotten that the poor and unemployed might begrudge £5 and that access to many services on the Internet involves a further fee.

For those who can afford the fees, yet who do not have their own access equipment, libraries are not the only means of access. Cybercafés, tele-cottages and other commercial services are springing up to provide access to the Internet for those who need it. Even some shops, Dillon's bookshop near University College, London for example, are providing facilities. One imagines that just as most people used telephone kiosks until they had a telephone installed at home, so the use of these commercial access centres will be a temporary phase until all offices and most homes are linked in to the networks.

The realization that information has economic value has led to our having to pay for many information services, and increased use of communication facilities needs further payment. At the same time, there is still a vast amount of information that is accessible free of charge. Some of it, such as social service information, has increased enormously in the last forty years. Radio also provides a wide range of informative as well as entertaining programmes and, in the UK at least, is free of any fee, though TV is not.

Monopolizing access

Some restrictions on the use of published information have already been discussed. Copyright and patent protection, which will be discussed in the next chapter, only restrict freedom to exploit information, not access to it.

However, access to information through networks can be controlled by the provider and so can the use of CD-ROMs. Approved users are given code words with which to gain access. Obviously this gives rise to opportunities to monopolize access to information which they have and either to charge exorbitant fees or to restrict access to bodies of which they approve. Even governments are concerned lest effective encryption systems make it possible for criminal or subversive organizations to transmit information and launder money without any fear of detection.

Books and journals are printed in many copies and are widely distributed. There is no monopoly of access, though getting hold of a copy through a library may be time consuming. A database, however, may exist on one host computer only though access through online networks can be worldwide and immediate.

The first anxiety arises over the systems used to access material through the networks. If the software needed for searching will function with only one type of computer software, both being made by the same firm, then that firm making is well on the way to controlling use of the network. This is an obvious commercial development but the implications of scope for monopoly, though probably unintended, justify careful scrutiny.

The second anxiety arises because the cost of creating and maintaining databases can be high. As happened some years ago in the legal sector, a merger took place between two services leaving customers with no alternative to use. Monopoly of access can also arise from making work easier for customers. If those publications which are at present also provided electronically cease to be published in printed form, then the database owners will have control of their use. Searching database online is now preferred to manual searching of print so that in the case of the major abstracting services, sales of the very costly printed copies is decreasing.

There is nothing unethical in these developments. They are a consequence of technical progress. Nor is there anything unethical in charging for access to database. The supplier and host service have to raise enough revenue to meet the costs of the service. But it does mean that instead of being able to look at a printed copy without paying any fee, one has to pay per use. If increasing the numbers of information poor is to be avoided, some fair means of subsidizing access will have to be found. Universities may choose to bear the cost as do commercial bodies but public libraries may have difficulty because budgets are very limited.

At the same time it must be remembered that there are good and legal reasons why access by all and sundry to some databases should be prevented. House agents, for example, would not want people to be able to use their database to find properties for themselves, thereby by-passing the house agent.

In press, radio and television services, the risk of monopoly control of news and information is obviated by having many channels under different ownership. Even the risk of dictatorial government control of the media is prevented by having

commercial channels. The very poor quality of some of the information that one gleans from some of the media (to say nothing of
the tedious trivia that passes for entertainment) is the price that
has to be paid for the safeguard. Those in Third World countries,
however, point out that the western world has a monopoly of the
major news agencies so that, except when a major disaster occurs,
there is a paucity of news about them in the world's press. This is
a different form of information poverty. The refereeing system used
by major scientific journals is also accused, probably unfairly most
of the time, of restricting access to the work of researchers in Third
World countries.

Policies to cope

For those in the UK that are really poor the public library provides
free access to newspapers and other publications. Other organizations provide free of charge a vast amount of basic information.
The concern that has been expressed at national and international
level that steps must be taken to avoid the creation of a new under-
class, the information poor is, therefore, primarily a concern that
all should be ICT competent. In some countries there is an additional worry about low levels of literacy.

In advanced countries a range of educational, social and cultural
policies has emerged to try to cope. These policies aim to ensure
that schools provide the right education and training, including use
of computers and networks, and that facilities are available for
lifelong learning, training and retraining. Other policies cover the
provision of social information, including ensuring that immigrants
not versed in the national language have access to information in
their own language. Cultural policies include ensuring that there
are public access points, e.g. public libraries, with ICT facilities
as well as conventional publications. Information policies are discussed in detail in chapter 14.

Governments are also keen that industrial and commercial enterprises, especially the small ones, shall not be among the information
poor. From the European Union and the UK Department for Trade
and Industry there come campaigns aimed at encouraging small
firms to make greater use of information and of information and
communication technologies.

The EU has an expressed a policy that everyone has a right
to use voice telephony systems, i.e. the telephone, subject only to
paying any necessary charges. This policy is implicit in the USA

and the UK in the terms under which the telecommunication firms operate.

Although there have been grants at various times from governments and the EU for innovative applications of ICTs, there have not been any direct subsidies except that for the French Minitel operation. The government there provided everyone who wanted one with a terminal free of charge to encourage the establishment of a large scale, nationwide information service.

As far as the developing countries are concerned, both UNESCO and the World Bank have been making efforts to make it possible for educational and other organizations to benefit from the opportunities the wired-society presents. All too often, it seems, the efforts amount to minimizing the extent to which they slip further behind advanced countries. One feels, without having researched the topic properly, that this is the consequence of a patchwork of well meaning aid efforts rather than planned and structured redesign of the national facilities and infrastructure.

For advanced countries, then, the need is to raise educational levels, to provide opportunities for everyone to become ICT literate and to ensure that adequate information resources are open to everyone and that access is not unfairly restricted. In theory the requirement in developing countries is the same but the starting point is rather different.

References

1. The General Medical Council (1995) *Confidentiality: Guidance from the General Medical Council*. London: The GMC

   There are other guidance notes including one for HIV and AIDS which is relevant.

2. Library Association (1996) *Code of Professional Conduct and guidance notes*. London: Library Association

3. British Computer Society (1992) *Code of Conduct*. Swindon: BCS (also published is a Code of Practice)

4. Froehlich, T.J. (1994) Ethical Concerns of Information Professionals in an International Context. In *New Worlds in*

Information and Documentation, eds. J.R. Alvarez-Ossorio and B.G. Goedegebuure. pp.459–469. Amsterdam: FID/Elsevier

5.   Pye, D. (1997) Changing the Corporate Culture. In *Understanding Information Policy*. ed. I. Rowlands pp.191–205. London: Bowker-Saur

6.   Haywood, T. (1996) *Info-Rich – Info-Poor. Access and exchange in the global information society*. London: Bowker-Saur

Ethical issues as they affect those working in the information sector, especially professionals, are discussed in more detail in: Hill, M.W. (1997) Facing up to dilemmas. Conflicting Ethics and the Modern Information Professional. *FID News Bulletin*, **47**(4), 107–117

The progress of the 1997 UNESCO programme on Information Ethics should be worth following for its attention to the problems of those in Third World countries.

CHAPTER NINE

Information ethics: intellectual property and data protection

So far, in discussing rights to seek, know and disseminate information, the only limitations to those rights considered have been those that would arise from misuse of the information. However, the rights of the owner are another important factor.

One might ask whether there can be ownership of anything as ephemeral as information? Assuming, for the moment that it is feasible to ascribe ownership, how can ownership be defined and what rights does it give? Can the owner do what he likes with it? Can the owner refuse to allow other people to make use of the information or are there public requirements which over-ride ownership rights?

In a society which admits that individuals have a right to personal property (although not all do), anyone or any organization that has revealed or created new information can claim ownership of it. Just as one enjoys being credited with a new idea, so one enjoys the credit for discovering new information. Unfortunately, information is intangible and difficult to protect other than by keeping it to oneself, in which case one enjoys no credit. So, one puts the information in some visible form in order to claim ownership rights.

Ownership rights and the type of protection given to the owner depend on the form in which the information can be expressed and recorded. When the information is expressed in words and numbers, either on paper or in an electronic form displayed on a screen or printed out, it is protected by copyright laws. Drawings, paintings and artistic works, and music are similarly protected. Recorded sound is also copyright protected supplemented by Performing Rights legislation. Designs and trademarks, created for commercial purposes, have their own protection if registered at one's national Patent Office. If the new information can find its physical form as an invention, it can be patented. The requirements for each type of protection and the nature and duration of the protection vary considerably. Most are now the subject of international agreements brokered by a UN body, the World Intellectual Property Organization (WIPO).

The subject of intellectual and industrial property, the latter being the term used to cover patents, trademarks and registered designs, plant breeders rights' and some other minor forms generally termed petty patents, is highly complex. What follows is only an outline of the main points of patents and copyright sufficient to facilitate a discussion of the underlying ethical principles and the information component.

Patents for invention

If one's new information refers to an invention, for example a new way to manufacture vitamin A, then one's rights can be protected by taking out a patent. One applies for a patent for the invention to the Patent Office of the country in which one lives and also to the equivalent Office in any other country in which one wants to protect one's ownership, i.e. where it might be used. Contrary to popular belief, being granted a patent does not confer any right to exploit one's invention. Rather, one is given only the right to prevent anyone else exploiting it.

Information dissemination is at the heart of patenting. The origin of patents for invention, lies in the idea that making information about an invention available will enable other inventors to build on the idea and come up with further inventions. A patent is granted only on condition that information about the invention is published. It is to this end, as well as to ensure that someone else has not made the same invention previously, that the Patent Offices publish details, called Specifications, of the patents they grant.

The first reported example of a patent occurred in the Greek colony of Epicureans in Southern Italy. It was the practice there to give anyone who invented a new and exceptionally tasty culinary dish a monopoly right to make it for a period of twelve months. After that other cooks could copy it.

In the Middle Ages, there were instances of patents being granted to foreign workers to entice them to leave their own country and come to work and teach their skills to the craftsmen of another country. Some early patents required the patentee, 'To teach apprentices the knowledge and mystery of the new invention'[1].

In theory one has to publish in a patent full details of the invention. In practice the law requires only sufficient details of the novelty to enable one skilled in the art to reproduce it. As a result, though the patent document is a very informative one, in many cases it gives insufficient information for anyone who lacks the know-how skills of those already in the business to reproduce it. The morality of this has been seriously questioned, especially by those in developing countries who, as a result, have to buy in know-how even though they have sent their students to be educated in technology in western countries. When one remembers that the original reasons for granting patents were stimulating more inventions or teaching the know-how, withholding part of the necessary information seems sharp practice. On the other hand, industrial and commercial cultures have changed and competition from firms in foreign countries is an all too real threat. This was not the situation when patents for invention were established. Modern industrial practice is so different from what it was even in the early 19th century, that the concept of patenting which prevailed then no longer applies.

Nevertheless, even a casual glance through the latest patent specifications published shows that a great many are easily capable of being copied for research purposes by anyone with the right equipment and a degree of relevant experience. It may be, though, that it is the most economically important inventions which are difficult to copy.

Another aspect generally overlooked or not appreciated is that it is only the new feature which is the subject of a patent. If someone invents a self sharpening blade for a lawn mower, the patent specification will not describe how to make a lawn mower, it will deal only with the self sharpening blade. Also, since such a device could find other uses, it will probably be widely indexed under cutting devices or even sharpening devices, not under machinery for cutting lawns, if there is such a heading.

Patent specifications are also, in places, highly stylized sometimes obscure documents. Nevertheless, they are a very useful source of technical information. There is commonly in the introduction a description of the 'prior art' which means related science and technology on which the patented invention draws. Their use can save lengthy literature searches, since that is what the applicant will already have done.

There is a great deal of specialized expertise surrounding patent protection and this account is a very simplified version. Anyone contemplating patenting an invention or copying or improving on an existing invention should seek professional advice.

Copyright

Two distinctions in principle between patent protection and copyright are worth clarifying. A claim for patent protection has to be lodged with a Patent Office; copyright exists from the moment the document, painting or piece of music is produced, no registration is needed. Second, the invention described in a patent may not be exploited without the patentee's permission but the information given about it in the specification can be copied or disseminated provided it is not republished – that would be a breach of the Patent Office's copyright in the document. The information in a copyright document may be exploited but may not be copied, performed, quoted, or translated. To give a trivial illustration: if an article in a magazine describes a walk between two places, then you may go and take that route. However, if you are writing a book about that district, you may not reproduce the content of that article without the copyright owner's permission. On the other hand, if a patent exists for the manufacture of nitric acid by a new method, you may not use the method to make nitric acid but you can describe the new method in a textbook you are writing.

Under copyright it is not the information *per se* which is protected but the combination of words or the diagrams and illustrations used to express it. If one can use a different set of words or different diagrams to express the same information, in theory one is not in breach of copyright. But there have been cases in which it has been claimed that the basic story or plot of a novel was plagiarized and a new novel written around it (Shakespeare did just that); if the similarity is very close it may be deemed breach of copyright.

As Parrinder [2] observes, 'The purpose of copyright law is not to restrict reading and interpretation, but to make activities such as textual alteration, appropriation, reproduction and quotation subject to authorial control.' Copyright was originally established to prevent pirate publishing of novels. Copyright laws exist for literary works, music scores and musical performances, broadcasts and pictures. Copyright applies whether the work is created on traditional media or in an electronic one. International copyright agreements exist so that a work which is copyright in one country is automatically copyright in all the other countries which are party to the relevant agreement. Unfortunately, as is well known, there are some countries which are not parties to it as well as others where, it seems, enforcement is lax.

Since the time of Thomas Jefferson copyright law has aimed to strike a balance between the interests of the creator of the work and those of the public. Opinion differs on whether it does. Following a period in which copyright enforcement seemed to be sliding into disuse in the face of the photocopy machine and the simplicity of copying computer discs and digital recordings, the recent revisions of the law, and new laws covering electronic publishing, seem to be moving firmly in favour of the copyright owner [3].

It is hardly surprising that publishers demand that authors vest their copyright in the publisher as their business carries the risk and bears all the costs of printing and distribution. The proper interests of multimillion pound businesses are at stake. To information workers, concerned with amassing information on a topic for a client, copyright rules are a nuisance and it is easy to regard the publishers as an enemy to one's work. On the other hand, the ubiquitous photocopy machine makes photocopying the pages of books or journals borrowed from a library so easy and so much cheaper than buying a copy of the publication, that publishers and authors need the protection of law since their fair reward from sales is at risk. For academic journals especially, there has been a vicious circle of photocopying reducing sales, prices rising to cover costs and yield a profit, leading to increased pressure to photocopy rather than buy multiple copies and hence further loss of sales. However, the publication of popular technical and fashion journals has increased enormously and sales do not seem to be affected by photocopying.

One really cannot blame the publishers taking a firm line against proposals to relax copyright law and wanting it strengthened. The clause in the 1956 Copyright Act which allowed specified libraries to make one copy of an article from an issue of a journal for a client's private study without seeking the copyright holder's permission, though at first strictly observed, was soon ignored especially in libraries with do-it-yourself copying machines.

Generally, most publishers readily give permission to copy and incorporate in another publication extracts from one of theirs. Even the copyright laws generally make provision for a small amount to be copied as what is called 'fair dealing'. To quote a short passage in a review of a book in order to illustrate a point would be fair dealing; to extract a complete table of data from a journal article probably would not. The new EU Directive on copyright [4] removes the fair dealing concession if the purpose of copying is commercial. Oppenheim [5] warns that 'fair dealing' is a defence, it is not a licence. It is to be hoped that it will still apply in the case of authors writing books of an academic nature or technical articles which are published by commercial publishers. Otherwise, the chore of obtaining permission for each of many tens, often hundreds, of references will have a severe impact on these publications and impede the dissemination of research results.

The option of publishing one's own material on the Internet without going through the traditional practice of finding a publisher has brought to light the willingness of a sizeable number of authors, particularly those who have opinions or unusual facts to express, to publish without bothering about enforcing their copyright.

What then about the ethics behind it all? In the case of a work of art, a piece of imaginative literature, a new piece of research or an invention surely there can be no doubt that the creator has a right to be recognized as the creator and to receive credit for it? Surely, those who create the work as a way of earning a living should, in these days when copying and mass production is so easy, be given a chance to seek a fair return for their labours provided doing so does not harm others? If the only way of giving that chance is to restrict the ability of others to copy it for a reasonable time, is that not fair? And by extension, if creators choose as their means of obtaining a fair return, to sell their creations to others to exploit or are paid, as employees, to do the work, is it not fair that the purchaser or employer should enjoy the same rights as the creators would have had to seek a return for the investment?

However, should this be the case if the research is funded by the State? The author should get credit for his contribution to knowledge but has he not already received his financial reward in the form of the grant or salary paid from the grant? In the USA, published government research is not copyright. Should not the same apply in other countries? If so, what would be the position of official research published in commercial journals? Presumably the publisher has copyright in his version but the content could also be published by a second publisher.

The duration of copyright protection is 70 years, not from publication but from the death of the author (this is in the EU only; the rest of the world sticks to the WIPO guideline of 50 years). In the case of patents, if one is not worked within a reasonable time, i.e. no return is sought, then it is possible to apply for the patentee's rights to be set aside. This avoids patenting simply to block progress by others. No such provision applies in copyright law. Again, the period of patent protection is limited to 20 years, that being considered long enough to get a return – though this is sometimes disputed, especially in the pharmaceutical industry. Is lifetime *plus* 50 or 70 years the time needed to get a return for a literary or artistic work? Such provision for an author's heirs seems out of step with an age in which bequeathing wealth is discouraged. Also , I find it very difficult to think of a justification where scholarly, scientific or technological publications are concerned. In these cases I would have thought that the same period as a patent, 20 years from the time of publishing the work, should be quite adequate. Of course it can be difficult to always distinguish between imaginative fiction and works of scholarship, some biographies being cases in point. But surely an effort should be made?

What about public interest? In the case of published information, are there public requirements which ought to be taken into account? This is where we find that imaginative literature and informative publications differ. Just as invention is stimulated by other inventions, so knowledge is advanced and the generation of further new information stimulated by the publication of new information. There is no bar to reading anything that is published, even if only one manuscript exists. Access may be difficult but the act of reading and so learning the new information does not infringe copyright. There is a valid public interest in any worthwhile new information, excluding the harmful categories discussed earlier, being made widely available so that people who live far from the creator can enjoy the same stimulus as those who live nearby. Should not copyright include a requirement to publish and disseminate widely?

There have been occasions to my knowledge when an important monograph has gone out of print and it has proved impossible to acquire a copy or to pursuade the publisher to issue a reprint or new edition. Reasons for that could be that it would not be economically worthwhile or that the possibility of either a new edition or a quite new work covering similar ground was being considered. In these circumstances, should it not be permissible to make single copies of all or part of the work or to quote it extensively in another work without breaching copyright?

Since knowledge builds on information and its expression as new information requires discussion of former information, is there not a requirement that one should be able to describe accurately the prior information? If so, is it not best done by being able to quote what its creator actually said? This is the normal practice in scholarly publishing and is why there is a 'fair dealings' clause in copyright law. Occasions when it is necessary to quote the whole of a publication, or even more than a small part, are rare and therefore, on practical grounds, it is not unreasonable to require that in those instances the copyright owner's permission must be sought. The most common occasions arise when a copy of a Standard or By-Law is needed as an appendix to a report and then one uses judgement whether to buy copies to attach or request copyright permission.

Many scholars and research workers who publish information about their discoveries are keen that what they have found should be as widely disseminated as possible, provided they are always given credit for the discovery. Their reputation depends on their work becoming widely known. They are keen that what they have written should be quoted in other publications. In this there is a fundamental difference between the interests of those who produce works of artistic creation and those whose work is largely investigative. It is unfortunate that copyright law applies equally to both. On the other hand, even the investigative worker will sooner or later write a book and then may be interested in preserving copyright. Were it not that announcements of new discoveries have normally to be published in professional or commercial journals, the publishers of which are understandably keen to maintain copyright, the authors could themselves introduce the required distinction. Indeed, academic authors are pressing [6] for a fairer balance between the *needs* of all the parties involved. However, the situation is a complex one with differences of requirement even between those in the same category. An early resolution is unlikely.

Copyright and electronic publishing

Electronic publishing has created a number of extra problems which are gradually being resolved, though not always with universal agreement. Both software and databases are protected by copyright, computer programmes being treated as literary works. However, there are two categories of database, one of which is causing serious concern for users. If it is judged to be an intellectual creation it will, under EU law [4] and the WIPO Copyright Treaty [7], enjoy the normal protection as a literary work. If, however, the database is merely a compilation, but one whose creation has involved much effort in obtaining, checking and arranging the contents, then a 15 year from creation protection against unfair extraction is given. However, there is, especially among academics, a firm belief that stored data should be freely usable, just as chemists have for many decades used the content of the *Chemical Rubber Handbook* [8]. This new category of copyright protection, which is analogous to a patent protection in that the period of protection is one which gives only time to achieve a financial return, would appear to limit the traditional freedom of academics and other researchers to make use of the world's store of data. It was reported at an ECIA meeting that in the USA the presidents of universities had protested to the government, and elsewhere FID, EBLIDA, ASLIB and the LA had been leading campaigns against this so called *sui generis* right. The situation needs to be resolved with fair dealing reintroduced and limits established.

It is common practice to convert a print-on-paper document into digital form. This makes it easy to communicate, store or amend. Just as a translator holds the copyright in the translation, though not in the work itself, so the person who digitizes a document has a copyright in the digitized form. Since much digitizing is done by direct reading machines, this is likely to become in future a purely academic point. At present the first person to digitize a Leonardo manuscript holds the copyright in the digitised version [9].

The question whether providing a means of communicating information through a network is a breach of copyright has, thank goodness, been resolved sensibly. Providing a communication channel is not a breach. It seems to be accepted that copyright in the content of Newsgroups and Chat rooms on the Internet is waived.

The Internet has opened up an opportunity for publishing widely without handing one's work over to a commercial publisher. A normal technical article can be published on the Internet at virtually no cost and a paper copy can be downloadied. Thus for those who believe that copyright should not be enforced on their publications, the Internet provides a means of disseminating them but a copyright disclaimer should be included. Copyright law does not distinguish between print-on-paper publishing and electronic publishing and downloading without permission does infringe copyright [5].

High energy physicists, among whose number are the originators of the World Wide Web, use it to keep an archive of brief versions of their papers which fellow workers can consult and copy without copyright restriction (the authors waive copyright but not moral rights) as well as being able to see the latest information long before the traditional publications or even in-house reports are disseminated.

Commercial publishing is also taking place on the networks, usually from a World Wide Web site. If they use the Web, publishers can arrange that the publication is accessible, i.e. can be read, only on payment of a fee. Parrinder and Chernaik [2] express the concern that 'the fact that material carried by the superhighway is subject to copyright law may mean that the only free material in future may be free advertising.' However, many official publications on the Internet can be downloaded free of charge despite there being a price to buy a printed copy.

For multimedia compilations, the situation is virtually chaotic [5]. Not only do copyright laws differ somewhat from country to country, but within a country those for text, still pictures, moving images and music differ, and it may well transpire that the copyright in each component is vested in a different person or organization. Commercial publishers of multimedia will no doubt sort this out, presumably getting all the individual copyrights assigned to themselves, but those needing to quote or extract from a multimedia publication will need to look very carefully at what it says about copyright ownership.

Copyright was complicated enough before electronic publishing and distribution came along. The problem is partly caused by a lack of distinction between types of publication. In this respect the distinction between the two types of directory database (intellectual creation and simple compilation) is encouraging because it indicates at last a willingness to admit the possibility of different types of copyright. If the distinction between works of imagination and works of information could be made and the very different interests of their creators treated separately, not overlooking the valid requirements of the commercial publishers, then a more appropriate system might evolve which would better meet also the needs of those charged with advancing our understanding of the world.

Right to withhold or restrict the use of personal information

Those of us who have made a discovery, no matter how minor, which has added to the total sum of information on a topic, usually feel that we should be given credit for it whenever it is referred to. To that end we support moral copyright, a new concept in UK law which meets that desire. But, where information about us as private individuals is concerned, most of us feel that any decision about whether it is noised abroad or remains strictly private is ours to take and should remain so. We regard ourselves as having a right to withhold personal details. This right, if it exists, has been greatly eroded this century though, in recent years, there has been some limited, very limited, restoration.

Attitudes to personal privacy vary considerably from country to country. In most western countries privacy is regarded as a right (the Englishman's home is his castle), invasion of which has to be sanctioned by law. However, not only have attitudes to what personal information one chooses to keep confidential changed but the reality of the extent to which we can maintain privacy is very different from what we would like to believe.

There are three distinct aspects of privacy. Privacy of activity i.e. not to be spied upon, privacy of information (i.e. a right to withhold it), and a right to a measure of control over the quality and use of personal information which is held by a third party. This last is the area of Data Protection.

There is in the UK a general right of privacy on personal information, which is supported in the Courts, breaches of which have to be sanctioned by law. However, laws do provide that when there is official need for personal information it must be provided, otherwise fines may be imposed or officials can come and get it. Thus electricity and gas meter readers have a right of access to premises where there are meters, though only for the purpose of reading them. Tax inspectors also have a right to enter houses or business premises to get information about financial dealings if we fail to give voluntarily the information they need.

Privacy can be invaded by bugging devices, hidden cameras and by tapping into telephone conversations and computer network messages. For the police to do this requires the authority of the Courts and an attempt to grant them authority to do this without going to the Courts has rightly been rejected, though they can do so in an emergency but even then must, as soon as possible afterwards, seek retrospective approval. However, there are other people who are not too observant of the law who use these devices to spy on people if there is potential for monetary reward for the information or pictures they obtain.

From time to time there arises a recommendation in the UK that everyone should carry an identity card as was done in the 1939–45 war and as is done in most other European countries. In the UK it is resisted on the grounds that it breaches personal privacy but in fact we have often to produce proof of identity; a driving licence is the most commonly used one but many of us also have passports. Whenever we use a credit or debit card there is potentially a record of where we have been. In the USA people have been startled to receive, on the day after they had visited a service station, advertizing of the type, 'Next time you get gas at XYZ service station why not also . . .'.

The privacy of one's home has been breached in other ways in recent years. The need to insure valuable items against theft or damage means that details of them are contained in the records of the insurance companies. One trusts that the companies' records, probably on computer, are adequately encrypted. The Land Registry holds details about one's house and land and about previous owners. The mortgage company's and estate agent's records contain much detail about the house and its value. If one has a listed house one has to give details of any proposed alterations and obtain permission for them. Planning consent for major alterations to any house means that details of one's intentions have to be revealed.

Privacy of activity, e.g. that I spent the day on the river, should not be officially monitored unless officials have good reason to suspect some illegal activity is occurring. There should be no Big Brother watching and recording what I do. But if my actions take place in public, others have a right to observe and note. Were my actions of public interest, the media are entirely free to report them and disseminate the information worldwide.

One's privacy to go about one's lawful business is infringed by the many cameras that, to enable lawbreakers to be apprehended, record one walking in the streets or entering buildings. The reasons are valid and most of us would endorse these cameras in this criminal society in which we live. What we must insist on, and be allowed to check, is that the regulations which require all film to be destroyed or wiped clean unless it contains evidence of a criminal activity are observed.

To trap thieves, we can install in our cars a device which enables its location to be traced immediately should it be stolen. In doing so we introduce a means of recording where we have been in the course of our lawful business. There is a need to be watchful lest such misuse occurs.

A few years ago in the UK a law was passed which removed the rule whereby a wife could not be required to give evidence against her husband. Pillow talk is no longer privileged, it would seem. The right to withhold information was further dented in the Criminal Justice Act 1996 by a clause which allowed juries to draw their own conclusions from an accused person's silence. Prior to that any accused person had a right to remain silent in order to avoid incriminating himself.

An aspect of this was at the heart of a case at the European Court of Human Rights in which Ernest Saunders, the former Chief Executive of Guiness plc complained about the pressure applied to him by the UK's Department of Trade and Industry and the Serious Fraud Office, using powers under the 1985 Companies Act, which empowers DTI inspectors to compel company directors to answer questions about their company, to disclose information prejudicial to himself. In a divided verdict, 16 to 4, the Court ruled that in this case the pressure to disclose was aimed at establishing the individual's dishonesty, not just the facts of the matter under investigation. The Criminal Justice Act of 1987 allows the Serious Fraud Office investigators to compel questions to be answered but restricts the use of the answers to questions asked during cross-examination in Court.

The Data Protection Act may limit the freedom of organizations to disseminate information about individuals in their records but if the information is stored on networked computers then, albeit illegally, it may be accessed by outsiders. A recent report (Associated Press) states that because the financial status of many Americans, as entered on Social Security records, has been made available on the Internet to make it easier for people to look up their own record, it is not difficult for criminals to exploit this, or so the Chairman of the US Privacy Council opines.

Data Protection legislation

Data protection is the term used for the regulation of the use which can be made of information about individuals. It does not apply to anonymous data nor is it concerned with any other category of data. Whether one agrees with legislation to limit the freedom of organizations to use as they wish data about individuals which they have legally and properly acquired depends, I suppose, on whether one believes that a person still has any rights over information about himself which he has freely given to someone else or whether one thinks such information once given is entirely in the public domain. A secondary consideration is whether, even if it is in the public domain, others should be able to exploit it for financial gain.

Although the original intention of Data Protection, as exemplified by the UK Data Protection Act of 1984, was the regulation of computer-held stores of personal information, the EU's Directive [10] extends its coverage to all stores of personal information whether on paper or in any other medium and has also introduced some aspects of privacy. The Directive will be taken into UK law by 1998 [11].

The original impetus arose from the problems that would be created in services trade between countries which had laws and those which did not. Even now, not all countries have data protection laws and there are still differences between those that do. Those of the EU, USA and Canada differ [12]. The moral need for legislation, as well as any trade requirement, has been brought home by some of the practices that were occurring before legislation came in. The exchange of files of personal data between commercial research firms, banks, mortgage lenders, insurance companies and credit card firms could result in a single piece of inaccurate information appearing in the files of all these organizations. The outcome of that could be that an individual could not get insurance or a loan and had no idea why. People generally were unaware of the existence of these databases which, for example, might have a note that in one case they had been very late paying bills or that they were not credit-worthy when neither statement was correct. Data protection legislation aims, among other things, to put these problems right and prevent their recurrence.

According to an EU Press release [13], the Directive aims to help ensure the free flow of personalized services in the information society by fostering consumer confidence and to minimize differences between the rules in member states. In addition to the rules that must be observed when processing personal data, it lays down the circumstances under which personal data may be lawfully processed without the specific and prior consent of the data subject. All seem entirely reasonable. They comprise meeting contractual and legal obligations, protecting the interests of the data subject, and for tasks carried out in the public interest or that of the data controller.

Other exemptions include data held for medical research, government statistics, files concerned with a company's career planning, personal social services, and the prevention and detection of crime. Journalism and the production of works of artistic and literary expression are exempted from the personal privacy provisions.

Not surprisingly since nearly every organization keeps its data on computers and these include records of staff, of clients and suppliers and many other people, there has been an outcry about the cost that implementing the Directive will impose. Some estimates put the cost as high as millions of pounds.

Lists of names and addresses have been available for many years. Local councils have maintained voters lists. Telephone directories give the address as well as the telephone number, though one can opt out of having an entry there (ex-directory number). Many other directories have been published in printed form giving more and more details usually of selected groups of people: *Who's Who*, the Army List and the Civil Service Yearbook are examples. The advent of computer printing created an opportunity, rapidly taken by some entrepreneurial organizations, to merge several of these listings to create a database or set of databases with more information about each individual than was in any one of the original sources. Such databases are portable and saleable to those who want address lists for targeting advertizing material. One outcome has been the mass of junk mail many people receive.

In addition to merging directory information, market research companies have been busy distributing questionnaires asking all sorts of questions about our shopping habits, where we like to go for holidays, what sports we indulge in and so on. Various incentives are given to encourage us to fill in these forms and most of us complete some of them, though few would do so for all.

It is by merging this information with that from address lists and directories that databases which contain a vast amount of detail about each one of us can be compiled. Under current UK legislation, and equivalent laws in other countries, if one wishes to create a computerized database which contains personal information, one must seek the permission of each person, known as the data subject, and one must register the existence of the database with the Data Protection Registrar. Furthermore, any use of the list for a purpose other than that originally intended (e.g. by selling a membership list of a club to a commercial organization) has to be agreed with the data subjects. Those compiling these databases usually meet this requirement by including, in very small print, a statement that those who do not wish information to be passed on to other organizations should put a mark in a box, or some similar wording. Those of cynical disposition will suspect that only a small proportion of those answering notice and mark the box.

What is happening is, of course, that much greater use is being made of this personal information. In the supermarket, and recently some other large stores, loyalty cards, issued on the pretext of giving discounts and special offers to regular customers, enable the store to record the buying practices and preferences of its customers. Does it really matter that the store knows you purchase every Wednesday two packs of Bonio, and hence have a dog, provided it keeps the information to itself? It certainly won't share it with competitors. If possession of the information were restricted to the one store, it probably wouldn't; after all most small shopkeepers memorize the same information about their customers and use it for their mutual benefit. But most supermarkets are part of big multinational multi-company organizations and if the information is processed centrally, it could be used by several different commercial enterprises, even some abroad ready for when you go on business or holiday.

One major problem with databases of people's tastes and interests, whether the information is given willingly and knowingly or not, is that human beings are wilful and inconsistent. We are free to change our minds and our practices quite abruptly. This year I am keen on holidaying in a distant, exotic place. By next year I've had quite enough of that and intend to holiday at home. On one questionnaire I may fill in that I drink on average so much wine, beer and spirits each week, omitting, since it was not asked, how much cider and liqueurs. In the next questionnaire I put down the number of standard measures of alcohol, a figure which does not match with the information put in the previous survey.

These are trivial examples but the point is a serious one. We change, we are not consistent, and, as pointed out in chapter 3, the questionnaires themselves often require a measure of interpretation – the questions as asked do not really fit us. 'Tick only one of the boxes', yet the real us is represented by ticks of varying strength in several boxes. 'Are you satisfied, partially satisfied or dissatisfied?' with some service we are asked. The answer is all three. We average as best we can but the result, for us, is highly unsatisfactory.

We may give the information willingly; after all there are people out there who are earning their living by gathering and analysing this information. The law will now require them to tell us who is compiling the data and on behalf of whom. Unfortunately, it does not require that the information be scrapped or updated after a given time. Presumably it is assumed that commercial organizations will update such information for their own benefit but I doubt if reliance can be placed on it.

In years past, it probably did not matter too much that our manager kept notes about our performance, that our bank manager kept a file on our credit-worthiness or that the newsagent knew we wanted the *Telegraph* and would not accept the *Mail* as a substitute if he ran out. Today it does matter because technology makes it possible for the information to be disseminated widely to other organizations, to be cumulated and for the results to affect the individual, sometimes in ways contrary to his interests.

The right of staff to see their annual reports has been given legal force with the Access to Personal Files Act of 1987 although such practice was normal in the Civil Service and many in companies before then. The new data protection proposals make it clear that not only facts and figures but also expressions of opinion about a person are to be treated as personal data. What information someone else holds about us is something we feel strongly we have a right to know and also a right to correct.

Medical records and health checks for insurance companies have been a source of concern. The Access to Medical Records Act of 1988 and the Health Records Act of 1990 both give individuals a right to see and correct their personal records. Presumably this will, therefore, cover our right to know what analysis of our genetic make up reveals.

Although these four Acts, the three immediately above and the Data Protection Act, represent a huge change in attitude to records of personal information the situation is messy and the pressure to reveal more and more continues. Data protection allows us to limit the use of files to which we have voluntarily or under compulsion contributed. The other Acts give us a right to see and correct files but we have to take the initiative. There seems to be no obligation yet for the holders of files to submit them to us at regular intervals for updating, as directories such as *Who's Who* make a practice of doing. Nor does there seem to be any possibility of being able to withdraw information, other than that in error, to do which surely ought to be a part of our right to privacy. Unfortunately, whatever right to privacy we may have, privacy of information about each of us is probably a lost cause.

References

1. Wittmann, A., Schiffels, R. and Hill, M.W. (1979) *Patent Documentation* p.8. London: Sweet and Maxwell

2. Parrinder, P. and Chernaik, W. (1997) (eds.) *Textual Monopolies: literary copyright and the public domain.* London: King's College

3. EU law will lead to imbalance. (1998) *Library Association Record,* **100**(6), 285

4. EU Directive on Copyright. (1997) Implemented in the UK as *Copyright and Rights in Databases Regulations.* Statutory Instrument S.I. 1997 No. 3032. London: Stationery Office

5. Oppenheim, C. (1997) *Copyright in the Electronic Age.* In Parrinder and Chernaik. See ref 2.

6. Hyams, E. (1998) Academic authors clarify stand on copyright in digital media. *Inform,* 205, 2–3

7. *WIPO Copyright Treaty.* (1997) House of Commons Command Paper. Cm3736. London: Stationery Office

8. Lide, D.R. (1998) (ed.) *Handbook of Chemistry and Physics* 78th edition. Florida: CRC Press

9. Le Crosnier, H. (1997) Lecture on copyright and new technology given at an ECIA meeting, Paris.

10. Commission of the European Union. Directive 95/46/EC on the Protection of Individuals with regard to the Processing of Personal Data and on the Free Movement of such Data. *Official Journal of the European Communities.* No. L281, 24 October 1995.

11. *Data Protection: the Government's Proposals* (1997) House of Commons Command Paper. CM3725. London: HMSO

12. Bennett, C.J. and Raab, C.D. (1997) The adequacy of privacy: the European Union Data Protection Directive and the North American response. *The Information Society.* **13**(3), 245–263

13. Monti, M. (1995) *Council definitely adopts directive on protection of personal data.* EC Press Release IP/95/822. 25 July 1995. Quoted by Bennett and Raab, see ref 12

Also of note are:

Oppenheim, C. (1997) Electronic copyright. *Inform* 199, 4

and EU DGXV Web site: http://europa.eu.int/comm/dg15/en/index.htm

CHAPTER TEN
Some social and cultural issues

'Social patterns usually get changed by technological progress'.

Naomi Mitchison [1]

To anyone who grew up before 1940 it is obvious that society and social attitudes have changed enormously in the last 50 years. Looking back further, to the change from an agrarian to an industrial society, one can see that a key feature is the size of the communities and groups in which people lived and worked. In the agrarian society, most people lived in villages, knew everyone they needed to know and worked in the fields in small groups. The opportunity to seek and exchange information and to learn what was happening in the world outside was provided by fairs, markets and itinerant tinkers and priests.

In contrast, the industrial society was characterized by very large numbers of people all working together. Thousands of workers poured in to the factory at a given time in the morning and poured out to go home in the evening. In offices large numbers of clerks and typists arrived together, worked together and left together.

In the 1980s much of this changed. Work forces in both factory and office were sharply reduced in size. Computers did more than anything else to make such changes possible though the underlying forces were economic.

Those of us who remember the period before 1940 are particularly struck by the change from the calm, ordered society of that time, a society in which everyone had and knew his/her place, to the frenetic, disordered one of today in which everyone has to compete to establish and maintain a place. Around us, previously stable organizations merge, demerge, disintegrate and disappear. Jobs for life become ever more rare, even in professions, part time work becomes more common and fewer and fewer enjoy the reassuring haven of a traditional family life.

One consequence for many is that their traditional sources of information have diminished. For the majority of the 'working classes' their principal source of advice and information was their workmates. There was always someone who could tell you the best way to ... or the best material for ... or you should go and see. ... The loss of the large group of fellow workers as an information source is not replaced by the cameraderie of the football crowd or the pop concert. It is something that present-day advice systems have not yet adequately replaced. There are plenty of specialized services but no one generalized one at which any sort of query can be thrown. If the Internet catches on with the descendants of these factory and office workers, it may provide a much needed substitute.

Changes in the size of working communities is just one among many social changes that have taken place in Western society in the last hundred years or so. In that time there have been the most profound social and cultural changes, more profound than those in the previous thousand years. They have been so extensive that it is difficult to believe that the anticipated information society can in the years ahead give rise to anything comparable. None of the changes is complete, not even those that have been underway for some time. Some changes one fervently hopes can be reversed. The list of developments that have affected us and make the way we live now quite different from that of a few years ago is lengthy:

- families are smaller, the adult members more widely scattered, and an increasing number of nuclear units unstable;
- relations between males and females have changed. The number of young women for whom marrying and raising a family are their principal aims is decreasing; more of them are career oriented; many marriages are ending in divorce; many couples do not bother to marry; many women do not have children; large families are rare; more people are living longer;
- women in general, not just exceptional individuals, are accepted as socially and intellectually equal to men;
- belief in the superiority of some races over others is gradually disappearing;

- there is an attitude of general social equality; respect has to be earned by one's achievements (wealth, power or media image); class distinctions still exist (they do in all societies everywhere) but in the UK we are in transition between class based on birth or upbringing, or on education and social behaviour, and one based on economic or media status;
- uncouth behaviour is no longer a source of shame; indeed, shame seems to be disappearing even if one is convicted of a crime;
- levels of crime have risen steeply; no longer is there the trust that allowed one to leave one's home unlocked; no longer can a woman with a baby and a bag of gold walk across England unmolested;
- youth and its tastes are treated as important; children have rights; the experience of age is no longer of value;
- personal wealth has increased enormously; though there are many categorized as poor, except for those who 'drop out' the grinding poverty many endured in the century before 1940 or is prevalent in developing countries is unknown now in the UK;
- linked to the general increase in wealth, there is a culture of discarding rather than repairing worn or broken goods and of acquiring the latest model, whether of car or computer programme, even before a new one is needed;
- we live in flats, semi-detached or detached houses with gardens rather than the long rows of terraces of the industrial age, which has contributed to loss of community spirit among adults and friendships among children (transporting children to nursery and primary school by bus rather than by car would deprive mothers of one of their principal opportunities to establish social contacts and informally seek information);
- dress has become much more informal, usually more comfortable;
- shopping has become a leisure activity rather than just a necessity; we prefer supermarkets to local stores; we buy in car loads rather than basket loads;
- eating habits have changed; we buy ready-prepared foods; we eat foreign foods as of norm; we eat out more;
- drink/drive laws have changed the practice of going far to a pub. Many pubs have established restaurants, and people go to eat rather than drink;
- most people take some of their holidays abroad preferring Tenerife or Thailand to Margate or Morecambe;

- religious beliefs are no longer held by a large part of the population;
- life is ever more phrenetic and time ever more precious;
- for many work does not provide any sense of stability; redundancy, part-time working, self-employment and unemployment are the lot of many who would in previous times have spent the whole of their working lives in one office or factory.

This is a long list and it is by no means complete but it serves to emphasize the extraordinary extent of the changes that have come about since 1945, many much more recently. It provides the background to changes in the information environment and includes many developments in which the growth of new information has been a significant factor. It would also be wrong to treat each change as distinct from the others. They are interrelated. The changes are, of course, not universally accepted; there is much conflict especially between the older, more traditional generation and those for whom change is excitement. This situation was admirably highlighted in David Hare's play *Amy's View* [2].

There is a general feeling that the pace of both technical and social change and of their acceptance is increasing. The motor car was invented in the last century but it is only since 1950 or so that it has had a major impact on the way the majority of people in the UK order their lives. The Kenwood mixing machine took only a few years, probably a decade, to change domestic cooking from a chore to a pleasure. Barsoum [3] has pointed out that it took about 28 years from the start of public service broadcasting before 40 million people had radios, only 8 years before 40 million people had TV sets, and a mere 3 to 4 years before 40 million people were connected to the Internet. Those are periods from the time when the services were first generally available: radio, TV and ARPANET (the origin of the Internet) were invented long before they became generally available.

Information alone is not the cause of these changes but it certainly has played a substantial part, particularly when it reinforces a change which is still tentative. Sometimes unusual circumstances have brought new information to light or have brought people in general to realize a fact that has been staring them in the face for a long time. For example, when in the 1914–18 war there was a shortage of labour, women stepped in and did 'men's work' and showed that in most cases they could do it just as well – and that information spread around.

It is not just information that leads to change. It is also the speed and extent to which it spreads. In previous centuries it was generally possible for new and unpalatable information to be stifled, at least as far as the uneducated majority was concerned. Children usually accepted what their parents said. Neither is entirely true but each is a fair statement of the situation. Universal literacy and the growth of the news media changed all that. Information spread rapidly and led people to feel that what they read or heard might have a relevancy for them.

Why should not women have the vote? If Jesse Owen can beat the best athletes Europe can produce, who says the Aryan races are superior? If the universe is millions of years old and human beings have evolved from simple life forms, the Biblical account of creation must be wrong. And if that is wrong, what credence can be put in the rest of the Bible? If other people can break through the social barriers and if those of higher social class are caught behaving badly, why should there be any class divisions at all?

This type of thinking is very crude and highly flawed but it is common. The consequences of the wide availability of information can be deeper and more dramatic than would at first be expected. There is more to the social and cultural changes of the last fifty years than just the massive amounts of new information, but those massive amounts have played and are still playing a major part. Whenever social mores are based on prejudice and tradition, as they so often have been, they can be put under strain by new information from any of a wide variety of sources.

Personal information

There are two categories of personal information: that which we possess about friends, neighbours, where we live, and events etc. in the world at large both past and present; and that which other people and organizations possess about us. Of the former, many of us have more than our ancestors ever did and more and more resources at our finger tips. Nevertheless, as indicated earlier in this chapter, for some of us gaps have formed. At the same time there appears to be a large group whom the education system has failed and which will be discussed in chapter 13.

The ethical aspects and the value to business of the second category, the large amounts of information about each one of us that are held in computer systems, and the importance of personal data protection generally, have been discussed in previous chapters. The dangers to our private lives posed by the new technologies and the masses of personal data have not been overlooked. But if there are dangers, there are also advantages, even if sometimes it is difficult to believe.

Computerized medical records, that most personal of information, make it easy for the GP to check past ailments and treatments and for the information to be accessed by a locum or conveyed to a specialist. They also make it possible to contact all the patients who have received a certain treatment if it should be necessary. In theory this could have been done from conventional paper files but in practice it was not feasible.

Another advantage of computerized banks of personal data is that it is easier to confirm one's identity when doing business by telephone. Already it is a common experience to find one's full address known as soon as one quotes name and postcode, thereby eliminating likelihood of error due to mishearing, and also to be asked for one's date of birth or for a security code such as one's mother's maiden name as a guarantee that you are who you say you are before a discussion involving personal information takes place.

There are other ways in which we can be identified. In the UK we have National Insurance and National Health numbers. The mobile telephone pinpoints its owner. Although in principle it can be shared and used by anyone with the permission of the owner, in practice it is used as a means of contacting one specific person. Next comes the personal e-mail address. It will not be many years before all but a very few have one. Already students in universities, Exeter University for example, are each given their own personal e-mail address to facilitate their studies.

As individuals, we are also labelled in unique ways by nature. The most reliable of these it would seem lies in our DNA molecules. Whenever we leave a scrap of ourselves – a drop of blood, of skin, of semen – somewhere, analysis of that scrap should reveal unambiguously that it came from us. That it does so only with a high degree of probability, not with certainty, is a failure of the analytical methods available as is explained in chapter 3. A fingerprint or a picture of the iris of one's eye can uniquely identify each one of us and experiments are being carried out to see if either can be used as a way of verifying an electronic transaction. There is evidence that one's voice is similarly unique but like appearance that can change with time or through accident. One's DNA, iris and fingerprints cannot.

In 1997 the concept of a national databank of photographic pictures was proposed. This, linked to observational cameras, would certainly provide an opportunity for the 'authorities' to know who was doing what at any given time. It can be argued that as long as the UK remains a democratic country there is little to fear. But what happens if criminals gain access to the films? Would it make it easier for them to plan a robbery, for example? As has been seen from the case of shopping data, information can be turned to uses which the information subject, to use data protection jargon, never envisaged.

One example was provided by BT's '1471' service which tells you the number of the person who last rang you so that you can, if you wish, ring them back. One wife used it to check her husband's office number so that she could phone him (he had just phoned her) only to find that he had phoned her from his girlfriend's flat [4].

So there is a need to be very watchful that new databanks and information facilities do not unacceptably erode personal privacy or freedoms. At the same time, these developments influence substantially the relationships between the individual and the society in which he lives.

The media and society

It is not irrational that one's train of thought progresses from a discussion of the benefits and dangers of amassing information about people to a consideration of the actions of the media, especially the news media. The Press and television are both a major determinant of many aspects of social behaviour and a revealer of social misbehaviour. But, perhaps even more important, news is a socially important category of information. It forms a significant part of everyday conversation and the majority of it comes to us through the news media. What is seen on TV or read in the papers and magazines influences the attitudes and tastes of a great many people.

The invention of radio dramatically changed our relation to news. Before that, news of far off events was very slow arriving. A war might be waged and be over before news of it appeared in the press. Now we can receive instant news from all around the world and, with TV, see events in distant places as they are happening. One recalls the war in Somalia where the TV crews were on the beaches watching the invading American forces come ashore. Now on both radio and TV there are round-the-clock news programmes so that no longer is it necessary to wait for the news broadcasts at fixed times. And news agencies still provide teletext services to those with receivers.

Although one may claim to treat all that one gains from the news media with a pinch of salt, and indeed, as discussed in chapter 3, there are many examples of errors and inaccuracies, in practice most of us absorb and make use of quite a lot of information from them. In fact, it may not have escaped the notice of readers that there are in this book quite a number of quotations from or references to items found in the Press or heard on the radio.

A recent development is that newspapers have become accessible via the Internet. Even more recently the BBC has started a free, 24-hour news service, called News Online, on the Internet. In the case of newspapers one can see them seeking a new readership, though the screen, even of a laptop, is hardly a convenient alternative to the printed copy for reading in the train or at the breakfast table. The BBC, with its 24-hour service, is presumably seeking to establish a presence in a medium that could otherwise reduce its listener/viewer ratings on traditional channels. However, the rate of change in this area is so great that any forecast of the outcome has a very low probability of being right. What does appear to be the case is that the trend towards news as entertainment is being to some extent balanced by greater accessiblity to the news. One can access the latest information all day long and through a variety of channels.

On the radio there is much information solidly presented, e.g. on Radio 4 and News Direct, while on other stations it is surreptitiously delivered in the course of music and chat. Virtually every London commuter listens anxiously to the travel news each morning.

Television programmes provide a vast amount of information, not only in news and documentary programmes but also in those which are primarily entertainment. Scenes of the Inspector Morse series set in Oxford have given those who have never been there a better idea of what the colleges look like than Colin Dexter's books could. The series 'All Creatures Great and Small' gave a lot of information about veterinary work, as 'The Archers' on radio does about farming life. For many people, television provides a principal channel of information and its impact can be considerable. Seeing something informative is more effective than reading about it, especially for those who lack imagination or who read only with difficulty.

The immense amount of information purveyed by TV as entertainment is illustrated by taking just one evening's programmes.

BBC 1 showed world news, regional news, a programme on fashion and beauty, 'Tomorrow's World' which deals with new inventions and trends, a programme on burglar alarms, more news, and a programme on ethics among holders of public office. Out of a total of thirteen programmes, seven were devoted to news and other forms of information. On BBC 2 the ratio was six out of ten, on ITV it was five out of nine, on Channel 4 five out of nine and on Channel 5 four out of nine. In total, 27 of the evening programmes were primarily informative though, of course, they included opinion and, in some, advice too. On top of that one has the cable and satellite channels, a dozen or so of which broadcast entirely informative material – I include live coverage of sport as informative. Of course such material is presented in an entertaining way. 'Mastermind' and 'University Challenge' are entertainment but they are also informative in that we all learn new facts from those questions we at home failed to answer.

However, as commented earlier, the presentation of information as entertainment arouses anxiety. Cronkite [5] observed, 'For those who cannot or will not read, television lifts the floor of knowledge and understanding of the world around them. But for others, through its limited exploration of the difficult issues, it lowers the ceiling of knowledge.'

For those who can and are willing to read, an important part of the leisure scene is the wealth of magazines dealing with all manner of pursuits from gardening and fishing to computing and music. Many of these, but not all, trivialise the field of knowledge that they cover. The serious magazines of the past have largely vanished and even those that remain, such as *The Spectator*, have a light-hearted style.

The number of these magazines has increased enormously since the 1950s and one feels that it must have reached its maximum. That it should have grown so much during a period when TV was gaining a greater hold on leisure time is interesting. It makes one feel that, though there will be always some ceasing publication, there will be new ones coming along to take their place and that the present level may well be maintained despite the Internet. It could happen that there will be a gradual switch to magazines on disc but somehow I doubt it. The printed format of the magazine is very convenient and comfortable to use provided it is not spoilt by deliberately nonstandard page sizes.

Advertising

'The primary function of advertising is, we are told, to introduce a wide range of consumer goods to the public and thus to support the free market economy, but this is clearly not its only role; over the years it has become more and more involved in the manipulation of social values and attitudes and less concerned with the communication of essential information about goods and services'.

Gillian Dyer [6]

A discussion of information and impact would be singularly incomplete without a consideration of advertising, since it can convey a wide variety of different sorts of information, many with social consequences. Advertisements have long been used to get over political and social messages. The various political parties all use poster advertising to disseminate their ideas. Anti-hunting and other lobbying groups use advertisements to persuade people to support their campaigns. But this is not all that Dyer is getting at. Advertising is skilled at changing our attitudes to certain types of goods which are related to specific lifestyles. Television advertising in particular, where one can tell a story with moving images, can develop an attitude that one must have certain goods to show one's status in society. Thus everyone who thinks himself someone has to have a 4×4 car to show his macho image. It is similar to promoting fashions in clothing which has been practised for many years with, for example, hem lines going up and down like yo-yos. The primary object is to sell goods, but it has the effect of creating a throw-away society; one no longer alters a garment or gets an old model machine repaired, one gets a new one and that has consequences for the pattern of employment.

Much advertising contains useful information. Local papers for example, contain advertisements for theatres and cinemas, for items which individuals want to sell or find, and announcements by local authorities of planning proposals inviting objections. *The Yellow Pages* directory is simply a source of information about which firms do particular types of job.

However, the main purpose of much commercial advertising is to give information about a product in such a way as to increase sales at the expense of a competitor's product. Thus to take two advertisements for Desktop PCs, one tries to encourage purchase with a claim that it has rated highly in customer satisfaction polls, while the other trumpets its interest-free installments scheme for payments. The technical specifications are also given: both machines have a 200 + MHz processor but machine 1 has a 3.2 Gb hard disk while machine 2 has 4.3 Gb hard drive. There are other differences and similarities in the specification details and in the package of goodies (programmes etc.) which come with each machine. This is advertising at its most helpful with the facts clearly distinguishable.

As everyone knows, not all (some would say, not much) advertising is like that. An advertisement for a watch that says no more than 'guaranteed for three years' or for a travel agent that simply offers 'generous discounts' would seem to do no more than draw attention to the name of the product or of the agency. The information content is minimal. However, most newspaper advertising does give some useful information, most poster advertising very little. Television advertising seems primarily to aim at creating a favourable impression. Presumably few viewers would jot down any details or even be able to in the short time that the ad is displaying.

Some information given is used, it seems, primarily to create the right impression. The ability of a car to accelerate from 0 to 60 mph in 5 seconds gives little guidance as to whether it is suitable for commuting day after day into central London where speeds rarely exceed 30 mph, and the real interest is in performance in circumstances of frequent stopping and starting.

The information impact of some advertisements is highly questionable. Many readers of newspapers and magazines develop a capacity not to see them, especially whole page ones. Although the advertisements on TV have been described as more interesting than the programmes, it is common either to switch off as soon as the programme ends or to go and do something else while they are on. Even if watched the key information may be lost. In my own case, I cannot recall the make of car the lovely Nicole and her father were advertising; my recollection is only of her and her father's appearance and the beauty of the town through which they drove.

Apart from the advertisements that one deliberately looks for, e.g. those for a film or concert, there is little doubt that quite a lot of information is picked up from that source by chance and not only from those on billboards, on TV or in the paper. Much advertising arrives unsolicited in the post, as loose inserts in magazines, by telephone, by fax and by e-mail . Though most is immediately thrown away or ignored, enough must strike a chord for it to be worth the cost of advertising, and whether a purchase results or not some of the information seen does add to one's store of knowledge. Telephone advertising and e-mailed publicity (commonly known as 'spam') is so irritating to many recipients that not only do sales not result but there may also be a positive failure to register any information content.

In the past, advertising has been sometimes quite misleading. Advertisements for remedies which were probably useless or even harmful were common in past centuries. In this century, advertisements for hotels 'within a stone's throw of the sea' which in practice were half a mile away from it were the subject of comedy. Successive governments over more recent years have taken steps to legislate against deliberately misleading advertisements as the following list of Acts and Regulations illustrates:

Trade Descriptions Act 1968
Fair Trading Act 1973
Business Names Act 1985
Control of Misleading Advertisements Regulations 1988
Property Misdescriptions Act 1993

It is not feasible to legislate to ensure that advertisements shall tell the truth, the whole truth and nothing but the truth, but at least the scope for deliberate error and intentional misinformation is reduced.

Support and advice: social services

Not all advertisements aim to sell something. Those in the Press, commercial radio and TV are used by official organizations and charities to give information about matters that affect people's lives. The local council publishes notices in the paper about planning applications and forthcoming roadworks. The government puts notices about all manner of matters and uses the media to make announcements, for example about elections. It uses advertising to run campaigns urging people not to smoke, not to drink and drive and not to abuse drugs. In the private sector, too, advertisements are used to convey a piece of information to a wide group of people. For example, individuals announce births, marriages and deaths, lawyers advertise to seek those who may be beneficiaries under a will and banks announce interest rate changes.

Awareness is a major concern. The Press, radio, TV, journalists and advertisers, public relations officers and official information services all do much to make members of the public aware of matters that affect them, issues on which they should have an opinion, changes in laws and regulations which they need to observe and benefits and services to which they are entitled. Yet despite the outpouring, the information does not reach everyone or it is not noted and remembered by everyone. In its first annual report [7] the Information Society Forum, a body set up by the European Commission, emphasizes this lack of awareness and proposes greater use of information technologies to fill the gap. Especially it is concerned that awareness of issues such as voting or consumer protection should be increased.

However, the ability of the better off ordinary citizen, let alone officials, to communicate with the have-nots and drop-outs is very poor. Probably this is due in large measure to the problem of understanding, of tuning in to each other's real interests and needs and putting information over in a way that will strike a chord. As Puttnam wrote [8], 'Our ability to communicate knowledge in ways which are technologically and conceptually more accessible is mocked by our failure to reach the people who need it most – the dispossessed and the marginalised'.

There has been a number of initiatives aimed at using information technology to assist those who are jobless and socially excluded. They have broadly taken the form of centres, very informally structured, to which people can just drop in, learn in their own way to use IT terminals and access information about jobs and social benefits. They are known as Electronic Village Halls, Community Resource Centres, Telecottages or other local term. An account of them and their very variable degree of success is given by Day and Harris [9]. Inevitably much depends on having the right people to put over technical matters without being patronizing and adequate, stable, long term funding. But the attraction of this new technology and the ability to communicate by machine, not directly with another human, draws many to gain an increased measure of self confidence even if not many get jobs as a result.

It used to be said that an educated person is not one who knows everything but one who knows where to find out. Many services exist to answer our questions and to provide help and advice but there can be not only ignorance of them but reluctance to use them. There are those who take their ailments to the local chemist rather than to a doctor. Solicitors exist to provide advice on legal matters but many regard them as a last resort. The local tax office will give much help on taxation matters but many choose not to avail themselves of that help. The local public library provides guidance towards self-help, e.g. reference books to consult, but not everyone is at ease explaining one's problem to a librarian even if one is sufficiently literate to use books.

Fully literate people, especially the growing numbers who have been to university, have a natural tendency to seek information for themselves in published sources, especially in those in which there is some evidence of research having been undertaken into the relative properties of comparable products or services. However, for the purchase of goods such as furniture one is often reliant on the advice of the salesman. Many of these are very good, well trained and knowledgeable; some are not, second-hand car salesmen having acquired a particularly bad reputation through the activities of a few rogues. A major problem users of information encounter is that the conclusions drawn from a small number of instances are assumed to apply to all cases irrespective of whether or not the sample is representative.

Newspapers and magazines have their advice columns ('agony aunts') which a few people use, though one suspects that some of the enquiries are not genuine but written in order to enable a point to be made, and that the selection published is chosen for its general interest. Some magazines – *Which?* is an outstanding example – offer advice in the form of comparative information so that one can judge whether the magazine's opinion of the best product among a range of different brands and models is likely to be appropriate in one's own circumstances and needs. The reasons for using or not using a particular service are many and often complex and very personal. One reason among the many is that people generally like to talk with people who 'talk the same language', i.e. come from the same background as themselves. There is an awareness problem and there is a communication problem.

There are now in the UK a large number of services, many voluntary, which attempt to reach out to those the existing formal services seem unable to contact. Possibly the best known of these are the Citizen's Advice Bureaux. Myers and McClean, in a paper [10] on the application of information management systems to them, describe succinctly the work of these Bureaux, which are to be found in most towns and which are manned largely by volunteers, backed by a small body of full-time staff, and local lawyers who give their services free. Calls on their services arise from many causes: 'Latter-day social systems are like cranky machines. At times, the machine fails members of society, or they fall foul of its workings. They run into debt. They find themselves in dispute with their bosses about their jobs, or with their spouses about marital problems. Red tape can snarl lives, and people find it difficult to make the system work as it should, and must. Race, colour, creed, gender and age can lead to unfair actions by others, who may hold power. Tenants, mortgage payers and debtors in thrall to purveyors of money can face loss of their homes, jobs, assets, firms, trades, credit, well-being and self-respect. When this happens, they may turn to their local CAB.' Problems with neighbours in this over-crowded country could have been included in the list.

It will be apparent from this account that the staff of the Bureaux need at their disposal a huge amount of up-to-date information on a wide range of matters to dispense to thousands of men and women each year. The larger Bureaux handle over 19 000 enquiries per year, the smaller ones about 5000. Altogether there are some 770 Bureaux so there must be in the order of 10 000 000 queries handled each year. Of course, these will be not be ten million different queries; many will be repeated many times and no doubt the staff can benefit from sharing with each other the answers they have found most effective. Nevertheless the advice and the help that is given, even that which can do no more than enable the sufferer to come to learn to live with his troubles, has to be based on readily accessible sound information.

Obviously ensuring, as far as is feasible, that the latest information is quickly available calls for computerized databases accessible online.

The moral of this vast amount of help that the Bureaux give is that the wealth of information put out from official sources directly and via the media does not have the desired impact on quite a lot of people. Whether this is simply a matter of timing (information received when it is not needed is not remembered), or whether it is not properly understood, or whether, despite the best efforts of the disseminators, it just is not seen one does not know. Most likely all these factors apply and perhaps others as well. Many people prefer to get information from another human being even if they are capable of looking it up for themselves and, in many more cases, even if they have looked it up they like to be able to talk it over in the context of their problem with some-one who is not involved. It is not only inadequate people who seek help.

A feature of modern society is the growth of counselling services and support groups to help those with personal problems. Some are provided officially but many are charities. Marriage guidance clinics and Alcoholics Anonymous have been well known for many years but many new ones have been set up, often related to particular ailments, handicaps and tragedies. One such is The Compassionate Friends, a support group for those who have lost a child. It was set up by some who had suffered such a loss and felt that they could offer experience and advice to others in the same trouble. Another is the New Variant Families Association, a support group of those who have members of their family suffering from CJD. The basic format is that of providing an opportunity to share one's worries with others facing the same problems, sharing advice and sharing information.

The need for these services must be, in part, due to the greater degree of isolation of people nowadays as well as to the speed of change. In past times information about the best vacuum cleaner, for example, would come from one's mother, one's sister or one's neighbours. When personal troubles arose the family, neighbours and friends would form a supportive community. This happens less often or is less effective now. Many families no longer live close together and, although the telephone makes frequent conversations possible, talking by telephone is less effective than gathering around the machine in question to look at it. Many people rarely see their neighbours and those who know them well enough to seek advice from them are lucky. Even if one has the advice to hand, manufacturers change their models so often that advice may be useful only in commenting on the quality of the after-sales service.

Lifestyle

Culture is defined either as the way of life of a society, i.e. a race or a nation, or as a body of imaginative and intellectual artefacts. A major part of the former is usually referred to as the lifestyle of people.

In the UK we now live in a market economy and a consumer society. According to official figures, the wealth of people in the UK, as expressed as Gross Domestic Product per person, had doubled by 1960 in real terms from the beginning of the century, had trebled by the early 80s and was almost quadruple by 1995. This increasing wealth, a major influence on changing lifestyles, has also increased the amount of information we acquire. All of us in wealthy countries know today very much more than our grandparents ever did.

To take an obvious example, foreign holidays, when mass tourism started in the 1960s, brought many for the first time into contact with foreign foods and foreigners' habit of drinking wine. As a consequence cookery books featuring foreign dishes became popular and gradually wine advice columns became normal in newspapers and magazines. Television has mounted programmes giving recipes, developing the interest into sheer entertainment, even including races to produce a dish from given ingredients. The habit that foreigners have of dining out has been noted and has spread in this country as people have perceived that they can afford it. At first there were guides to where suitable eating places could be found. Now there are guides to which are the best of the innumerable eating places that exist. Some even advise on the right dress to wear. Of course, there have been other influences, among them the drink–drive laws, which have forced out-of-town pubs to add a restaurant to the establishment. Reinforcing interest in new foods has been the arrival of the immigrant communities who have set up their own restaurants which have then become popular with the indigenous community.

Ridley [11] cites research by Hirshleifer and colleagues who claim that decisions, such as what skirt length to wear or what film to watch, take into account two sources of information: one's own independent judgement and what other people have chosen. 'After all, other people's behaviour is a useful source of accumulated information.' Unfortunately, this is, as Ridley notes, a very unreliable source. 'With only the slightest new piece of information, everybody abandons the old fashion for a new one'. The information, it seems, is not that A is better than B or that it has certain good features but simply that more and more people are using A, and fewer are using B.

But discussing lifestyle is not just a matter of recording new tastes or even improvements in the quality of life. Life's drop-outs also have a lifestyle, even if it is one that few would wish to know about, let alone experience. Anyone who has read George Orwell's *Down and out in Paris and London* will have noticed how those at the bottom of society share information among themselves, information about how to do the most menial job in a hotel or about the features of each lodging house and how to evade some of the rules and regulations. For them exchanging information is one way in which they can help each other when they have little else to offer.

One's lifestyle makes clear to others one's position in society. Our dress, our homes, the way we decorate them and tend the front garden, the cars we own, whether we have a swimming pool or just a barbeque in the back garden (terribly *démodé* now), and even our style of speech conveys to others information about us. For many people presenting the right impression is deemed to be very important; only those who are rich, self-sufficient or supremely self-confident can ignore the impact on others of one's possessions, one's pattern of behaviour and one's appearance. 'Life is quintessentially about symbolization, about exchanging and receiving – or trying to exchange and resisting reception of – messages about ourselves and others. It is in acknowledgement of this explosion of signification that many writers conceive of our having entered an information society' [12].

Signs of this sort have a very short life. They are very closely linked to fashion. You buy the latest style of car; within two years 'with it' people have changed to a different vehicle and either you change too or you risk giving the message that you are one of 'yesterday's people'. Speech patterns (not to be confused with accent or regional dialect) also convey information about whether or not you belong to a particular group of society. Belonging is important to individuals, despite our much vaunted love of freedom, and each group has its own ways that its members must follow. The speech patterns of teenagers are deliberately different from what they perceive to be those of older people, especially in their invention of new words, new meanings of old words and new phrases. There is as much information contained in the fact that they use these words and phrases as there is in the sentences themselves.

One sign that is often a very sad one is when individuals try to give the impression of belonging to a group to which obviously they do not. Best known is when older people wear clothes which are the latest youthful style, but one also finds it in speech patterns. There are politicians who have modified their speech to give the impression that they are 'of the people'. There is at least one TV reporter who changes his speech according to the likely audience for the type of programme he is on.

Dress and speech have always been related to one's place in society. When one lived in small communities and never left one's village, dress and speech were whatever was normal for one's work and for the area. Everyone knew everyone else, one's status never changed and no 'messages' were necessary. Only those who travelled to the cities, especially London, had any need to impress. Even there it seems that it was not until the late eighteenth century that accent and pronunciation began to matter among some, not all by any means, members of aristocratic society (Sheridan parodies attempts to copy 'posh' speech in his plays). Even so, it was only in recent times that 'received pronunciation' was considered important anywhere save in the circles of fashion-conscious dilettantes who tried to maintain what was essentially an exclusive club.

One great difference today is that one is constantly meeting strangers. Giddens [13] makes the point, 'In modern social life many people, much of the time, interact with others who are strangers to them'. In addition, most people are aiming to move up the business and social hierarchies. No longer is there acceptance that one's position in life is immutable. Quite the contrary, few people are able to retain the same job and live in the same home throughout their lives even if they want to. Even one's friends change and a part of making new ones is conveying to them the information that you are a suitable person to be a friend. Real friendships still develop but they start not only from proximity at work, in residence or in leisure but also from appearances, from the information thus conveyed. Those who seek to move up the social hierarchy need to acquire information about both the obvious and the subtle differences of behaviour with which they will have to conform. The mark of an exceptional person is to ignore such requirements and set the standards oneself.

At work one is competing. There is a strong similarity between the way male birds put on a display to win a mate and the way employees put on a performance to impress their colleagues with their superiority. The 'Alex' cartoons in the *Daily Telegraph* are based on just that.

Even at school the pressures to conform, thereby establishing status, are intense. There has been the interesting change from the situation of establishing status by being different, by wearing better or more flamboyant clothes than the other children to that of doing so by being the same. Clothing shops are rejoicing, if parents are not, especially when the 'in' style or colours change. Parents need to know just what is right at any time, not only what their children should have but what they themselves should be wearing lest they 'let down' their children by not being 'with it'. Only when they reach retirement do people as a whole relax and cease to worry about keeping up appearances and not all do even then. There is a constant pressure to keep one's information on these matters up-to-date.

Health and diet

It has been said that because in today's world we lack the emotional security and comfort of tradition, religion, stable jobs and families, and because the major catastrophes of global warming, nuclear disaster, terrorist attack and rising crime are beyond our control, we turn or are directed to worrying about the things we have some hope of controlling. Two connected topics in this category are health and food.

The news media and many magazines contain accounts in each issue of the latest researches into medicine and diet; suggestions for new dishes to eat and wines to drink abound; health clubs and fitness centres multiply; and those who can afford it take out private health insurance. Bawden and colleagues, at the end of a review of health information in magazines [14] comment, 'The advantages of encouraging people to change their health behaviour are vast, both for financial reasons and people's well-being in general.' From the government's point of view a healthier population reduces the expenditure on the National Health Service. From an employer's point of view fewer working days are lost. From commerce's point of view there is scope to encourage much greater spending on foodstuffs.

However, three serious worries arise. The first is that some people take the advice given to extreme. Told that a particular vitamin is beneficial, they take excessive quantities with harmful results. Second, perhaps because some information given has been contradicted by later research, many are sceptical about what they read or hear and ignore it. An example of changing information was a newspaper report on a Friday on the harmful nature of common salt, corrected the following Tuesday in a doctor's column. Changing reports on the effects of caffeine is another example.

The third, because of the way televised cookery programmes are conducted, is that the topic of food and drink has become for many people more a matter of entertainment, though from time to time, genuinely serious worries do arise. Even then, as in the case of BSE in cattle, many choose to make their own assessment of the risk rather than relying on often conflicting reports.

Incidentally, Bawden and co-workers revealed that there are marked differences between men's and women's magazines in their treatment of health matters. Among other differences it was noted that in men's the most frequent topic was exercise, whereas in women's it was medical advances. More surprisingly, men's gave greater coverage to matters of diet than did women's. One problem created by the affluent society is that of overeating. At first, more and better food increased health. Then too much and the attraction of very tasty but unhealthy foods spoilt the improvement.

The presence of a relationship between diet and health has long been suspected. However, a number of official campaigns aimed at improving the health of the nation, such as keeping one's weight down to reduce the risk of heart attack, stopping smoking to avoid lung cancer and so on, allied to research which revealed that radiation, foods containing cholesterol and the dust of asbestos were all potentially dangerous, has gradually led to many impressionable people and even some phlegmatic ones becoming anxious about health and diet generally. A major problem with health research is that not all human beings respond the same way and also it is often a question of degree. A modest quantity of X is beneficial, an excessive amount harmful and the boundary between the two states varies from person to person. Often incomplete information is disseminated, and it can be very misleading.

Information has spread about ailments, diseases and health risks few had ever heard of until recently. Cases of anorexia nervosa and bulimia, serious self-inflicted eating disorders, have made news. A government minister warns that *Salmonella* in raw egg dishes may be dangerous to the elderly, the very young and pregnant women and near panic sets in. Sales of eggs, which are a very healthy food, slump though the risk is small and can be eliminated by avoiding dishes containing raw eggs.

Of course, it is absolutely right that people should be told whenever any food or substance poses a risk, that there may be *Listeria* bacteria in unpasteurized cheese for example, but it is crucial surely to explain what is known about the degree of risk and ways of eliminating the trouble. Only if the degree of risk is high or cannot be estimated and there is no way the individual can treat the food to eradicate the trouble should official action be taken, as in the case of BSE.

In a very thoughtful article [15] Leith discusses the food scares and shows that many of the problems arise because of our changed lifestyle, food handling practices and legislative requirements. For example, to make mayonnaise raw eggs used to be mixed freshly opened with generous amounts of vinegar which kept any germs at bay. Now our tastes call for less vinegar and often the opened eggs are kept for some time before the mayonnaise is made. Indeed, time of keeping around seems to be the key factor. Many foods contain some harmful bacteria but if the foods are eaten up quickly, i.e. while fresh, the bacteria do not normally have time to multiply to harmful levels.

Whether this is accurate or not, I do not know because I am neither a bacteriologist nor a dietician, but when scares arise from the media one does need to acquire quickly the best information one can. For those who can understand technical articles, access to the journal or report which has given rise to the scare may enable one to judge for oneself the strength of the evidence. In this, electronic publishing will help by improving readiness of access. However, not many do find technical articles understandable and some other way must be found to avoid unnecessary alarms and on–off scares such as that on the use of wooden implements. The announcement that wooden implements pose a risk, because they can transfer germs from one food to another even if washed, was shortly after followed by another statement that wooden implements were in fact safer because wood has mild antiseptic properties which other materials lack.

Officials need to find a way of informing the public of possible hazards without causing panic response. The way the media like, it seems, to dramatize news or give prominence to 'human interest' stories adds to the difficulty. It seems as though the cult of the individual, that great feature of modern society, has reached the level that the lives of two or three individuals are deemed to be more important than a major part of the economy.

Leaving scares aside, we are inundated with advice on healthy eating and healthy exercise. One sees people, looking thoroughly miserable pounding drearily around the streets or jogging circuits but, other than in their case, does the information and advice have much effect – except to form a topic for conversation after that of the weather has been exhausted?

Usually information which is repeated over and over again does have some effect, at least for a while, especially if it is taken up by a campaigning group. Smoking tobacco, once an almost universal practice required for social purposes as well as to soothe those working under pressure, has decreased very much among British and American adults. In the UK in 1947 45 per cent of those over 16 smoked; by 1994 the proportion had fallen to 27 per cent [16]. On the other hand the proportion is now said to be increasing, especially among young girls.

The extent to which information is believed, even such widely publicized information as the risks involved in smoking, is always surprisingly small, especially when people don't want to believe because to do so would upset their pleasures. A survey carried out in March 1997 found that of those sampled, 50 per cent did not believe that smoking causes lung cancer and 75 per cent did not believe that sunshine can cause skin cancer. The figures may not be strictly applicable to the population as a whole, but they do suggest that a sizeable number still do not accept the oft published information.

Recent reports that the number of overweight people in Britain is increasing suggests that either information weariness, boredom with all the talk of watching calories, is creeping in or, as suggested earlier, the information is being treated as little more than entertainment.

Information has an impact, however, when it is used to justify a new law. The information that drinking more than two units of alcoholic beverage affects one's sense of judgement has been known for a long time, but had no effect on people drinking far more and still driving. However, when it was publicized that in many car accidents the driver had been drinking excessively and a law introduced a penalty for any driver who had more than a certain level of alcohol in the blood, the law was accepted with hardly any demur. Questions such as what percentage of drivers who drink have accidents, what percentage of accidents do not involve drink driving, in what percentage of drink–drive accidents was it the driver's fault probably were asked, but the answers, if given, were not generally noticed. In this matter, as in many others, there is a public acceptance that the avoidance of accident or risk of accident to a few takes priority over the freedom of the many.

One important by-product of all the research that has gone into foods and their benefits and drawbacks is the labelling of foodstuffs. It is normal now for the contents of prepared foods and for their calorific value to be given on the pack. Also given is a 'best before' or 'use by' date. Although the contents label is ignored by most people most of the time, the best before date is checked by many shoppers. Cynics may claim that its main role is to increase sales. It is probable that it does reduce the incidence of poisoning from food kept too long.

Those with allergies find the labelling invaluable. For example those allergic to peanuts need to be sure that traces have not been used in made-up dishes. Those to whom chocolate gives migraine equally need to ensure that cocoa has not been included in products where one would not expect it from the name, e.g. as a flavour enhancer in coffee cake.

As said in chapter 3, when faced with reports of health research, one feels sometimes a need to look at the original research paper. Sometimes a newspaper will quote its source, e.g. the scientific magazine *Nature*, and one feels fairly confident that it is correct. One is less sure when the information comes from a reporter or news agency, especially if no source is cited. Not all reporters have the background knowledge of scientific disciplines to be able to précis a report accurately. One newspaper account said that a study of 900 Scotsmen found that those taking a new drug had 36 per cent fewer heart attacks compared with men on cholesterol-lowering diets. What proportion of the 900, all of whom apparently had slightly raised cholesterol levels but no history of heart disease, had a heart attack? Obviously not all of them since they were comparing rate of absence of attack. What was the confidence level in the significance of the data?

One questions whether such information should be published in the popular press. It can be of value only to doctors since only they will have access to the drug; but what about the report that men who get angry are twice as likely to have a stroke as those who diffuse their rage? This information came from a study of 2110 men of average age 53. Did they annoy all 2110 in the same way but make half become angry while the other half were somehow enabled to diffuse their fury? And how many had strokes? One hopes not many or the researchers would soon run out of subjects to study. However, if it leads to more people diffusing anger, it will be no bad thing.

Communicating socially

In the 1950s possession of a television set was a status symbol, indicated to one's neighbours by a prominent aerial on the roof. Since the 1960s nearly everyone has had one, even those who receive income support from the State. Probably welfare services accept the need because television is so important as a channel of communication, as a way of getting information to people as a whole, not because it is also a very cheap form of entertainment. It is also important in providing topics of conversation; those who have not seen a programme others are talking about feel socially excluded.

Among the visible ploys used in recent times has been that of wielding a mobile telephone, though this has quickly lost its prestige impact, as so many people now own one. Yet it had an eminently sensible purpose of enabling one to send urgent messages when one was not within reach of a public telephone. Perhaps it was not envisaged that one side effect would be that of being at the beck and call of one's employer at any time of day or night.

Until the telephone became widespread, letter writing was the normal way to communicate information to friends and relatives. Doing so was limited necessarily to those who were literate but since the beginning of this century the majority of inhabitants of the UK has been literate, even if standards have fallen in the second half. Letter writing and the office memo were not eliminated by the telephone. For a long time it was viewed as an additional facility, particularly in business where a telephone discussion would normally be followed by a letter for the obvious reason that it provided a permanent record. In recent years, the telephone has been much used instead of the social letter and it may well be that in many cases it has led to a greater degree of contact with distant friends and relatives than letter writing did. It also has the advantages of speed and the capacity for interactive communication. One result, among others, has been a greater and more effective exchange of information on matters of mutual interest.

The sort of social information that one transmits by telephone is the same as that which one would write. The great difference, of course, is that one goes into greater detail and explores side avenues as well. In other words the content of a telephone call is much richer than that of a letter. One feels instinctively that, if the Internet should replace the telephone, the content will become poorer. Having to use a keyboard is as great an impediment to lengthy and rambling intercourse as is the pen. The subtle inflexions of speech will also be lacking.

The telephone remains a social boon (and occasional curse) and is also an invaluable tool for obtaining information. It has long been a maxim of information professionals that one can get almost any piece of information with three telephone calls: one to identify the right organization, the second to identify the right person, and the third to get the information itself. This is true for anyone, not just information professionals. Recently, of course, the option has arisen of putting a query to a Newsgroup on the Internet or on an electronic Bulletin Board and it is reported that the results are often very encouraging. This is a sophisticated version of 'if you've got a problem, shout it around'.

The drawback to the telephone, not entirely solved by the answering machine, is that one must be there to answer it. Fax and e-mail do get over this problem but then one is back to 'letter' writing or typing or drawing sketches. It remains to be seen whether they will have the same degree of effect on social interchange as did the telephone. My guess is that they will not since more people enjoy talking than enjoy writing and the latter is slower and needs more care.

However, as if to contradict this, e-mail messages by Internet and intranets are having an enormous impact on business life and on social contact in the office. Cases are reported of employees sending e-mails to colleagues at the next desk in preference to speaking to them. Art Buchwald comments [17] on the way the terminal is killing office life and he tells a depressing story of a couple dating each other by net rather than by telephone.

References

1. Mitchison, N. (1990) *You May Well Ask*. London: Fontana Paperbacks

2. Hare, D. (1997) *Amy's View*. London: Faber and Faber

3. Barsoum, K. *Information in the Electronic Age*. A talk given on 2 October 1997 to the RSA Forum for Ethics in the Workplace

4. Knowsley, J. (1997) BT puts finger on the cheating spouse. *Sunday Telegraph*.

5. Cronkite, W. (1997) The Guardian. 27 January 1997. Quoted by I. Watson, 'The Information Society', *Managing Information*, **4**(3), 12

6. Dyer, G. (1982) *Advertising as Communication*. London: Routledge

7. Information Forum (1996) *Annual Report 1996*. Brussels: European Commission, Information Society Activity Centre

8. Puttnam, D. (1996) Information in the living society. *RSA Journal*, 5472, 33–42

9. Day, P. and Harris, K. (1997) *Down-to-Earth Vision. Community Based IT Initiatives and Social Inclusion.* Hursley: IBM

10. Myers, J. and McClean, J. (1997) *Knowledge management for citizens' advice in the 21st century; an innovative strategy.* London: Solon Consultants

11. Ridley, M. (1997) *The Origins of Virtue.* pp.184–5. London: Penguin

12. Webster, F. (1994) What information society? *The Information Society* **10** 15

13. Giddens, A. (1995) *The Consequences of Modernity.* p.80. Cambridge: Polity Press

14. Graham, S-C., Bawden, D. and Nicholas, D. (1997) Health information provision in men and women's magazines. *Aslib Proceedings*, **49**(5), 117–148

15. Leith, P. (1996) A Peck of Dirt. *RSA Journal*, 5473, 25–31

16. The Economist (1997) *Pocket Britain in Figures.* p.138. London: Profile Books

17. Buchwald, A. (1997) Isolated on the Internet. *International Herald Tribune*, 8 April 1997

CHAPTER ELEVEN
Economic factors

Economics is the study of the material wealth of a country, of a region or of people in general. It deals with questions concerning the production and distribution of wealth. Wealth is measured by the ability one has to pay for what one wants to buy and is measured in money terms, in pounds sterling, US dollars or, soon, euros.

A country's wealth includes its mineral deposits, its farm produce, its manufactured goods, the services it provides, its holdings of gold bullion and the value of its investments abroad. Each country aims for a positive balance of trade, i.e. that the total income it receives from other countries, from the sale of goods and services and from investments, is greater than the sums it has to pay out to foreign countries for similar requirements.

Obviously, information services, among which I include fee-charging services on the Internet and conventional publishing of non-fiction material, are a factor. The UK makes considerable use of American services but its own are widely used abroad. There is a deficit in the UK's trade balance with the USA but a considerable surplus in its trade with the rest of the world, thanks largely to the prevalence of English as a world language. The position of information *per se* is less clear. The country generates much new information but also imports much new information from abroad. But, except as a component of information services including publications and as technical and professional knowledge, patented or know-how, there is no trade balance expressible in financial terms.

To a large extent information serves as a raw material, contributing to what we do and make. The information we have at our disposal and our ability to exploit it fully to create new products and services, to improve existing ones, and to reduce costs and operate more efficiently are crucial to our economic success.

It is popularly said that a country's wealth lies in the skills, mental and physical, of its people. Obviously that includes the knowledge they possess and their power to utilize it. As Rutherford said on one notable occasion, 'If we haven't the money, we shall just have to think'. The UK lacks mineral deposits and its exports of farm produce do not balance its imports, so it is on our creative, manufacturing and intellectual skills that our prosperity depends. Employment is, therefore, a good point to start exploring some economic aspects of information and ICTs.

Employment

The two greatest changes of the past in the way mankind lived and worked were brought about largely by his ingenuity. One implement, namely the plough, was the principal cause of people being able to abandon a nomadic hunting life and settle down to farming. Two factors, sources of power – coal, oil, electricity – and the invention of machines brought about the industrial revolution but also had a revolutionary impact on farming methods (the tractor replaced the horse). Now a combination of four influences – computers, microprocessors, telecommunications and information – is at the heart of dramatic change by creating new ways of working and earning a living. The four are, in their turn, having a huge effect on manufacturing and a lesser one on farming.

Two of the features which most distinguish human beings from other animals are a large brain and the ability to make and use tools (a third is a sense of humour, which does even more than either of the other two to make life tolerable). For several thousand years both brain and tool-making abilities were exploited to make the tasks of living easier – pottery to cook in, ploughs to cultivate the soil, animals harnessed, farmed and domesticated – but at no stage did such inventions and new practices reduce the number of jobs available for people to do (it was not so much that tilling the soil was made quicker and easier but that a larger and more adequate area could be tilled).

Perhaps the first serious hint that new inventions might reduce the amount of available work was provided by the invention of the printing press. The large number of scribes who had been engaged in book copying were no longer needed for that work.

The Industrial Revolution meant that cottage industries disappeared. However, the factories needed a large workforce, so large that not only women but even children were pressed into service. There was a demand for a rising population and for many years, even as late as the 1950s, it was in some circles accepted economic dogma that increasing prosperity could be achieved only with a rising population. However, it was not many years later that computerized flow lines and word processors started to make their impact on employment.

The first major decrease in available jobs was that in the Great Depression of 1929–35. The reasons for it were complex as Hobsbawm [1] explains. They were not the advent of any new technologies and in the event proved but a blip, though a large one, in the long-term steady economic growth.

The impact of the Depression was such that after the end of the 1939–1945 war there was a determination not to let the circumstances that had caused it return and to put in place a welfare system that would look after any individuals that, through no fault of their own, fell on hard times. Full employment, maintained or created by government spending, the Welfare State, and steadily rising Gross National Product (GNP) were the panaceas and for a while they succeeded. However, by 1980 the cost of subsidizing overmanned industries was becoming unsustainable and new technologies had reached the level of sophistication, especially as used in Japan and the USA, such that manufacturing processes could be operated by remotely controlled robots. The computer made large labour forces doing simple repetitive jobs in factory or office a feature of a past method of working.

For example, computer type-setting by editors and reporters resolved eventually the long running industrial disputes of the newspaper industry by enabling most of the printers to be laid off. To take another industry, between 1950 and 1970 the number of long-distance telephone operators fell by 12 per cent but the number of calls rose five fold. Between 1970 and 1980, even though the number of calls tripled, the number of operators fell by as much as 40 per cent [2]. And the same story is heard in job after job.

Nor was it only artisan and clerical jobs that were affected. The decrease in the armies of workers also meant that many supervisors were redundant. Those managers whose work consisted of little more than passing instructions down and information up, to use Drucker's description, became surplus to requirements. Only those who could manage information survived. Information flowed up and down, and in other directions too, along wired circuits. The management structure of organizations changed to one with fewer layers but many more types of expert, a more horizontal structure, and in many cases individual workers acquired a higher level of responsibility by their own efforts. Another change has been a considerable increase in the numbers of part-time workers.

However, despite all the changes that have taken place, there are still large numbers of people working in factories making goods, and there are still large numbers working in offices, many with PCs rather than typist support. There are still large numbers in sales, especially 'on the road'. There are still many working in shops and stores, and many still do low-level manual work. In all categories, workers have had to learn to use new equipment or to learn new practices, new health and safety requirements and new ways of relating to those with whom they interact.

Fortunately for the UK, the financial centre, the City of London, was earning enough income from abroad to keep the country afloat while its industries and other profit and loss-making activities sorted themselves out. During the 1980s and 1990s service industries, all highly dependent on information in one way or another, have blossomed. So too have professional and expert services and a number of other information generating, supplying and exploiting activities; not enough, however, to absorb all the educated unemployed and providing no haven at all for the inadequately educated.

If ICTs have resulted in a substantial decrease in traditional low-skill jobs, they have contributed to the growth of some new jobs of the type that can be done by some of those who in the past would have sat at a factory flow-line. In the supermarkets, for example, there are the rows of check-out operators, simply passing bar-codes under a laser scanner and calling for a senior person whenever a problem arises. Even for these there is an extra requirement of suitable personality which would not have been needed in a factory. Shopper-operated scanners may, if trials prove successful, reduce the numbers even of check-out staff.

Government, a huge employer of labour, has reduced its requirements, and hence its tax-payer met salary bill, partly by hiving off some departments to form agencies (Quangos) which have to operate within fixed budgets and partly by privatizing those that could be operated commercially. This is not, however, a consequence of the new technologies or new ways of individuals working; it illustrates that there are other influences at work on the labour market and emphasizes the need for care in allocating causes for any particular change.

The greatly enhanced ability to communicate easily to any part of the world, not only makes it easier for multinational companies to get work requiring only a computer or telecommunications terminal in any country; it also makes it easier to transfer their business from the high wage economies to the low wage ones. In practice the equation which determines where to site work is much more complex than this, especially where manufacturing is concerned. If quick delivery of goods is crucial, as when just-in-time ordering is involved, there will be a strong argument for the supplier locating his manufacture near the principal market. On the other hand, the very high standards of pollution control required in Western Europe provide an incentive for manufacturers to establish plants where the requirements are markedly less stringent. A substantial number of other factors are involved, some information-related, some not.

Haywood [3] draws attention to one serious added disadvantage to firms moving to other countries, leaving only a small office with a terminal in this country. It is that if manufacturing, such as ship-building, is lost then so too are the associated expertises which underpin other jobs and, in this case, produce experts in marine insurance.

At the same time many individuals in high salary countries have established new working patterns. Some find they can work from home or from telecottages set up locally and can develop new agencies which undertake work previously performed in-house in large organizations. It has been reported [4] that laws in California controlling the number of employees that may have cars has sharply increased the incidence of teleworking. Numbers of self-employed people undertaking casual contract work, often for the firm that made them redundant, have increased sharply. There always was a large body of small and one-person enterprises but now their numbers have been increased by freelance information workers. Secure, life-long, pensionable employment, though there is still much of it, is becoming less common. It is perhaps an irony that the age of the 'common man' is becoming the age of the 'individual man'.

Professionals, many of whom have always been highly independent, have no difficulty continuing to work much as they always have done, provided they have adapted to the greater use of the information technologies and can make time to keep up-to-date with the flow of new information. Medical practitioners, for example, can use their PCs to look up the best treatment or drug for whatever complaint the patient may have. Lawyers can use their PCs to check national and international laws and court decisions, though in their case most use printed documents when possible.

However, the skilled and semi-skilled workforce, whose skills are still relevant to the firms which they have left but who now have to work as casual contractors, are having to learn to run themselves as a business, doing which involves acquiring information skills. Those who can be retrained face also the same requirements. For those who lack the sort of intellectual or manual skills that are in demand and cannot retrain, the outlook is at present gloomy. Part-time or short-time working at relatively low wages is the most that can be hoped for. To maintain these people at the standard of living which has become normal in this country will require supplementing what they can earn with some form of state hand-out, the funding for which depends on higher taxes on companies and better-off individuals. Whether in the long term an increase in demand for low level manual skills will arise it is impossible to say. For the moment, the main demand seems to be for those who can exploit information, can operate to advantage the new ICTs, and can plan, advise and direct.

Since many of those in employment are using computers and communicating over one network or another, efforts are being made to equip the unemployed with ICT skills. The use of ICTs to bring those who seem to be excluded from society back into it was mentioned in the last chapter. Cyberskills training centres have been established in various parts of the country to provide short courses for the unemployed. Although many employers say that these skills are not what is needed to ensure employment, they will be a help provided that the other requirements can be instilled as well. Employers are mainly concerned that employees shall be basically literate and numerate, and have the right attitude to work, i.e. will work hard and intelligently, have the normal social skills and will co-operate with fellow workers to make a team. Given those basic requirements, ICT skills will be a bonus [5].

A new financial situation

In 1992, Wriston, an eminent American banker gave a lecture to the RSA entitled 'The twilight of sovereignty' [6]. In it he made the following points:

> 'In the last few decades the information revolution is changing the very source of wealth. The new source of wealth is not material, it is information, knowledge applied to work to create value. The pursuit of wealth is now largely the pursuit of information, and the application of information to the means of production. . . .
> the information economy changes the very definition of an asset . . . changes everything from how we make a living to how and by whom the world is run . . .
> how does it [national government] track or control the money supply when the financial markets create new financial instruments faster than the regulators can keep track of them?
> the convergence of computers and telecommunications has created a new international monetary system . . .
> the global market makes and publishes judgements about each currency in the world every minute and every hour of the day. The forces are so powerful that government intervention can only result in expensive failure over time . . .
> what becomes of the great mission of modern governments: controlling and manipulating the national economy?'

That lecture was given just a few months before currency movements forced Sterling out of the European Exchange Rate Mechanism and caused devaluation despite heavy government intervention. At the time the Bank of England had in its reserves $44 billion. Each day an average of $300 billion was being traded on the London Foreign Exchange Market. The total nongold reserves of all the industrial countries together amounted to about $500 billion but about $900 billion was being traded daily across the nine major foreign exchange markets [7]. As Handy [8] comments, 'There are now 70 multinational companies whose revenue is greater than that of Cuba. They are important because they can transfer technology and know-how and spread this intangible property around the world to where it does most good and is most profitable.' It was noteworthy that the Uruguay round of the GATT negotiations laid special emphasis on trade in information services and products.

As long ago as 1989, Jussawalla, Okuma and Arak: [9] were drawing attention to a connection between the volume of trade between countries and the level of exchange of information between them. This is, of course, just what one would expect. Trade is not just a matter of buying and selling. Even in a street market there is some exchange of information between trader and customer about the quality of the goods. International trade involves the manufacturer, for example, learning as much as he can about the tastes of foreign customers and the nature of any competitors and their products. Firms who use agencies in foreign countries expect a considerable input of information from them. Trade may still follow the flag but it is conducted by cable.

The Stock Markets have felt the effect of the way the ICTs enable information to be moved around virtually instantaneously. The three great Stock Exchanges of the world, London, New York and Tokyo, are almost operating as a single 24 hour stock exchange, the time zone spread of the three enabling the brokers at each to get some sleep. Similarly offices around the world are able to operate as a single office, intranet links meaning that information on a project can be accessed and dealt with at any location.

Handy [8] makes several relevant points including: 'Because the new form of property is intellectual, not physical or even financial, there is no limit to the amount of this new, intellectual, property that can be created in this world by all of us,' and 'most of the new knowledge markets and service markets that have been created are low-entry-cost markets.'

So can information be examined by the same criteria that are used for physical artefacts? Has it value that can be expressed in monetary terms?

One definition of economics is the study of the arrangements that societies make for the use and development of their scarce resources [10]. Taken as a whole information is hardly a scarce resource, though the package needed for a specific project may be unique. Complaints of information overload are loud and frequent. As Handy comments there is no limit to the amount that can be created. A large part of information management is concerned with reducing the flood to manageable proportions or, to change the metaphor, extracting the pearls and leaving the oysters for others to harvest.

Doubling the amount of money in the economy, other things remaining constant, merely halves the value of money. Doubling the quantity of goods increases wealth though the monetary value of each specific item of goods may halve. What about information? Doubling the quantity available probably makes little difference to value or price unless in the extra information is something which negates, modifies or amplifies an earlier piece of information. In general, value, such as there is, lies in a specific piece of information not information in general and even then only in how the piece of information is used.

A partial analogy is books. Even putting aside the existence of multiple copies of each and considering only individual titles, there is an excess of them; far more exist than any person can want. To an individual most are of no interest; some have sufficient interest to be worth borrowing; some sufficient to be worth buying a copy if the price is reasonable; a few, a very few, of such rarity to be worth specialist collectors paying considerable sums of money for them. The analogy should not, however, be taken further. Monographs are a form of commoditized packages of information and databases likewise. They are marketed at preset prices and each hopes to find enough buyers to make its production profitable.

The commodity model

Sometimes it is said that information itself is a commodity. It has many of the properties of a raw material. It is an essential ingredient of services and even manufacturing methods as well as of decision making. Also it can be traded in bulk as in data books and on CD-ROMs. The bulk is, however, of many different pieces, not of many identical pieces. Consequently, there would be difficulty trading it on the commodities market. It is not a homogeneous product that can be traded by the ton like wheat or oil. It can be, and has to be, managed in modest quantities of selected items in compartmentalized information systems from which single items, or small tailored packages, can be produced as and when required.

Heine [11] looked very critically at the concept of information as a commodity. He considered several of the conventional economic aspects of a commodity – benefits and disbenefits of acquisition, excludability, non-rivalrous consumption, and public/private goods distinctions – and concluded that these 'features of the high-rhetoric of economics' have little to offer information management.

One argument that is advanced against treating information as a commodity is that it can be shared without loss of value. This is true of some information; that published in directories is an example. In that respect perhaps the economic comparison should be a shared experience such as watching a theatrical performance or a football match. On the other hand some pieces of information, confidential ones, may lose all value once shared with a wider group of people. Information that company A is about to make a takeover bid for an ailing company B may be very valuable if you are able to buy shares in company B before other people try to do so and push the share price up. Other information can be published without losing its value provided that others are prevented from taking action on it, e.g. information about a patented invention.

The raw material analogy has some merit when considering how information is used but it is not helpful when trying to value it.

Valuing information?

Since the 1960s much has been written about the value of information and many efforts have been made to put a monetary value on it. Much of this has been excellently surveyed by Badenoch *et al.* [12]. In reading the literature it is necessary to maintain a clear distinction between efforts to value information and those to value information services. Non-commercial services such as libraries and within-organization information departments have found it very difficult to put the sort of value on their services that accountants and cost-conscious managers recognize. Griffiths and King have tackled the problem in two ways: first, by examining what the cost of outsourcing the operation would be; and second by comparing the cost of the service with that of the time spent by its users.

In the case above of the takeover one can put a monetary value on the information the investor had. It is the profit he made on the share dealings. But another investor with the same information would probably have made a different profit and so the value is not an absolute amount. Also there is a judgement factor involved. The investor made a profit on the basis of his judgement that the price of the shares would rise. He could have been wrong and then the value of that same piece of information would have been a negative one. The value of this sort of information is the value it acquires from its use and that depends on a prior judgement of what its value may be.

Watson [13] explains why the cost of using an online database is commonly seen to be greater than the value of the piece of information retrieved. As he says, the costs of creating the database, keeping it updated, and keeping it up and running online, plus the usual administration and marketing costs, have to be distributed over the usage made of the service. Pricing each single piece of retrievable information would be impracticable. Pricing by time taken to search is much easier. Pricing other goods by the length of time it takes to acquire them is not likely to attract favour.

Most attempts to put a value on information run into the difficulty that the term covers too great a variety of different things. As such, information has no intrinsic value. A piece of information is given value by the use to which it is put. Hence the same piece will have a different value in different uses. It cost a certain amount to produce the piece but there is no standard relation between cost and value. If information is stored, many pieces in the same store, any customer for pieces from that store would expect to pay a share of the total cost of the store, cf. Adam Smith, *The Wealth of Nations* Book 1, Chapter VI. There is also a cost to supplying information from the store but that is a communication cost; it does not indicate value because supplying useless information by the same method would cost as much. The Government's share of the cost of creating new scientific and technical information in the UK in 1990–91 was £12 100 million. It is hardly surprising that there was pressure for the majority of this to be spent on producing exploitable information but what the actual financial return was on the information produced we shall never know.

Much information is valuable but cannot be properly priced. Thus if you have decided on a course of action despite many doubts and anxieties, and a piece of information arrives which confirms that you have made the right decision, its value, which is great, lies only in reassuring you, not in any extra financial benefit. To take another example, in most circumstances to know that the width of a set of windows is x cms and not x + 5 is scarcely any value. But if one is measuring up for curtain material, to know that it is x cms rather than x + 5 cms may mean that only four widths of curtain material rather than five will be needed, which saves an expense that might have been incurred had one not measured carefully. Know-how, which is only information, has immense value to those making a product for which the information is necessary; it is valueless to those not in the same business.

Sometimes one can put a monetary value on a piece of information, but more often one cannot; one can never put a value on something as unspecific as information in general. Perhaps it is more helpful to talk in terms of the importance rather than the value of information or to think of value in a qualitative sense, as we do when we value friendship for example. The importance to a palaeontologist of information derived from a newly discovered fossil and that of a new recipe to an enthusiastic cook may be equally great though otherwise impossible to compare. In fact it may be easier to compare importance in terms of the enthusiasm generated than to use an unemotional measure such as money. Value in the abstract sense can be economic, social, cultural or even intellectual.

Free or cost plus?

Until quite recently there was a widespread belief that information should be free and a consequently reluctance to pay for information services. Reality, of course, is that it is never free; the only question is how it is paid for and by whom. The how arises because on occasions when one goes and finds the information oneself, payment is in time which, as has often been repeated, is money. Also information is commonly an object of barter, both barter for more information and barter of information in return for influence – not forgetting singing for a 'free' lunch. Is the level of barter such that the information economy is leading the way to a world-wide 'dual-economy' which is already to be found in some developing countries and even in small localities of developed ones?

Of course, we expect to receive official information and to use the basic public library service without any charge being imposed, i.e. both are paid for from taxes. There seems to be general acceptance that the community should share the cost of some aspects of information supply, irrespective of who benefits most, though under most tax systems richer individuals contribute more than poorer ones. Whether socially beneficial or not, this practice distorts the market-based economy which the classical economists, Adam Smith and Ricardo, considered should be based on unimpeded competition if proper prices for goods and services are to be established. However, not all official information is free. One has to pay for printed copies of most official reports, even those available free in electronic form over the Internet. Basic library use may be free but a great many of the additional services, including reserving a book or borrowing one from another library, incur a fee.

An example of an apparently free information service (actually it is subsidized from the TV licence fee but if one has no TV set it is free) is the news service on BBC radio. Anyone who has a radio set can listen to the news, and all the other programmes, some of which are informative, without paying any fee. To watch television one pays an annual fee or, for some commercial channels, according to the amount one watches.

However, one feature of the information society has been a growing recognition that, if information is valuable, it must be paid for one way or another. If it has to be paid for, does it then represent a capital asset or a perishable good? The Hawley Committee [14] was quite clear that it is the latter. As their report says, 'Information frequently loses its value over time, sometimes over very short periods.' In the scientific field, studies have been made of the decay over time in interest in journal articles and it was found that the pattern was closely similar to that of radioactive decay. Consequently the concept of journal articles having a measurable half-life was introduced. Even with journal articles there were exceptions; for example a new discovery could generate a sudden surge of interest in a past theory. On the other hand, much general everyday information, and much of that concerned with business and social matters, very quickly suffers loss of interest or value.

It would be so beneficial if one could attach a 'use by' date to information as one puts it into store but this is rarely possible. Patenting and copyrighting preserve one's rights for a specified period but they do not guarantee value is maintained. A new invention may render an already patented one valueless. An out-of-date timetable is useless, though it may have some value as a historic record. Well known is the way sentiment on the stock market swings as each new scrap of information about a company's progress supersedes the last. In contrast, a compilation of information about an individual employee, which is built up in a company's staff files, remains of relevance until the employee leaves and quite often for a while thereafter.

As a rule, information adds value to goods. To give a trivial example, putting a sell-by date on a product speeds up turn over and increases sales from the manufacturer since out-of-date stock will be discarded. Putting instructional and content information on goods may add to the labour of producing them but clear information gives the product nowadays a competitive advantage over one with vague information. Many customers do check the labelling.

Economic life

It is an obvious truism that information is the lifeblood of industry and commerce. Trying to manufacture something without any information would be like trying to play bridge with blank cards.

Anyone trying to strike a deal without information would end the loser. Hutton [15] brings the situation out clearly when he decries the concept of free-market economics based on a level playing field principle. 'The trouble is that in reality no such level playing field could ever exist. Information is distributed unfairly between the players. . . . The starting point is that market participants have to spend time and effort acquiring information about the transaction they are entering into before they can judge whether it is worthwhile. . . . This information is an investment in ensuring that the transaction will work out as intended. But this knowledge is necessarily distributed unevenly between the parties to any transaction. The borrower will always know more than the bank about his true creditworthiness . . . The point is that if information is held asymmetrically, and your welfare depends in part on other people's strategies, the prosecution of undiluted competitive self-interest is often self defeating.'

Hutton's polemic seems to aim at showing that a competitive market economy is not in the best interests of supplier or consumer or of organization or sub-contractor whom he in this case seems to be treating as competitors. Competition is more usually considered as between two organizations selling the same product to the same market. Hutton's conclusion that it is better for organizations to collaborate rather than compete would seem to apply only to the instances he quotes. Otherwise collaboration would be deemed contrary to monopolies and price fixing legislation. Nevertheless, his point that acquiring information ahead of any business deal is vital, is expensive and even if shared openly between them will not leave both parties equally well informed (because the knowledge base from which each starts is different) is important. The difference between market success and failure will, in many cases, be dependent more on the quality and extent of a firm's information than on marginal differences between its products or services and those of its competitors.

The report of the KPMG Impact Programme on Information as an Asset (report of the Hawley Committee) [14] emphasizes the importance of the Boards of companies and other organizations ensuring that information acquired, generated and disseminated by them is handled with the same care and attention to detail as are their financial, staffing and other major resources. Drucker [16] and Marchand [17] make the same points. Businesses have always acquired, generated, exploited and disseminated information but it has happened in an unstructured way. Now that it is seen as a resource it is managed (see chapter 6) so that it can be retrieved when required, it is systematically added to, and it is scrutinized and manipulated to look for new information to help improve the running of the business, its profits, its image and so on.

It is now recognized that information can and should be harnessed by companies and other bodies which operate competitively to give them an advantage. One conference on the topic [18] led to Reuters, well known for their *Reuters Business Briefing*, publishing a *Guide to Good Information Strategy* [19]. The general outcome – see what information resources you have, make sure everyone in the organization is fully aware of the benefits of the strategy and willing to participate, and establish ways of monitoring progress – seems fairly obvious, but, as those of us who have for many years past been encouraging the adoption of such strategies know, top management has been very slow to appreciate it.

In business today, it seems, there is a belief that customers have an insatiable demand for new products, a hunger from which the information industry is not exempt. New models of cars, new TV sets, a new upgrade of computer software, new styles and materials for clothing, a new type of chocolate bar or of breakfast cereal, a new type of information management; and so it goes on. To meet this demand companies must have the latest technological information, details of market trends, the views of potential customers, the results of market tests and so on. Novelty seems to be paramount in some sectors though, to keep a sense of proportion, there are still a great many products that have changed little over 50 or more years.

In the course of achieving company aims policies and strategies are designed and implemented, processes, physical resources and people are managed and markets are established and maintained. New information is generated and disseminated, existing information is utilized and additional information is acquired and put to use. Information about the business, its activities and its progress is given to each category of stakeholder.

Information always has been used in these ways in businesses but doing so has involved costly and cumbersome tasks. Armies of clerks typing and filing copies of letters and internal memoranda, keeping files of staff records, maintaining libraries, finding and despatching to an enquirer the right set of files and so on. It was very slow and cumbersome. Consequently there was a strong disincentive to use information thoroughly and efficiently. One benefit that the new ICTs have brought is the ability to retrieve and communicate information easily and quickly. At the same time a new awareness has arisen that information is a vital resource and that in the present, highly competitive, environment one would be very foolish not to make the maximum use of this resource just as one does of all one's other resources.

Talking about businesses involved in the electronic marketplace, Barsoum, Chief Executive of IBM UK, observed [20] that there were four lessons to be drawn from events so far: the first that electronic business is about people; second that observance of sound ethical standards is crucial for the development of the market; third that access management is vitally important; and fourth that proper security of electronic systems is also vital.

Marchand [17] said that information systems are found in object oriented programming, in knowledge maps (e.g. where in the company expertise lies), in knowledge repositories and in data warehouses. These last two have attracted much hype [21]. At heart a data warehouse is a large collection of data which an organization has accumulated in the course of its day-to-day operations, organized such that it can both deal with *ad hoc* queries and analyse the data to reveal unexpected correspondences and trends. Store loyalty cards are a popular way of gathering data, and large retailers and travel companies have been successful users. A classic case was the US supermarket Wal-Mart which spotted a correlation between sales of packs of cans of beer and babies' nappies [22], not a pair of items a human analyst would choose as sufficiently likely to yield any information of value to be worth expending any effort.

The information industry

All enterprises nowadays use information intensively but there are many whose business consists solely of creating and exploiting information. Others give the information added value by proferring opinion and advice based on it. Financial services such as banking, stock broking, insurance and commodities marketing fall into this category. Even individuals can operate in these markets and cause problems for nation states as Mr. Soros illustrated when his dealings proved the final straw and the UK was obliged to leave the ERM in order to prevent further speculation at the expense of the pound.

Other businesses that are almost entirely information processing are booking agencies for theatres or holidays or flights. The media, or at least those that deal in news and documentary material, are largely information industries though in their case there is the physical product of the TV programme, newspaper or magazine. Supporting them are the teams of reporters and the news agencies such as Reuters and Associated Press which are information industries in themselves.

The presentation of information provides another large and wide ranging industry, its exponents including advertizing executives, official and company information officers, public relations firms etc. Interpreting information with explanations and often advice occupies the time of firms of solicitors, of advice bureaux and of many other agencies.

Information is the core component of some forms of entertainment especially quiz shows of one sort or another and games such as *Trivial Pursuits*. Some of these games sell for quite substantial sums.

Not surprisingly, with so many businesses dealing entirely or largely in handling information, the Internet has come to play an important part. It has been estimated that by 1996 there were already about 10 000 electronic businesses and that by the year 2000 business dealings on the Internet will amount to $100 billion. These figures probably seem modest but that is because they do not include conventional businesses that include electronic activities as part of their operations, nor does it include the large-scale money transactions of banks and insurance companies. At the same time the ability to advertize one's products or services on the Internet does yield business one might otherwise fail to acquire, and the advertisement is viewable world-wide. The requirement of one US state that all bath fittings should be lead-free resulted in firms that installed bathrooms surfing the Internet to find possible suppliers.

The new ICTs have dramatically added to the ways information compilations can be presented to the market. The first development back in the 1960s and 70s was that of being able to search, first in batch mode, then online, computer-stored databases of abstracts of journal articles. This was the outcome of using computers for the printing process. It led to the specialized services of the great database hosts, Dialog, Questel-Orbit, STN etc. Now, the practice of having one's data held on computers but available to each office through a network and the opportunity by linking the network to the Internet of providing public access, enables organizations either to publish information that previously they would not or to publish it in a new way. Web sites are proliferating. Even such a staid institution as the United Oxford & Cambridge University Club in Pall Mall has one.

One example of taking advantage of the opportunity to publish has already been mentioned, that of an insurance broker publishing its directory of international law, but there are many more. The market for products of this type on the Internet is instantly worldwide and publicity for it to a known market, e.g. other insurance brokers and major international legal firms, can be achieved by e-mail.

Another application has been the provision of electronic versions of newspapers and magazines. This seems successful but must have a new or specialized market. For a number of years experiments were carried out to test the viability of an online journal. In general the results were disappointing in that user response was unenthusiastic. It seems that with the Internet attitudes have changed; looking at text on the screen is now 'cool'.

Before the advent of the Internet, the information industry was fairly easy to define. It comprised the online services from the database hosts and from a few specialized outlets such as the FT and Reuters, and professional information searching services including those provided by major libraries. Sometimes market research and analysis services like Frost and Sullivan and the pollsters and opinion research organizations like Gallup and Mori would be included depending on how broad one's definition needed to be.

Now the Internet and especially the World Wide Web have made it so easy to market information products that it no longer makes much sense to try to define an information industry. Anyone can offer their product for free or for a fee (usually a fee to allow access to the product). This, in a way, mirrors what is happening in the retail market generally: supermarkets sell financial services; garages sell groceries. The old divisions are disappearing; a new structure has not yet become apparent.

And new products are appearing – an inevitable and welcome by-product of new ways of marketing. Discussion lists are one example. Multimedia is also opening up new opportunities. A glance at the monthly lists of new products and services in the Institute of Information Scientists' magazine *Inform* gives some idea of the nature of what is happening. The scale may be indicated by the publicity for the Internet Search Engine Lycos. It claims to hold in its index 70 million URLs (site addresses). They are needed because there is so much material accessible on the Internet that simple search terms lead to an overwhelming number of hits. It must be expected that over the next five to ten years there will be much coming and going of both new and traditional products and services before a new balance of use:product:service emerges.

Although there is no longer any hope of defining the information industry as it exists today, it is worth looking back at the sector which was regarded for some years as the heart of the information industry in order to get an inkling of the scale of the market.

Reuters, for example, had in 1996 revenue of nearly £3000 million. Reed Elsevier paid US$1.5 billion for LEXIS-NEXIS, a major legal online service, while in 1995 TRW Information Services had a turnover of US$604 million. MAID (now the Dialog Corporation since its take-over of Knight Ridder), a major company in the business information market, was reported [23] as paying some £2 million to link to a major Internet provider. This company was, indeed, one of those that led the way into providing database services through the Internet.

According to the LISU data [24], revenue in the UK electronic information industry totalled £2881 million in 1994. There can be little doubt that this figure will have been greatly exceeded by now. The same source reveals that in the same year the revenue from the sale of non-fiction books was only £2000 million. However, it would be wrong to deduce that print-on-paper was overtaken that year by the electronic sector because the figures do not include revenue from publishing magazines and journals.

These figures give meaning to the efforts of the European Commission to develop the information market. Europe has not been very successful in either the hardware or the software components of the new industries but, as the Commissioners say, Europe has a wealth of information which its commercial information services can exploit to earn foreign exchange and to improve the performance of other indigenous manufacturing and commercial activities. Liberalizing the communications networks should help but whether the database and copyright directives will prove beneficial or counter-productive, it is impossible yet to tell. They certainly do not help information repackaging and may, in the long run, discourage generators of new information.

Information work

Information is, as we have seen, a crucial component of all businesses and most provide as well as use it. Even a handyman, like a plumber, offers information and advice although his essential work is mending or installing pipework. Car dealers, estate agents and travel agents are doing little but acquiring and giving out information even though they have a product to sell. One would not call these people information professionals, nor would one insurance or stock brokers. Perhaps to emphasize the point, there is a category of people known as information brokers though they seem little different from searchers.

Generally, though, as a result of the pervasiveness of information and the increasing numbers of activities which are information-based, it is becoming very difficult to distinguish between those who deem themselves information professionals and those whose work is largely handling information. Probably librarians and computer programmers are the only two categories that remain distinct and even the latter are not as distinct as they were.

The members of the major professions are almost exclusively information workers. They gather information and match it to their clients' needs. They include lawyers, auditors, accountants, surveyors, teachers and doctors (GPs). Others of somewhat more recent origin have increased in numbers and become more prominent in the second half of this century. Of such are bankruptcy practitioners, head hunters and counsellors of many types. They are all information professionals yet none would normally be categorized as such.

Some of the large companies in which many of these professionals are based have moved further into consultancy, which is, after all, essentially giving information and advice. Management and accountancy firms like KPMG and Deloitte Touche are typical examples. Their involvement emphasizes the point that put to the right use information can have very considerable value.

Just as the marketing of goods brought into existence a host of middlemen to facilitate the activity, so in the information age there have grown up a number of intermediaries of one sort or another. Insurance agents, independent financial advisers, and tourist boards are among them. Changes in society and the growing wealth of the population have increased the need for some of these as they have done for a range of jobs in the social services, e.g. counselling. At the same time the ability to hold information in computer, to accept new information and to match the two to provide a programme for action or to give advice is leading in some fields to 'disintermediation' – a horrid but expressive word!

Thus made-to-measure clothing can be produced at a factory as the result of a few measurements of the customer being input at the shop into the factory computer system. Similarly, the possibility exists of inputting one's symptoms of an illness into a computer expert system and getting back a diagnosis and recommended treatment. But it is still wiser to let the doctor do this as individuals vary so widely in their responses to a disease. Already, however, some intermediary professions have been feeling the impact of expert systems. Quantity surveyors, for example, are needed far less than used to be the case.

Authors of informative monographs and textbooks, compilers of encyclopaedias, directories and dictionaries and journalists are information workers of long existence. Those who compile documentary and news programmes for radio and television or for publication on videotape or multimedia disc are merely a modern variant, not anything radically new.

The wealth of publications increased the number of indexers needed and brought about the need for an army of abstractors to write brief résumés of journal articles for publication in abstracting journals and then in online bibliographic databases. Most of those who wrote these abstracts did so as a part-time sideline to their normal work in the same subject field. These are information activities that have a long history behind them. In modern times they have exploited ICT as a means of enhancing the range of sources or ease of access to them and in many the number of people involved has grown enormously. Essentially, however, they are still providing the same service as before, making information accessible, but they are using the new technologies to do it.

As mentioned earlier, many of the abstracting journals became so large and unwieldy that their transmutation into online databases came only just in time. During the 1970s and early 1980s online searching of these large systems became a vital part of scientific and technological research and development. Many databases had peculiarities that made it advantageous to employ a searcher who was experienced in their use. So there grew up together the online industry and the profession of information searcher.

The searchers used the online sources to trace journal articles, reports, patent specifications and other documents which they then studied in libraries. The cost of online searching could be quite high by the standards of library usage and there were cases of some commercial databases being bought and mounted in-house by universities. The advent of optical disc systems, notably CD-ROMs, which could carry large quantities of data, bibliographic or otherwise, and be mounted and searched on one's own computer was welcomed as an answer to high online search costs.

Many of those searchers are members of small companies which search information sources of all types, not just online ones, to produce information packages for clients. Such companies also act commonly as consultants on information management and set up training courses for the staff of larger organizations.

Researching, amassing and publishing information has become a sizeable business. Newspapers such as the *Daily Telegraph* exploit it as a sideline. The *Financial Times* has gone into it in a big way. So have news agencies like Reuters which create databases from the information they have gathered to provide online access to news, business, market and financial information.

Companies that used to specialize in undertaking polls to forecast the probable outcome of elections – pollsters – have expanded their range of activities to surveying a wide range of activities. Market research companies have proliferated; though, to judge by the way some of the newer ones phrase their questions and the seeming lack of careful anticipation evident in the absence of provision for variant choices, the results must be suspect. This stricture does not apply, of course, to the highly professional companies like Gallup, Mori or Frost and Sullivan.

The expansion of employment in the leisure industries has been greatly aided by the demand for information. Tourists, for example, expect a great deal of information about where they are going and what they are looking at when they get there. The knowledgeable tour guide is an essential component of a package holiday and so too is the official guide at tourist sites. The entertainment industry, as commented earlier, is another huge user of information not just for quiz programmes. Much research is carried out for its better commentary and documentary programmes.

Evening classes, and daytime ones for the unemployed or retired, are a modern leisure activity which creates an opportunity for those well informed on a topic of general interest to earn some income from lecturing.

Another large information industry is that which is concerned with presentation. Advertising and public relations are not new but the scale on which they operate nowadays is quite unlike that in the first half of this century. As discussed earlier, much advertising is genuinely informative: the advertisements in technical magazines, the readership of which is well informed, illustrate this well.

Advertising has spread onto the Internet, particularly with Web sites. It can be incorporated into the screen display in a way analogous to advertisements in a newspaper. Many Web and other network sites contain little but publicity material, though it can be useful – an example being the levels of monthly payments for a loan.

Some organizations link their database to the Internet for their own use, just as some motorists use the London Orbital M25 as a convenient way between two adjacent junctions. Consequently there are occasions when one can glean useful research information by scanning these sites. Keiser has pointed out [25] that, in the USA at least, universities often have Web sites with helpful data such as insurance information.

The information industry is vulnerable to claims for damages arising from the consequences of using incorrect information. This is because it is using second-hand data; it did not generate the information. Information professionals, even those specializing in a subject, are able to reveal information to be false, though generally they do. It is noteworthy that the old rule of *Caveat Emptor* is no longer deemed an appropriate or adequate safeguard and that where wrong or misleading information is given the sufferer should be compensated. There is no doubt that today there is a considerable pressure to ensure that information that is provided by commercial bodies to individuals is sound and reliable. Advertisements on commercial radio, for investments for example, are accompanied now by quite remarkably discouraging disclaimers.

On the Internet there are probably no enforceable safeguards. Where is the site from which the advertisement is coming? Some examples of Internet fraud and possible leakages of information in the securities market [26] have been causing anxiety, but such problems are to be expected in the early days of a new facility in an era when, it seems, so many people are looking for a way to make a quick buck, whether by ethical means or not. As using the Internet becomes more and more a part of everyday business life, people will make the necessary adjustments and the systems themselves will become more carefully geared to their purposes.

References

1. Hobsbawm, E.J. (1994) *Age of Extremes: The short twentieth century 1914–1991*. p.85. London: Random House

2. Ibid. p.413

3. Haywood, T. (1995) *Info-Rich – Info-Poor: Access and Exchange in the Global Information Society*. pp.100–104. London: Bowker-Saur

4. Switzer, T. (oral presentation) The Web and its impact on Teleworking. Globalization of Information. The Networking Information Society FID Conference and Congress, Graz, 1996.

5. Appleyard, D. (1997) Skill centres irrelevant to jobs. *Daily Telegraph, Connect*, 7 October 1997

6. Wriston, W. (1992) The twilight of sovereignty. *RSA Journal*, 5432, 568–577

7. Featherstone, K. (1997) A single currency – Good for Europe? Good for Britain?' *RSA Journal*, 5476, 52–53

8. Handy, C. (1996) What's it all for? Reinventing capitalism for the next century. *RSA Journal*, 5475, 33–39

9. Jussawalla, M., Okuma, T. and Araki, T. (1989) (eds.) *Information Technology and Global Interdependence*. New York: Greenwood Press

10. Burningham, D. et al. (1991) *Economics* 3rd edn. Sevenoaks, UK: Hodder and Stoughton

11. Heine, M. (1994) But what kind of commodity?. In *Changing Information Technologies*: *Research Challenges in the Economics of Information* eds. M. Feeney and M. Grieves, pp.156–171. London: Bowker-Saur

12. Badenoch, D. et al. (1994) The value of information. In *The value and impact of information*, ed. M. Feeney and M. Grieves, pp.9–78. London: Bowker-Saur

13. Watson, I. (1997) Recycling information. *Managing Information*, **4**(6), 56

14. KPMG (1995) *Information as an Asset: the Board Agenda*. (The Hawley Report). London: KPMG

15. Hutton, W. (1995) *The State we're in*. pp.248–9. London: Jonathan Cape

16. Drucker, P. (1993) *Post-capitalist society*. pp. 38, 47, 96–98. Oxford: Butterworth-Heinemann

17. Marchand, D.A. (1997) Managing the I in IT: creating business value with information and technology. *RSA Journal*, 5481, 61–64

18. Dieckmann, H. (1997) Information for Competitive Advantage. *Managing Information*, **4**(7), 19

19. Reuters (1997) *Reuters Guide to Good Information Strategy*. London: Firefly Communications

20. Barsoum, K. (In press) *Information in the Electronic Age*. Lecture to the RSA Forum on Ethics in Business, October 1997

21. Cheng, P.S. and Chang, P. (1997) Transforming corporate information into value through Datawarehousing and Data Mining. *FID News Bulletin*, **47**(5), 157–161

22. Bird, J. (1996) Data in, Knowledge out. *Management Today*, Sep. pp.70–72

23. Thomson buys LEXIS-NEXIS rival. *Information World Review*, 110, 3.

24. Library and Information Statistics Unit (1998) *Library and Information Statistics Tables*. Loughborough: LISU

25. Keiser, B.E. (oral presentation) How the use of global networks is changing the face of the financial services industries: insurance, banking, securities. In *Globalization of Information*.

The Networking Information Society. FID Conference and Congress, Graz, 1996.

26. Pretzlik, C. (1996) Regulators concerned over fraud on Internet. *Daily Telegraph,* 27 July 1996

CHAPTER TWELVE

Information and the environment

Of all the topics on which information has had an impact, two must stand out in the mind of most individuals in industrialized countries: care for the environment and improving human health. During the last thirty years the attitude of many of us to the environment, in Western Europe especially, has changed enormously. Prior to 1970 only a few people worried at all about the possibility that irreversible damage could be happening to the atmosphere, the land and the oceans, or the species of plants and animals. Local damage was recognized and schemes such as the Green Belt round London were put in place to minimize the risk of further harm. But they were mainly schemes intended to retain amenity rather than protect nature. The thought that harm on a global scale was happening did not occur to most of us.

The change is an outstanding example of the dramatic impact information can have. It also provides an interesting example of the manner in which information makes its impact. On the one hand there has been the continual drip, drip of more pieces of information. Almost daily in the papers and on the TV and radio there is news of some discovery: it may be a polluted water supply; it may be a list of endangered species; it may be a forecast that the weather patterns are changing. Each new piece adds to an overall feeling that the environment is changing and that something needs to be done before the changes run out of control.

At the same time, there have been groups, Greenpeace, Friends of the Earth, Council for the Preservation of Rural England and so on, campaigning against practices which, they claim, cause harm to the environment. Some groups' activities seem extreme but they do serve to keep the problems in our minds. So there have been two features: a continual supply of new information which has increased our understanding of our planet, its environment and the relation of life to the environment; and constant publicity to ensure we do not overlook or ignore the information that we are getting.

It is not just the very great increase in our knowledge of the structure of our planet and of the systems that support life on it that have led to serious concern about the way the environment is being damaged. It is that the unexpected features of the new discoveries have generated a fear that we may not yet know the full effects of what is happening and that further information, yet to be found, will reveal irreversible disasters are already in train. Information has indeed revealed how poor our understanding was and has generated an urgent need for much, much more information.

Of course, anxiety about the future is not the only outcome. The public understanding of natural processes and the way animals behave and plants grow has increased enormously. Weather patterns for the whole world are visible from satellites and provide much better data on which to base forecasts than was previously available (even if the forecasts in the UK seem as unreliable as ever). We are learning how events in one part of the world, e.g. El Niño, can affect the climate elsewhere.

It is generally felt that the first warning of troubles ahead was that given as long ago as 1798 by Malthus in his 'Essay on the Principle of Population' [1]. He pointed out that the planet cannot support an ever increasing population. It is, perhaps, ironic that although his claim that populations increase geometrically while food supplies do so only arithmetically was wrong, his basic concern, overpopulation and competition for resources, led Darwin to propound his principle of survival of the fittest. Malthus' mathematics may have been faulty but the fact that there is a limit to the resources of this planet, that one after another they will become exhausted and that the larger the population the sooner this will happen, is now generally recognized and accepted. It was brought forceably to public notice by the Club of Rome Report *Limits to Growth* published in the 1970s. A more sophisticated analysis published by the same team in 1992 [2] had less impact but painted a very gloomy picture of economic collapse and environmental disaster on a large scale occurring by the middle of the next century.

Predictions of this kind are beginning to have an impact on the way some people in industrialized countries behave. The most obvious changes are attempts to reduce the consumption of mineral fuels, by insulating buildings and making engines more fuel efficient, and the recycling of paper, glass and metals.

Similar to the anxiety about depleting resources is that about the extinction of species. In this case it was Rachel Carson's book *Silent Spring* which awakened public awareness of what is happening. Research has shown that every year a few species of plants and animals become extinct. I am not aware of any counterbalancing evidence of new species coming into existence, unless mutated bacteria and viruses count. Of course, over the millions of years since life started on this planet a great many species have become extinct from the dinosaurs to the dodo. One sees reports that the rate of loss of species seems to be increasing and that the principal cause is man's actions. We are still in the process of learning what the consequences are.

Already ecological research has revealed much about the way in which communities of plants and animals are interdependent and that if one disappears it has an impact on the others. Animals feed on other animals or on plants. Thrushes feed on snails which feed on plants. Eliminating snails, eliminates thrushes. It has been observed that loss of habitat, as when hedges are removed or forests destroyed, may lead to a reduction in the numbers of some species of mammals and birds. The consequences of changing the animal population by importing species from one place to another have been known for some time: the impact of rabbits in Australia, where there is no predator to keep them in check, and of the grey squirrel on the indigenous red squirrel in Britain are well known.

Our knowledge of how changes in, for example, the extent and nature of woodlands and copses can affect the bird population, sometimes helping one species, sometimes harming another, is gradually increasing. But the realization that detailed studies of such events need to be undertaken is relatively recent – since 1950 – and the length of time that is needed to carry out most of the studies is very long. Studies of the effect of weather changes on plants and hence on animal life in Wytham Woods near Oxford have been carried out for over thirty years and are only now beginning to yield meaningful results. Ecological research requires a very long time. Ecology is not a discipline like chemistry in which each experiment generally takes no more than a few days to design and implement. It is also very difficult to carry out controlled experiments, as distinct from merely observing events, over an area of more than a few acres.

Nature itself, if left alone fluctuates. Information on global warming is unconvincing to many because over time, a year, a millennium or a geological age, very much larger changes occur. Melting of the Antarctic ice cap is occurring but in past ages the ice cap in the Northern Hemisphere has covered much of Britain and has then receded again. Anxiety about the Antarctic, however, is partly because the change is happening so quickly, because it may be related to atmospheric changes, because the consequences for other parts of the world may be very significant and because it is unlikely we can do anything to reverse it. Increases and decreases in the population of creatures as food supplies vary with periods of high rainfall and of drought are known and so is the ability of some species to adapt to new conditions.

Obtaining enough reliable and complete information to be able to forecast events and to plan action to prevent disasters is difficult. Nevertheless, a large number of pieces are coming in. We have learnt that removing trees causes desertification, that the use of the insecticide DDT, apparently harmless to birds, in fact makes their eggs infertile, and that factory emissions are a major cause of thick fogs and of acid rain which damages some trees.

Other research has revealed that there are growing areas in the upper atmosphere where the amount of ozone has decreased. Further research has indicated that the probable principal cause is Chlorofluorocarbons (CFCs), gases thought to be inert and therefore used in refrigerators and other equipment. The loss of ozone allows more UV radiation from the sun to reach the earth and, it is believed, increases the risk of getting skin cancer. The consequence has been a sharp reduction in the numbers of people sunbathing and an increase in the sales of anti-sun creams of high blocking power. This is an illustration of a different type of how one thing affects another which in turn affects another and so on.

There are many other pieces of information about actions and events which are affecting, usually adversely, the environment and, sooner or later our lifestyle. Let us end the list by returning to Malthusian worries. Despite all that is known about contraception and the need to reduce the birth rate, data shows that the world's population is still increasing rapidly. The outcome must be increasing consumption of non-renewable resources, greater output of waste products and more generation of carbon dioxide.

The publicity given to the information as it appears has led among some people to a feeling of fear, fear that the world is running out of control. Pressure groups, such as those referred to earlier are receiving a great deal of support. The Green Movement has had an impact on governments and Green issues are prominent in their programmes, even if one sometimes cynically thinks it is only to get votes.

Evidence of the acceptance by some governments of the urgent need for more information on all these problems is given by the amount of research being funded. Just one example is provided by the European Commission which has announced 306 new projects under its Environment and Climate Research Programme. Some 205 million ECUs will be spent on projects which range from waste water and ozone depletion to the effect of greenhouse gases on climate change.

These problems are widely recognized not only at the scientific and political levels but, thanks to the media, by most people in industrial countries and a fair proportion of those in developing ones. There have been in the 1990s two major top level international meetings on the environment, the Rio Earth Summit and the New York Ungass meeting, and one in Cairo on the population problem. Action has been mooted but there is strong opposition to some of the proposals. Not everyone is willing to put the welfare of future generations before their own, not everyone is convinced that the evidence is strong enough to justify dramatic action.

For example, as the Tokyo meeting of Environmental Ministers showed, while the EU countries and Japan have been willing to set targets for the reduction of greenhouse gases (by 15 per cent by 2010 using 1990 levels as datum) the USA is not. The reason is that to do so will have an adverse economic effect on the oil and motor car industries, and on all the other industries that depend on them (it will have a similar adverse effect on EU and Japanese industries). It appears that US industrialists either do not find the evidence of irreversible harm convincing or are prepared to ignore it. Whatever the reasons, the same information is being differently heeded by different parties; its conversion into decision making knowledge is different according to the existing knowledge and prejudices of different individuals and groups of individuals.

The Rio Earth Summit, one of the meetings referred to above, gave rise to a programme of local actions, known as Agenda 21.

In Western Europe many local Councils, encouraged by their governments, have taken this to heart. The principle propounded is that of achieving a sustainable local economy which, though not an achievable target, especially for an urban community, does provide a focus for a series of actions whereby individual citizens can feel they are doing something to reduce harm to both the local and global environment.

Local Agenda 21 discussions often run into difficulties because of lack of data, both about the existing situation and about the consequences of various actions. Getting data, reliable data, to put into the computer model costs time and effort and that usually requires money. There is a limit to voluntary work. There is also a limit to available money. I have known discussions on acquiring the indicator data needed for monitoring reduced to the absurdity of deciding to measure those parameters that can be measured for little or no cost even though they would be of little use for the problem they were needed to solve.

One important change that results from information about a few cases of harmful effects of chemicals on the land and of traces of them in foods, is a move towards so-called organic farming. In this no artificial chemicals are used to enhance the crop-bearing potential of the land or to eradicate insect pests or weeds. Nor are animals given growth promoters. The cost of the product is higher and often is not as perfect in appearance. Nevertheless there are a growing number of people who buy 'organic' foods in preference to the others despite the higher price.

The huge amount of information that research has brought to light about the impact our technological activities, our farming practices and our lifestyle are having or may have on the environment has undoubtedly struck home to many of us. It is one field in which the results of research can be displayed in documentaries on television. Natural history programmes are very popular, including those of David Attenborough on all sorts of animal life and of Bill Oddie watching birds. The impact has been considerable and the public perception of how nature works has been greatly enhanced.

Gathering more and more information is facilitated by the new technologies. Time lapse photography can be applied to watching plants grow or, mounted on a satellite, to watching movements in the oceans and how the emissions from volcanos spread. Radio tagging of birds and fish is used to track their migratory pattern, yielding much more information than did the old style tags which depended on the bird or fish being caught and the fact reported. Microcameras transmitting the pictures TV style can reveal events inside a bird's nest.

All this is bringing to light a wealth of new information about our environment and the plants and creatures that inhabit it. Most of it does not raise cause for anxiety. A great deal of it will enable us to improve the way we and other forms of life can co-exist on this planet.

References

1. Carey, J. (1995) (ed.) *Faber Book of Science*. London: Faber and Faber. Contains the gist of Malthus' article.

2. Meadows, D.H., Meadows, D.L. and Randers, J. (1992) *Beyond the Limit: Confronting Global Collapse, Envisioning a Sustainable Future*. London: Chelsea Green Publishing

CHAPTER THIRTEEN

Education Now and in the Next Decade

'The nicest child I ever knew
Was Charles Augustus Fortesque
He sought when it was in his power
For information twice an hour.'

H. Belloc [1]

Growth, change and new technology

It is estimated that by the year 2000 AD there will be in the UK 5.3 million children in nursery and primary schools and 3.9 million in secondary ones, an average of 0.7 million children in each year between the ages of 3 and 16 needing schooling. To cater for them there are about 30 000 schools of which only about 2 400 are independent (different sources give anything between 29 and 39 thousand as the number of schools and a similar degree of variation for the number of independents). The proportion of pupils staying in full time education after the age of 16 is 38 per cent in the first year and 28 per cent in the second. Thereafter about 23 per cent continue in higher education full time. However, many more continue part time.

Since the last century there have been tremendous changes in state schools. Pupils have to stay longer, the curriculum has expanded and keeps changing. Vocational subjects have increased in number and in the complexity of the equipment needed. The same increase in sophistication has been occurring in the sciences. New theories of teaching have come, some for just a short while, others changing permanently the approach adopted.

Population changes have created further problems. The huge number of immigrants since 1950 has brought first a group of children whose mother tongue is not English and then a group, born in this country and therefore speaking it well enough but whose cultural background is different from that of the indigenous children. Thus the background knowledge of those in a class will vary to a far greater extent than used to be the case. Care has to be taken with the teaching of subjects to allow for different sensitivities. The history of the growth of the British Empire is an obvious example. Those of Indian origin may not see Clive's 'glorious victories' as anything like glorious.

A further complication for teachers has been the growth of political correctness. The terms used in normal English language for many years are suddenly not acceptable, sometimes thereby restricting the clarity of instruction as happened for a while when the word 'black' became taboo, sometimes improving it by eliminating unhelpful metaphors, but always adding to the teacher's load.

Teaching then is not just a question of what is taught and why but also to whom and how. At first teaching consisted of a few pupils grouped around the teacher, learning from what he said and from watching what he did. In various ways this is still the cornerstone of education whether in the one-to-one interaction of parent and child, of university tutorial and of workshop practice or the one-to-a hundred exposition of the lecture theatre. The difference lies in the degree of two way discourse that is possible.

From early times, too, the listen, or watch, and question sessions have been supplemented – reinforced might be a better term – by reading, by written exercises and by practical work. And at the end, whether daily, annually or after completion of a course, there have been examinations to find out how well the student has understood and how much he has learnt. The ability to recall facts, to repeat parrot fashion what was taught, has never been deemed adequate. The ability to exploit the information has been equally, often more, important. At school originality is praised, at university it is required – or should be.

As new technologies have been devised, suitable ones have been pressed into service in the classroom; the epidiascope, overhead projector and the movie projector were early examples. Schools' broadcasts have been commonplace since the 1920s and schools' television in the last thirty years. The use of CD-ROMs and other videodiscs is now normal practice. One difference in degree if not in kind from the past is that the latest technologies, the ICTs, are not just aids to learning but the subject of lessons.

Radio and television have opened up opportunities for learning in places other than schools and this has been further enhanced by networked computers. Books and correspondence courses have long provided this opportunity for those who have been taught to read. The Open University carried distance learning a stage further using radio and television. Now multimedia systems can even teach reading and a measure of interaction between system and student is possible though not as personalized as with a teacher. Whether video-conferencing and virtual reality systems will achieve the degree of personalized instruction each pupil needs for fully effective learning it will be interesting to see.

The UK Government has announced plans for 'A National Grid for Learning' [2]. It is envisaged as a computer network linking all schools, colleges, universities and libraries. Announcing it the Minister stated that it would give 'the opportunity to access up-to-the-minute information on a whole range of subjects.' The proposal opens up interesting possibilities which some, already connected, are exploring. An example is provided by a videoconference style link between classes in two countries to provide a new type of language and culture lesson. In many schools which already have computers it is being found that they are generating an enthusiasm for lessons even in subjects previously deemed boring. Computers are fashionable and 'with it', books are old fashioned and dull. The computer is enabling new ways of teaching to be introduced, thereby giving the teachers themselves a new interest. Skills of reporting can be carried through to the design, editing and production of a newspaper for example. Essays can be entered onto an intranet and marked, not edited, by the teacher online and be easier to read than handwritten ones.

Gradually developing in pupils the ability to search for information has always been an important part of education. Familiarising them with the use of reference books and libraries and how to carry out projects is standard practice. It is now necessary also to get them used to using the Internet to find information and to know the skills necessary to find required information in the huge mass there available.

At universities the use of the Internet has become part of the normal way of life, especially among research workers. Professor

Bundy observes [4], 'These online discussions often do then inform my face-to-face discussions and *vice versa*'. Later he goes on, 'when they [his students] conduct literature surveys, not only can they collect the latest versions of papers quickly and easily via the Internet, but they can also readily ask the authors how each paper fits into the overall picture and what their latest thinking is on the topic. This provides a richness of educational experience which has not previously been available'. Most people thrive on communication with friends and colleagues. The Internet gives an opportunity for academics, to whom the interchange of ideas and information is virtually the bread and butter of existence, to exchange thoughts with those engaged in similar work all over the world in a more relaxed way than by fax, a less intrusive one than by phone and a quicker one than by letter.

Broadband networks are gaining new teaching uses at the practical level. For example, using closed circuit TV, a specialist physician at a location remote from the operating theatre, has been able to guide and advise a surgeon during the course of an operation. The same system has been used to enable students to watch the details of an operation without needing to be present in the operating theatre – and probably learning more by being able to see more clearly. Question and answer is possible as the operation proceeds.

The computer, whether networked or stand alone, will pose some of the problems that have been encountered with other devices which have found educational roles. In mathematics the hard work of numeric calculation was made easier first by log tables, then by the slide rule, then by the mechanical calculator, then by the pocket electronic calculator and now by the PC. At each stage the teacher has faced the task of instilling fundamental arithmetic skills to youngsters who can see no reason for not just relying on the current latest device. In chemistry a similar situation arises when teaching analysis: modern automatic methods such as chromatography and spectroscopy, render rare at work the need to carry out classic analytical processes, yet there is merit in learning the manipulative skills required.

It could be said, therefore, that the argument about the extent to which computers should be used in schools is just another stage in the long process but there is a new aspect. Whereas other new equipment simplifies doing a sum or an analysis but the answer still has to be found, the computer can cover up student error and even produce the answer on behalf of the student. Thus the spelling checker may hide the student's need to learn how to spell. The problem the student has been set to work out can, in some cases, be fed as it stands into the computer and the answer read on the screen. Given a connection to the Internet, the student can place the problem on a bulletin board and have it answered by others.

The ability to do this sort of thing is invaluable and should be learnt by everyone though in general and especially during exams the student should work out the answers to problems for himself. Nevertheless, teaching pupils to be at ease at the computer is important and communication skills should encompass both conversational ones and those needed for Internet discussion groups.

It is not all straightforward, of course. There will be the need to keep the equipment not just the content up-to-date, (some Open University films seen recently seem very dated). There will be a need to guard against viruses entering the system and deal with those that do, already in many universities a very time consuming and costly task. Nor will computers and networks completely revolutionize education. Just as videos of literary classics are no substitute for reading the novels, so is the ability to quickly look up information on the Internet no substitute for training one's memory to store and rapidly retrieve large amounts of information. As everyone knows, the ability to recall and present relevant facts when involved in any sort of discussion establishes one's position and in negotiation gives one an immense advantage by enabling one to substantiate one's opinions and to disprove rather than merely dispute opposing arguments and claims.

Who teaches the teachers?

A teaching profession full of inspiring, knowledgeable, up-to-date members is fundamental to providing the education system needed. No matter how good the techniques for distance learning and self-tuition become, with but a small number of exceptions children need the input and stimulation only a teacher can provide. At university level there can be substantial reliance on self education but even there guidance from a tutor and the stimulus of seminars is needed. Multimedia could replace some lectures, especially those given routinely and unchanged each year, but even now such lectures are often better read in books.

Unfortunately inspiring teachers, like inspiring people in any walk of life, are not as plentiful as one would wish. Nevertheless, the majority of teachers, like the majority in any other profession, do a very sound job. Keeping up-to-date is, however, a problem for them. A solicitor, for example, expects to spend a part of his time keeping abreast of the latest laws and judgements. A university don keeps up-to-date by being involved in research, being surrounded by other colleagues similarly involved and by attending conferences as part of his way of life. For the school teacher, lifelong learning, which is what it amounts to, requires more effort on his part; it is not built in to the job in the same way.

But it is not only keeping up-to-date with new information about the subjects one teaches that is necessary. Now there is also the need to keep up-to-date with the technologies that are used in the classroom. Scientific apparatus and mathematical calculators have advanced but those used in schools have never been difficult for teachers to master. This is not true of IT apparatus. The point is illustrated by Collingridge [3]. Talking to teachers about using the computer to provide visual images in geography she found that, 'It was only when it came to the questions that I realised what I had taken for attentive interest was actually stunned bafflement'. The information and communication technologies, their applications and their content are developing so rapidly that the teachers have to be kept up-to-date as well as the equipment. The National Council for Educational Technology (NCET) is very active in this as well as recommending standards for the equipment for school use.

There can be little doubt that one of the major requirements for national success in the future will be a well educated population. To get everyone up to the maximum level of which they are capable and to instil an urge to continue throughout life adding extra information to keep one's knowledge up-to-date and learning new skills whenever necessary will require the best teachers we can produce supported by the resources they need. Whatever shape future society takes, information will be a key resource and those who have it, can find any more they need and can utilise it will be the ones who are most successful. However, serious problems are being encountered with some teenagers and those in their twenties.

The problem of the poorly educated

Aristotle said men have a craving for knowledge. Perhaps, but as surveys of the output of our state education system would appear to show, Charles Augustus Fortesque is an exception: modern teenagers have a craving for ignorance. Mantel, in her novel *Fludd*, writes [5], 'The girls had learnt nothing; or if they had, they had forgotten it, immediately and as a matter of policy.' She was, I am sure, writing from experience. Lightfoot [6] reports that research in Devon schools finds that boys believe that they gain 'street cred' by not working and that carrying bags of crayons and pens is 'naff'. Kelman wrote [7], 'When working class people leave school they never want to see another book in their lives. Reading seriously is a form of punishment'. This used not to be so. At one time education was seen as the way out of the poverty trap. Times have changed.

Of course the situation is not as bad as the reports would make it seem. The majority of children do as well as they always did but there seem to be some, too many to ignore, that, in modern society, are having and are causing problems.

Very young children do ask questions, do seek to find out, but it seems that in far too many of them that natural inquisitiveness is killed off early. There are several reasons and no doubt the balance of the factors varies from person to person. Nevertheless, for many teenagers there is no pleasure to be found in learning and their peers encourage only apathy. The consequences are disastrous both for these youngsters and for society in general. Considerable effort is required to change the situation; fortunately, recent governments have shown awareness of it and a determination to tackle it but much more than government effort is needed.

Concern about educational standards in the UK is based, it seems, on a variety of tables which show that compared with other industrialized countries British children are, on average, less advanced age for age or that a higher percentage are performing poorly in various tests [8]. The consequences are apparent in adults. *Social trends* recorded in 1995 that 40% of 21 year olds have literacy problems. A survey by the Organization for Economic Co-operation and Development confirms the gulf that exists between the top and bottom 25 per cent in the UK. It is also reported that young adults find it harder to read and understand newspapers and brochures than do those in their 30s, but that 45 to 60 year olds are, on average, less literate than the youngest adults. There seem to be conflicting messages in these figures but one can conclude that all is not well.

Obviously more than just national pride is at stake. If the reports are correct part, at least, of the education system has been failing to meet the needs of both present and future society. It is not enough to be satisfied that the top 50 per cent of the population is well educated since a poorly educated bottom 50 per cent will be a millstone around their necks. Britain has too large a population to earn its living by exporting agricultural and mineral produce. Our wealth depends on manufacturing goods and providing services for which those in other countries will pay. Therefore, to earn our living we must do things better and/or more cheaply than do other peoples. Inventiveness and high quality are essential. Commercial skills and acumen, not usually strong in the UK, must be acquired. The proportion of jobs for which a high level of education or of skill is required is rising while the number of those classed as unskilled or only semi-skilled has fallen since 1980 and continues to fall.

That is the economic imperative. There is also a social one. It must be the wish of all of us, excepting only a few curmudgeonly or criminal types, to live an interesting, full and worthwhile life, to enjoy it to the full and to contribute in generous measure to enabling others to enjoy their lives. The depression of unemployment, the boredom of having too little to do and the growing culture of drugs and crime spoil the enjoyment of life for all of us, not just those who perforce are trapped into those ways. Education is not the whole answer, it cannot be, but it can provide, among other things a sound foundation for finding worthwhile ways of spending one's leisure time – enforced as well as earned – and for learning how to behave in a way that is compatible with the expec tations of the society which one lives.

But in the UK, it is not just poor results from our educational system that are the concern. It is now clear that our ability to maintain our economic prosperity will depend not just on rectifying the situation but on raising standards to a higher level than ever before and on developing the content. In 1997 Sir Geoffrey Holland, Vice-Chancellor of Exeter University and formerly Permanent Secretary at the Departments of Employment and Education, identified [9] the strategic need. He observed the huge technological advances in communications, the impact of the global market place, changing employment patterns and social developments as placing a demand on the education system which must be met if both country and individuals are to flourish.

A system which provides, for those who left school at age 14 or more recently 16, only an adequate level of education for unskilled and semi-skilled jobs in manufacturing industry, for clerical and junior managerial posts and for simple service jobs such as shop assistants, is quite inadequate for today's needs. The level of knowledge and the skills of each individual need to be raised to the highest level practicable. Drucker [10] observes that society will be divided into two classes, knowledge workers and service workers, and that 'service workers, as a rule, lack the necessary education to become knowledge workers'. He may be right but he should have added that even the service workers require a higher level of education than in the past.

Aims of the system

Giving students a sound and extensive store of information on which to base manual and intellectual skills and powers of judgement, the ability to acquire more when needed, the skill to select, evaluate and utilize information and an understanding of how knowledge advances are at the heart of any education system. So too is stimulating students' imagination. It is now important, following the precepts of Drucker, Holland and Moser, to rethink the role and function of school and schooling to make sure that the resources we devote to it are directed to produce the optimum results. This includes examining how the education system can cope with the ever increasing amount of new information, and how it can best utilize for teaching the new information and communication technologies as well as enabling students to become proficient in their use.

If we are to discuss the interaction of information and education, then it is necessary to remind ourselves of those aims of the system which are relevant. Education is much more than learning the 'three Rs'. One is no more educated having learnt only them than one is a carpenter after learning to saw a piece of wood accurately. The UK's education system should result in everyone by the time they reach adulthood:

1. being able to communicate effectively in English in speech and in writing;
2. being able to read and understand any piece of English literature and a wide range of informative and technical writings;
3. being properly numerate, not merely able to do arithmetic but also to appreciate the significance of numbers and of quantity, so that at least one knows instinctively that, for example, 2.4×53 cannot amount to 1272;

4. possessing a substantial and sound fund of general know-
    ledge about the geography, history, political structure and
    culture of both the locality and country in which one
    lives, and a broad background of general knowledge about
    the same features of the other regions and countries of the
    world;
5. having a sound general knowledge about each of the arts,
    humanities, sciences and technologies;
6. having at least one practical skill, e.g. woodworking or playing
    a musical instrument;
7. being able to read and speak a foreign language and having
    an appreciation of the way different languages affect the way
    ideas are expressed and understood;
8. having a desire to learn more about the things that interest
    one and a willingness to learn new ideas and skills;
9. having the habit of examining all new information critically,
    relating it to existing knowledge and, if accepting rather than
    rejecting it, reappraising the state of one's knowledge in the
    light of it;
10. having a knowledge of how to find information using both
    traditional and modern searching techniques;
11. having familiarity with current information and communica-
    tion technologies and the ability and willingness to keep that
    familiarity up-to-date;
12. last, and far from least, a high level of social skills.

These are, of course, only the basic requirements, the aim of
which is to enable each individual to find work in the service or
manufacturing sectors of employment, to be able to acquire, understand and make use of the wealth of information that will be
needed in all areas of life, to assess the merits of all that which
will assail him/her whether bidden or unbidden, and to enjoy
leisure whether earned or enforced. As employers keep emphasizing, it is vital that, even if 'education is still to be for the old
high purposes, to make people more whole, so as to understand
better the world or society or themselves, so as to broaden their
minds, so as to have fuller lives, more enriching experiences' [11],
it is equally if not more vital that it results in people who possess
the necessary abilities and attitudes to be first rate employees
throughout their working lives. Recently some employers have
been pointing out that their requirements of new employees are
that they are able to read and write clear English, are numerate,

are able to communicate and have a positive personality. Computer skills are welcome but only in addition to these qualities.

A change of recent times with a considerable effect on the education system is the increasing insistence on qualifications for all manner of jobs. On-the-job training and experience are no longer enough. Diplomas are required even for such jobs as domestic catering service and waiter in a restaurant.

There are many other requirements not listed above – the development of proper moral values and the ability to stand up to life in a highly competitive world for example. However, we do need in society to decide whether the school is the proper place to learn them. If there are, for example, failings by parents ought we to leave repairing the damage to schools, thereby distracting from the proper role of the school, or should we find some alternative way.

Mitchison observed trenchantly [12] that, 'whatever schools are like, there is no real equality, and not much fraternity, so long as one child comes from a home with books, telly and radio used not as background noise but for furthering knowledge and appreciation, [and with] intelligent adult conversation he is allowed to join in, while another child comes from a home with none of these things. So it is more than education that needs changing.'

Raising the educational impetus

It is apparent that the need to educate people to the much higher level required by our future society is such that the traditional pattern of Primary (ages 5–11), Secondary (11–16 or 18) and Tertiary (18-early 20s) education is no longer sufficient. Changes are occurring, some of which have been in train for several years, notably the addition of pre-school education and, at the other end, facilities for lifelong learning and for taking up tertiary courses at whatever age suits the individual.

One is the addition of nursery education for all who want it. It will be vital that the opportunity this creates for starting the learning process is not squandered through over-much emphasis on getting the children to work in harmony. Educating out anti-social behaviour is very important but so is starting the love of books and of learning and of training the memory. Research has shown how vital for future mental performance is brain development in the child's early years.

As commented earlier, government and many other institutions are well aware of the need to improve the general level of education in the UK. For some years there have been efforts to ensure that the curriculum gives a proper level of attention to basics. The spur of competition has been applied to schools by publishing league tables of how well the children do. Schools have at last been given the authority to dismiss ineffective teachers. At the same time a start has been made to find a way to remedy the results of poor teaching and help those who have experienced difficulty. Thus, the introduction of remedial classes during the summer holiday, for children who do not seem to have reached the level of reading and arithmetic they should, seems to have been a success.

A major consideration is that of meeting the needs of the individual child. The bright need to be given the opportunity to race on without making those who learn at a slower rate feel failures. Anti-elitist attitudes may be good in their way but they must not be allowed to hold back the intellectually good. Kemp writing in his 'A Father Writes . . .' column [13] comments that at both primary and secondary school there was an attitude of expecting, i.e. requiring, pupils to give of their best and to achieve. Brighouse makes a similar point as a Chief Education Officer [14] when he urges expectations of success and setting standards for school success.

National curricula are fine as minima but not all pupils need the same education. There must be room for substantial variation. As a former headmaster put it to me [15], 'I feel we are in danger of heading towards everybody being taught the same and losing the input to the child of individual teachers'. Were distance learning and excessive use of TV in schools to become popular, there would be a serious danger of uniformity.

Changes are being made to meet the need to continue universal education beyond the age of 16 and to create a learning culture. In addition to the usual fare of day and evening courses at the local college of further education and evening classes run by the local council, there are schemes being tried out by the Department for Employment and Education to train those without jobs. Other efforts include a number of programmes initiated by the European Commission. Among them are schemes to promote mobility of students, in particular grants for the interchange of students in secondary and higher education (Socrates), for language education (Lingua), for vocational and training apprenticeships (Leonardo da Vinci) and for the Training and Mobility of Researchers (TMR). All these schemes emphasize that the aim is not only to promote a European rather than national approach but also to promote the necessary background to thrive in the 'Information Society of the future'.

Recently the Royal Society of Arts has, by starting a Campaign for Learning [16], added its weight to efforts to achieve a culture shift, to get the UK to become a learning society, i.e. one in which everyone regards undertaking learning as just as normal a part of life as taking a holiday. Obviously this ties in well with the oft expressed need for life-long learning in the Information Society and with the requirement that leaving school or university should not be seen as the end of one's education. Unfortunately a MORI poll commissioned by the RSA [17] showed that while a large majority of those polled acknowledged the importance of lifelong personal development, only a few intended to do anything about it for themselves. Continuing education and training, like moral behaviour, is a great thing – for other people. Despite this discouraging start, a demand for post-scholastic education and training is apparent among a large number of those in their late teens and twenties. It is crucial now to amass sufficient evidence to convince the others in that age group that it pays off and similarly to get the same message, backed by hard evidence, across to those in their thirties and forties.

Looking at the upper end of the educational ladder, even PhD training has come under scrutiny. It has changed considerably already since the middle of the 20th century. Arguably many holders of the degree are mediocre research workers rather than outstanding ones as they used to be. A recent European chemistry conference has been discussing [18] new approaches to produce sufficient numbers of PhDs of the calibre needed to match employers' needs. One approach is to create an additional qualification, DChem, to indicate a substantial contribution to the application of existing knowledge rather than the generation of new knowledge. A second suggestion is to make flexibility of field of specialization a feature of training so that movement between different areas of research and even different industries is facilitated. However, this latter could defeat the aim of raising the standard of expertise.

The benefits of absorbing large amounts of information, provided it is relevant, and of learning necessary facts and figures, will not be lost on those who see paper qualifications as essential for a job. It is not only professional work that requires much learning of facts and absorbing a great deal of information. Consider, for example, someone who wishes to be a gardener. He or she needs information about what plants flourish in what conditions, about the nature of soils and how to improve them, what chemicals are needed to nourish plants and what can be used to eliminate diseases and pests. Some training in garden design is also useful. Without this sort of training all the person is useful for is mowing, clipping hedges and digging.

However, broader general knowledge may not be seen as useful and will have to be learnt later if the schools cannot impart it effectively. Of course much is acquired as life progresses but the vast amount of information that assails us every day and needs attention is such that learning by chance and experience is unlikely to be enough. Of course there is a fashion for general knowledge quizzes on TV and in pubs, from which something will stick but this is hardly the information from which, for example, a judgement of local environmental initiatives is likely to be made. Nor will gossip with friends be likely to yield adequate sound information unless at least one of the friends is well informed on the topic.

Learning or learning to use?

The value of requiring pupils to memorize large amounts of information and data has been questioned. The reason given by some of those teachers who hold that opinion is that the rate at which facts are disproved or superseded is so great as to make memorizing information a waste of time. Far more important, it has been claimed, is to teach them the ability to think rationally, not to accept ideas uncritically and to seek information for themselves as and when they want it. As a headmistress said, 'Teach students how to make use of information rather than filling them with knowledge'.

No-one would deny the importance of these abilities but it is necessary also to have a thorough grounding in general information in the subjects one is studying in order to build up knowledge and ability therefrom to judge other information. It is very difficult to appreciate properly news about crises in, say, Ethiopia and Sudan and the extent to which they are or are not connected if one does not know that the two countries adjoin each other in the same continent but have very different populations and cultures.

There is also, which must not be overlooked, the importance of training memory. How this is to be done, whether memorizing one's nine times table, French irregular verbs, or Shakespeare's sonnets, is a matter for the teacher and child but it must be done. A good memory is a valuable asset and it needs to be trained and kept fully active.

It is always a challenge for educators to be able to strike the right balance between all the things that ought to be taught, the time available to teach them and the ability of individual pupils to take them in. Dismissing the teaching of facts because facts can change is, however, no answer. The need is to bring home to students that some information can be taken as reliable, some as usable for the time being and some as needing corroboration. It is the same problem as that which has caused so much dispute over the years: when do you take on trust what a senior person tells you and when do you treat it as open to challenge?

That pure common salt is a crystalline lattice of sodium and chlorine ions is a fact that can safely be taught as truth. That one needs common salt in one's diet is also a fact but one open to misinterpretation. The amount needed changes from one dietary theory to another and probably depends on the individual and on the circumstances, e.g. whether the person has recently been perspiring heavily.

The study of history is invaluable for training students in handling information. Historical research consists essentially of obtaining a body of facts and a body of accepted beliefs, showing the possibility of relationships between them and devising interpretations. One cannot have all the facts, one cannot ever know what all the people – or even any of the people – involved in an event thought. One can only know what happened, what was recorded at the time and what events preceded the happening. One is unlikely to have all the facts; some historians, it seems, are even selective in the facts they use, so that the theories or interpretations which they produce are unlikely to be the last word on their subject. With luck successive studies will bring us closer to an understanding but the key point is that the facts remain the facts even if more and more are added; it is the interpretations that change. Both are information but whereas the facts are information as such, the theories are information only when expressed as 'Professor Jones' interpretation is . . .'. This way of distinguishing the two is not often expressed and the student needs to be trained to make the distinction automatically for himself.

For example, that Elizabeth Tudor came to the throne in 1558 and died in 1603 is fact. It is also fact that during her reign the Spanish authorities sent a fleet of ships with orders to transport Spanish troops from the Low Countries to England. Whether the attacks by the English ships inflicted serious damage (a few Spanish ships were sunk or damaged) is open to interpretation for most of the fleet reached harbour in France where they could meet the troops. That fire ships were sent in is fact and so is the rapid departure of the ships without waiting for the troops to arrive and embark. Since many ships never got back to Spain, some being wrecked while trying to sail round the north of Scotland, it is not unreasonable to interpret the result as a defeat for Spain and as saving England from invasion; but one can argue about the extent to which the result was due to misfortune, to bad tactics by the Spanish Admiral, or to the good tactics of the English. National pride can bias one's interpretation of historical events though the facts may be incontrovertible.

The development of historical study is interestingly recounted by Evans in his *In Defence of History* [19] but note my interpretation. That word 'interestingly' is my opinion and can only mean 'interesting to me'. I cannot know whether it will be interesting to anyone else but I offer the piece of information that in my judgement it will be to a number of people.

The immense outpouring of new information, which seems so often to contradict what was reported only yesterday, is very challenging for young people until they have learnt how to distinguish fact from theory and how to respond to change in a mature and balanced way. Teachers themselves are inevitably not fully up-to-date in everything and those in secondary schools face the challenge of retaining their authority as mentors as they lead pupils from the 'learn from teacher' situation in the primary school to the university approach of 'find out for yourself and build knowledge by sharing your findings with the tutor'. In my own experience, many years ago now, the transition was well advanced in the 5th form (i.e. age 15) and virtually complete in the 6th. Good teachers work towards this goal throughout the years of secondary education.

It follows that a major challenge for schools is teaching pupils how to set about finding the right information needed to cope with any situation they encounter, in an environment in which everyone has to face a torrent of all manner of information with but a trickle of instruction, where one has to work out answers for oneself and where one does not do the same thing day in day out for most of one's life. At present we just do not know what life and work will be like in twenty years' time but it seems that mastery of information will be an invaluable asset and that our education system must instil this into pupils as the best preparation it can give for the unknown future.

Herring comments [20] that how to find a book in the library or to use CD-ROMs and the Internet are low-level skills; the real challenge is posed by the range of formats in which information is presented and especially by the overwhelming amount that one may find in the electronic sources. The ability to discriminate on the basis of quality is difficult to teach when even relevance is inadequate to stem the flood.

Nevertheless, a key requirement for the education system is that of preparing us for a life in which, as far as can be seen, change will be the dominating theme. Gadgets change, rules change, jobs change, skills change, qualifications needed increase. The typewriter has been replaced by the PC with a word processing package which is easy to use only after one has mastered its complexities. For many trades, such as plumbing or building, new or revised standards and safety rules keep appearing, new materials are available, new fashions appear and disappear. Keeping up to date is crucial and this involves, when each new job comes along, being able to find and understand information. Of course the old methods of finding out and getting advice, e.g. asking at one's suppliers' counter, still provide the answers to some problems but the proportion is decreasing.

For everyone the need for forward planning is increasing whether one is buying food for a week or ordering stock for a business. On the other hand 'just-in-time' ordering systems, splendid when they work, replace the planning need with communication skills. The skill needed to manage one's finances has become greater with the advent of credit and debit cards. The old technique of simply spending the cash one had in hand until it ran out, though still possible and still used by a few people, is rare now that bank accounts and mortgages and other forms of loans are normal for the majority. Tax self assessment may not be obligatory yet for everyone, but it must be possible that it soon will be.

So the conclusion must be that despite all the simplification of procedures that occurs as a new device matures (motor cars and computers are much easier to use nowadays than during the first years after they were available to the public) the complexity of life is increasing, that the extent of knowledge needed to cope is increasing, and that the nature of the skills needed is changing. Lifelong learning appears to be essential for everyone. Learning to use information technologies is a key requirement for the immediate future; longer term there will be other new skills to learn.

Learning to handle, evaluate and exploit information, both new and old, is essential both for the short term and the long term future.

References

1. Belloc, H. (1997) *Cautionary Tales and other verses*. p. 39 London: The Folio Society

2. Standage, T. (1997) All schools set to be wired by 2002. *Daily Telegraph, Connected*, p.3. 7 October 1997

   The DFEE *document Superhighways for education: the way forward*. 1995 is also interesting in this context.

3. Collingridge, V. (1997) Mayday call in the classroom. *Daily Telegraph, Connected*, p.7. 22 April 1997

4. Bundy, A. (1996) Education uses of the Internet. Letter. *RSA Journal*, 5470, 14

5. Mantel, H. (1990) *Fludd*. p.29. London: Penguin

6. Lightfoot, L. (1997) Report of the Annual Conference of the Secondary School Heads Association. *Daily Telegraph*, 26 April 1997

7. Kelman, J. (1992) Some recent attacks. AK Press 1992. See J. Pateman, (1997) Breaking the information blockade. *Focus*, **28**(2) 115

8. Moser, C. (1996) Our educational future: priorities and politics. *RSA Journal* 5471, 60–73

9. Holland, G. (1997) Are we educating our young people for the 21st century? *RSA Journal*, 5478, 43–47

10. Drucker, P. (1993) *Post-capitalist society*. p.5–7. Oxford: Butterworth-Heinemann

11. Hoggart, R. (1993) *An Imagined Life: Life and times 1959–1991.* p.214. Oxford: Oxford University Press

12. Mitchison, N. (1986) *You may well ask.* London: Fontana Paperbacks

13. Kemp, T. (1998) Much ado about education. *Daily Telegraph,* February 1998.

14. Brighouse, T. (1996) Avoiding failing the future – the need to go beyond the National Curriculum. *RSA Journal* 5470, 62–72

15. Youngman, R.T. Private communication.

16. Greany, T. (1997) Reaching our potential in a learning society. Campaign for learning. *RSA Journal* 5479,

17. RSA (1997) *Annual Report 1996/7.* p.15. London: RSA

18. The Royal Society of Chemistry (1997) PhD training in chemistry. *Chemistry in Europe,* **5**(3), 4

19. Evans, R.J. (1997) *In defence of history.* London: Granta Books

20. Herring, J. (1997) Enabling students to search and find. *Library Association Record,* **99**(5) 258–259

CHAPTER FOURTEEN

Information in politics and government

'Information is not in itself subversive, and knowledge is not necessarily power. On the contrary, information can be used to manufacture consensus'.

Melanie McGrath [1]

Government and information are inseparable. However, all governments have an ambivalent attitude towards information. On the one hand they require citizens and institutions to make available all the information that government officials think they need as and when they, the officials, think they need it. On the other hand they do not believe, notwithstanding the provisions of a Freedom of Information Act, that citizens and institutions should be informed about all the plans they and the government are preparing or enquiries they are making until they deem it timely to release the information. At the same time it does require citizens and institutions to make themselves fully informed about what they, the citizens etc., are required to do and what has been done for their benefit.

One mistake is to think of government as an entity. In fact it consists of a large number of individuals in many departments working not only as individuals but in groups, and each may take part in several different groups. Each individual has his own ambitions and prejudices and will choose to serve these as well as departmental aims. Personal aims should not give rise to conflict with departmental ones nor departmental ones with government ones but in reality there will be occasions when they are not entirely in harmony with each other. As Bierce [2] put it, 'Politics: a strife of interests masquerading as a contest of principles'.

In official and government circles, there is an intricate web of diverse information sources, channels and needs, each with a different set of concerns. Some – the politicians – are dependent on voters' whims to retain their jobs; the majority are employees of the state with career interests as well as a sense of duty to the politicians and the citizens to whose needs they minister.

There are four major areas of involvement between government and information, not to mention several more minor ones. First and foremost it must gather information. A government without efficient and full input of information would soon fall. It could not know what its supporters want or its opponents are plotting. Laws cannot be made, or even the decision taken not to make a law, without proper information about the matter to be regulated, what options exist for regulations and what will be the effects of each option.

Second, government must provide information. Even the most secretive government has to inform those it rules what it wants them to do or not to do. Enlightened governments keep the citizens well loaded with information about what the government is doing, what services it is providing and what plans it has. Well informed but not completely informed; the latter is neither practicable nor desirable. Freedom of Information, as said earlier, has its limits.

The third major area of involvement is in the provision of information for institutions and the public to use for their own purposes. Much of this information will come from the stores government departments and agencies have amassed for their own use, but presented in ways which meet known public needs. Thus the Office of the Government Actuary produces demographic data which helps, *inter alia*, social research and the Ordnance Survey publishes its Pathfinder series of maps for hikers.

The fourth major area of involvement is in the interchange of information between its citizens and between them and the citizens of other states. Of course, every government, just like any other institution, would like to have control of the flow of information in and out of its domain if only to avoid the leakage of highly sensitive material. A totalitarian regime, or one which aims to preserve its culture from pollution by foreign influences, may try to prevent transborder communication, or may try to jam broadcasts from other countries. However today there are so many channels of flow of information that preventing inter-nation communication is quite impossible. Encryption can, of course, render international communication secure, blocking out government – the opposite almost of official jamming. Currently there is concern that the UK has chosen to introduce some controls on the freedom of organizations and individuals to use encryption systems without keeping government informed [3].

It is claimed that it was the flow of information from western countries into the Soviet Union that played a large part in generating the disenchantment with communism that led to the dismantling of the Berlin Wall and of the Union itself. On the other hand, when there is a revolution within a country, one of the first acts of rebels in modern times is to seize the radio and TV stations. It was the failure of the rebels in Spain a few years ago to do this (they seized only the Madrid stations but there were many others in the country that remained in government hands) that enabled the King to rally support and defeat them. As Theodore White commented in the context of America, 'power is control of the means of communication'.

Information, it would seem therefore, can have a dramatic effect even on the stability or otherwise of a political regime or a party. In an adaptable country like the UK, a flow of information derogatory to the government is likely to lead to its failure at the next election and a change of party in power, as happened in the UK in the mid-1990s.

Managing the information flow is therefore an aim of most governments and political parties, if only to minimize the flow of incorrect or adversely biassed information and to be able to present in time an accurate or more favourably presented version. But there are now so many and such sophisticated means of communicating, that control is impossible even when, as in the case of pornographic material, the vast majority of people want the flow prevented. Such control has to be exerted by the receiver. The most official effort can do is to pass laws so that those who communicate immoral or antisocial material can be prosecuted and their equipment or books seized. But that action cannot prevent transmissions from another country via TV or the Internet, unless there is international agreement to do so.

The nature of government

To go back in time for a moment, when Western style democratic government was first introduced in 5th century B.C. Athens, issues were debated and decisions taken by the people as a whole – or rather by those people whom we would now classify as the well informed commercial and managerial classes: the labouring classes, i.e. slaves, were excluded. Today everyone (except Peers and those certified mentally deficient), whether well informed or not, gets a vote but only for a person to represent him. Referenda, the nearest equivalent to Greek style democracy, are rare in the politics of most countries.

One of the anxieties of recent years has been the growth in effectiveness of pressure groups which, with a singleness of purpose which originates from having only one objective and no interest in the consequences for anything or anyone else of achieving it, make great play of any information which seems beneficial to their cause and attempt to decry any which is contrary to their theme. Instead of rational debate, considering all the available information, bullying tactics are all too often used.

De Tocqueville, writing in the 1840s about the growth of democracy in America [4], points out that the people of a democratic nation become totally dependent on their government, though the system of voting to elect their leaders gives an illusion of independence. In this fashion, too, he claims , large numbers of people spread over a wide area can be made subordinate to petty rules and regulations. This, apparently, was not possible in former ages because 'the want of information, the imperfection of the administrative system and the natural obstacles caused by the inequalities of conditions would speedily have checked it.' In the UK today these checks are not present, though that is not to imply that the administrative system is perfect. We have indeed become highly, though not quite totally, dependent on government. This was recognized by the Thatcher Government whose programme of privatizing many activities and official organizations aimed to reduce the extent of that dependence. Most people have become dependent on the government for education, health services and many social services. We expect government to protect us from noise and nuisance from our neighbours, to provide counsellors to solve our domestic problems and hold our hands when we are frightened or shocked, to regulate adoption and abortion, and to protect us against pushy or unscrupulous traders.

Little of this is blameable on greater or better quality information. However, the growth of information is leading to governments, local councils and the EU Commission increasing restrictions on our freedom of choice and pressurizing us to change our normal habits as they 'care' for us and prevent us from harming other members of the community.

Of course, we have to leave it to government to negotiate on our behalf with other governments, to protect us from hostilities, to provide a police force to ensure that criminals are apprehended, and to provide a justice system. We welcome the use surveillance and tracking devices to ensure that lawbreaking is detected and that the activities of other governments which we distrust are monitored. However, we do not want government to use them to watch us and we require government to ensure that our fellow citizens and commercial institutions do not misuse them. A problem is that misuse has to be allowed to occur before it can be banned otherwise initiatives of a beneficial nature might be stifled.

The philosopher Hamann and his followers, according to Berlin [5], considered all rules and precepts deadly; they may be necessary for the conduct of everyday life but nothing great was ever achieved by following them. English critics were right in supposing that originality entailed breaking rules. Rules, he declared, are Vestal Virgins: unless they are violated there will be no issue. On the other hand, to quote de Tocqueville again [6], 'As every man sees that he differs but little from those about him, he cannot understand why a rule that is applicable to one man should not be equally applicable to all others.'

The requirement in practice lies, as it usually does when extreme positions are opposed, somewhere between the two attitudes. If people live together in large communities, there are basic rules of behaviour that must be observed if life is to be tolerable. On the same time, major developments which though at first repugnant eventually benefit most people are achieved only by being different and thinking differently. Progress is rarely much to write home about if it comprises just carrying on as before.

The roles of government

It is worth reflecting for a moment what it is basically that government, any government, should do. Surely, the fundamental roles are:

1. to preserve national security and organize defence against foreign attack;
2. to ensure internal safety and security and enable citizens to live and work together;

3. to maximize national economic prosperity;
4. to ensure an adequate standard of living for all citizens;
5. to ensure the provision of those services and infrastructures that are required on a national basis (e.g. roads, railways, telecommunications, postal services, libraries).

To achieve this central government is empowered to be the supreme law making body and to impose taxes in order to raise the money necessary to carry out its tasks. We must not forget that there are three levels of government: international, national and local, or in the USA federal, state and local. Law making and tax raising powers will vary somewhat from one region of the world to another and from one country to another but in general the federal/national body is supreme.

Even as recently as the last century, governments did little more than deal with the above five roles. Modern goverment is quite different. It is deeply involved in the running of many aspects of the daily lives of citizens and institutions. The extent to which government tries to manage activities directly or to facilitate and encourage depends on the political system. Each country differs. In the UK in the 1980s there was a marked swing away from dirigiste management of enterprise to a free enterprise/market economy culture. The outcome has been what is called a mixed economy. Some work that might have been undertaken by public sector bodies is left entirely to a competitive private sector, some is contracted out by the public body to the private sector, some is done in partnership and some entirely by the public sector. The information requirements for light regulation on the activities of competitive private sector companies, e.g. for establishing the information superhighway, are, obviously, very different from those needed for actually running an activity such as the communications monitoring centre, GCHQ. A notable feature of modern governmental control of its agencies and privatized activities is setting targets for performance and then publicizing, especially in comparative tables, how well they do.

In many respects government is a business, the chief ministers acting together in Cabinet more like a board of directors of a conglomerate company than the management of a factory. Their function is to direct the economic, cultural and social working of the country and their information needs are those necessary to establish or revise policies and strategies. Yet both national and local government is deeply involved in administering, managing and executing tasks from national health services to local employment centres, from postal services to public libraries, undertaking which requires more and more detailed information.

Information gathering

Modern government, then, has had to build up a huge information gathering infrastructure over the years. It used to be said with truth, that government tried to direct tomorrow's affairs with yesterday's information. Demographic data is a key component yet, even now, censuses are held only once every five years. Fortunately trends can fairly safely be extrapolated over a five year period. It is not a field in which sudden discontinuities in the data are at all likely. Even more fortunately, the data for most activities is acquired from more frequent returns, at least annually, some quarterly or monthly.

Nevertheless, all too often the data required to meet some task are not immediately available and have to be gathered. Instant decisions are not always possible (and are rarely wise). To take a trivial but common example, recently the Minister of State for Culture, Sport and the Media, Chris Smith, was reported [7] to have said that it would be some time before the necessary information concerning possible future uses of a specific piece of land could be gathered in order to be able to take a decision on its future. In such situations it may be sufficient to send out a questionnaire, it may be necessary to designate someone to go and gather data and opinions, it may be necessary to engage an expert organization to conduct a survey or it may require a commission of enquiry to be established. Different information needs call for different modes of acquisition.

A brief listing of some of the Ministries will emphasise the wealth of information that the state must amass:

- Trade and Industry: output and demand at home, potential markets overseas, competition, etc.;
- Defence: new weapons, strength of foreign forces, etc.;
- Education and employment: birth rate, numbers of pupils at each age, supply of teachers by subject expertise, numbers of forthcoming jobs and skills required, etc.;
- Health: supply of doctors, nurses, ancillary staff and hospitals; numbers of various categories of patients; length of waiting lists, performance against targets etc.;

- Social Services: numbers in need in each of many categories, demographic data, availability of homes for the elderly, etc.;
- Environment and Transport: numbers of families and dwellings, change in acreages of open land, criteria for listing buildings, expected growth in numbers of motor vehicles, etc.;
- Agriculture, Fisheries and Food: acreages of various types of farm land, size of fishing fleet, quantities of fish landed, trends in demand for various food stuffs, etc.;
- Treasury: gross national product; estimated yield of a penny on income tax, expenditure requirements of other government departments, etc.

This is a very brief and superficial list but even as it stands it reveals what a considerable amount of work must be involved in getting together all this data and other types of information. Fortunately the advent of networks of computers makes the work of compiling and analysing very much quicker, though the task of gathering the information in the first place and examining it to see if it is valid, i.e. answers the questions asked without misunderstanding, is as laborious as ever.

To get the information there are numerous forms and surveys which have to be completed. Individuals have to complete tax returns, voters' registrations, forms for dental treatment and for prescriptions. Those in professional practice or in business have many more to fill in.

There are many thousands of organizations of all types, official and private sector which have to gather information for their own needs and make it available to government. Local government is one such. Embassies and Overseas Commissions supply information, some regularly, some one off in response to a specific enquiry. Many official bodies have to make annual reports to Parliament which contain much data. The Audit Office makes reports to Parliament on the activities of those official bodies.

The Meteorological Office has a series of weather stations around the country which send in frequent reports each day. The police spend much time and effort gathering information in order to bring to light wrong-doing of various sorts. If the consequence is to be a prosecution, the information has to be sound and as complete as possible. Government intelligence services keep a watch on foreign countries and on the activities of political terrorists, both one's own and those of foreign nations. There is also much exchange of information between countries in these and many other respects.

Gathering information to deal with a particular problem may involve a special inquiry. Where information about public opinion is important the government may publish, in its Command (Cm) series, a document giving known facts, outlining its intentions and inviting the submission of views. The paper on Freedom of Information proposals (see chapter 7, ref 5) was one such. This commonly presages a Bill.

Information on particular topics will be submitted, and usually published, by various 'Think Tanks'. Some are established by government; others are semi-official and yet more private. The Adam Smith Institute,the Royal Institute of International Affairs and the Policy Studies Institute are active in this way. Another way is to set up a Committee to enquire and produce a report with all the information that has been acquired by commissioned research and by submission from interested parties. The information all these provide is very useful but like any other it needs to be examined carefully. Anyone who reads the Report of the National Libraries Committee and then the two volumes of evidence [8] would be as likely to reach a conclusion different from that of the committee as he would be to reach the same one.

At the same time, individual politicians have their researchers and input from individuals and associations in their constituencies. On a matter of special concern to them, they may well add information additional to that gathered officially. Members of Parliament also have their library and the services of the staff there, often invaluable for asking awkward questions. In the USA the Library of Congress, though often thought of as the national library, is in fact primarily the library which serves the members of the Congress.

Not all the information gathered officially is for policy or law making. Much detail is used by junior civil servants in the pursuance of their administrative duties. Much, too, is distilled into briefs for ministers or senior civil servants representing their Department at national or international conferences. Government, national and local, is a complex business and a wealth of information has to be available from which to draw what is necessary when it is needed or delay ensues.

The value of information to government as a means of stimulating action or keeping performance up to standard should not be overlooked. The Audit Commission has already been mentioned, its reports much feared goads. Submitting evidence to a Parliamentary Committee is also a 'stimulating' experience for those who have undergone it. The *Citizen's Charter* [9] had a strong information component: 'Every citizen is entitled to expect that full accurate information should be available, in plain language, about what services are being provided. Targets should be published, together with full and audited information about the results achieved. Wherever possible, information should be in comparable form <u>so that there is a pressure to emulate the best</u>', (my underlining). The league tables we now see published for school or hospital performance are a consequence of this approach. Arguably, to stimulate an effort to improve, they may serve a useful purpose; I am in no position to judge. As a source of information about a school or hospital league tables are of very limited value. They reflect only one or two aspects of performance and will not reveal other features which may be of greater importance to a particular pupil or patient.

Publicizing government actions

A government that does not keep the nation adequately informed cannot expect citizens to behave as it would wish. There may be considerable differences of opinion on what is adequate but at the very least it has to tell them what laws must be obeyed, what has been done for their protection and what is being provided for their welfare. It must inform commerce and industry what the national economic strategy is to be and of any standards their products or services must meet; it must inform privatized services what standards of performance are expected. It must publish information about international agreements which will affect their citizens. It must put out much more information besides on an enormous range of topics. Much general information is issued by the Central Office of Information and by each of the government departments, quangos and agencies.

Government also needs to distribute information about how well the government itself is doing. Public relations work is becoming a more and more important aspect of government and the introduction of professional public relations experts (spin doctors) into government departments has started. Until recently PR work was generally contracted out to the private sector, the Information Officers in the Civil Service being expected remain politically neutral. As has been discussed earlier, the way information is presented can affect considerably how people respond to it and if government is to be pro-active it has to get people to respond.

Various tactics can be used, or adventitious circumstances exploited, to help a government with information problems. A good scare story – infected blood used in many operations, even a risk of BSE from cattle bones – which is correct information can distract the public's attention sufficiently from matters more worrying to a government. A common tactic in some former colonial countries where the press is not entirely free is to give prominence in the papers to news of events in other countries, especially the UK. In British, European and American papers domestic news takes clear priority over foreign.

Returning to government's need of positive PR rather than a smokescreen, even a consultation document will serve the purposes of putting over its aims, giving a certain amount of information and creating an atmosphere of a government concerned with the needs and interests of the citizens. Thus the transport consultation document [10], contains statements such as:

'The Government's Objectives: A strong economy, a sustainable environment, an inclusive society'
'And, importantly, we want to see safe services which take full account of the needs of all sectors of society, including the disadvantaged and those with impaired mobility.'
and gives information:-
'Since deregulation, local bus fares have risen by some 22% in real terms, and the standard of passenger information in many places has been deficient.'
'There has been a steady increase in freight traffic using UK ports over the last 30 years, and 95% of all UK trade now passes through our ports'.

However, information given in such documents is likely to be incomplete as a footnote in the Discussion Document admits, 'A fuller description of the key facts and figures against which this policy review is taking place is available on request ...'. Until the advent of air freight, did not 100 per cent of our import and and export freight pass through our ports? Or does it mean that only 5 per cent of UK trade (in goods presumably, not services) is confined to the UK?

A graph in the document shows the rate of increase of motor traffic against the rate of increase of Gross Domestic Product, the former increasing more rapidly. No explanation is offered why there should be any connection or why it is wrong for motor traffic to increase more rapidly, which is the implication of including the graph. The number of mobile phones has also risen faster than the GDP, very much faster, but that is not usually deemed wrong.

These are examples of correct facts presented in a way that will create a particular climate of opinion and encourage recipients of the document to view the Government's intentions favourably. The same statements and information could have been presented in a less dramatic way but probably would have aroused less response. It is a typical example of the fact that both understanding of and reaction to a piece or pieces of information depend on the manner of presentation and on the environment in which presentation occurs.

Facilitating and encouraging use

Governments have accepted that they have to take the lead both in regulating citizens' and institutions' use of information and, more recently, in facilitating and even promoting its more effective use. A Command Paper [11] published in 1995 jointly by several Departments including Treasury and DTI says:

> 'Access to, and analysis and exploitation of, information will be crucial to competitiveness throughout industry and commerce. New information delivery services and major new infrastructure businesses will provide growth in hardware, software and services. The countries with the best infrastructures will have an advantage.'

Although there is the usual emphasis on the infrastructure, here is clear admission that technology is only a channel and that the key agent is information. There is much that government can and does do by way of supplying it. In the UK there was the Tradeable Information initiative in the early 1980s which seems to have fallen foul of pressure on government departments to earn revenue. The Vanguard Initiative to promote electronic trading seems to have had much more success and, in a different mode, there was the One-Stop-Shop programme which among other things aimed to provide new firms with information and advice.

The Commission of the EU has long been working to encourage greater use of existing information (12). In the 1970s it set up EURONET to encourage greater use of online services and two working parties had the task of encouraging small and medium sized industry to exploit technical information and patent information. The intention was early signalled by the creation of a Directorate General (XIII), originally entitled Scientific and

Technical Information but which in recent years has changed its title almost from document to document. It still seems to be responsible for the Information Market and Information Industries, for Innovation, for the Libraries Programme, for automatic translation and other details of information use.

One of the major EU programmes has been 'Developing the European market in electronics, telecommunications and information services'. The major programme of developing a European telecommunications policy and electronic infrastructure has been taken over by DG III. The outcome has been the so-called Bangemann Report [13], and an Action Plan [14]. The Research Programme FP5 from DGXII includes the aim of 'creating a user friendly information society' [15].

Also at the international level the 1994 G7 Economic Summit included 'the development of an open, competitive and integrated worldwide information infrastructure' among its decisions and a subsequent set of objectives included 'to create a critical mass to address global information society issues; and to promote, through information exchanges, further developments of the information society' [16]. In pursuit of these aims a number of projects were set up focussed on such themes as Maritime Information Systems, Government Online, Global Emergency Management Information and Worldwide Library Services (Bibliotheca Universalis).

Government accepts that it is responsible for ensuring that the necessary infrastructure exists for public access to and the communication of information. The responsibility is discharged in one or more of several ways. The provision of national and public libraries has long been supported both through state funding, direct or indirect, and through Acts which mandate their provision (e.g. 17 and 18). The existence of these and academic libraries, also state funded, act, intentionally or otherwise, to support the publishing industry which is a major source of information. More recently the provision of much free official information on Web sites is encouraging access to information via that channel, just as in France where the provision of free receivers encouraged the development of the commercial Minitel service.

The infrastructure for the sending of information or other sorts of message has a long history. A network of Post-houses where messengers could exchange a tired horse for a fresh one existed for several centuries. Official postal services existed well before Rowland Hill conceived the idea of the Penny Post. Telephone services were originally a public service; now they are provided by commercial organizations but with a Commissioner appointed to keep a watch over them to ensure that the service is efficient and that fair competition prevents excessive prices.

Now, of course, interest is in communicating computer to computer via telephone or broad band channels. Creating super-highways has had the support or at least encouragement of governments, the USA setting an example to others. Probably mindful of how notably unsuccessful official attempts were to develop computer industries in the UK and France, in Western Europe the private sector or the educational/research sector has been left to develop the channels they need. The Commission of the EU has said that in its view 'The creation of the information society should be entrusted to the private sector and to market forces' [19]. Nevertheless it has still tried to influence the development of a European multimedia content industry through its INFO2000 programme.

The UK Government in 1994 made it clear [20] that its role in facilitating the development of broad band communications should be limited to:

- establishing and maintaining the regulatory framework;
- promoting competitiveness;
- setting an example by purchase and use;
- supporting research;
- determining the effects on economic and social activities;
- being watchful to ensure that the needs of special groups of the community are properly catered for.

In other words, the aim is not to direct developments but rather to clear unnecessary obstacles out of the way, monitor what is happening and try to ensure fair play, the exact opposite of a dirigiste approach. It is not yet clear whether the current government sees itself following the same path or whether it will wish to take a more interventionist approach. Its plans announced during 1997, most notably those to network public libraries [21] and to link schools [22], are in line with encouraging rather than attempting to direct but the provision of funds to assist is a measure of involvement.

The educational programme, discussed in the previous chapter, is also part of creating the right environment by ensuring that the country has a population with the skills necessary for the computerized, communicating, information exploiting society of the near future. While there is a laudable effort to raise the level of those at risk of unemployment, unfortunately there seems to be at the same time a strong element of discouragement of the education for the exceptionally good students, those who are original thinkers and creative workers and potentially will do more than anyone to bring economic success.

In addition to ensuring that there is an infrastructure in place for access to and transmission of information and for increasing the capacity to utilize it, government is also a major supplier. Much of the supply is a by-product of information it has obtained for its own purposes but it is commonly repackaged to provide for the needs and interests of the public at large. Agencies such as the Central Statistical Office (Government Statistics Service), Companies House, and a large number of government departments publish a vast amount of information both in print and more recently on Web Sites. The government funds research, some at centres such as the National Physical Laboratory and those under the aegis of the Medical Research Council, much, through the research councils, at universities and colleges.

Arrangements for publishing official documents vary from country to country. In some it is entirely in the hands of a government agency, in others very largely in the private sector. In the UK publication of all the vast amount of information is entrusted either to the Stationery Office (formerly HMSO) or to the agencies etc themselves. In the USA the supply of official reports, mainly emanating from the Government Printing Office, is provided by the National Technical Information Service. The scene is however complicated, even more so when the outpourings of other countries are taken into account [23, 24]. Public access to copies of official publications, other than purchasing them, is entrusted to public libraries. In the USA there is a large network of Depository Libraries which receive copies free of charge. In Europe the EU supplies some depository collections free of charge. In the UK the libraries purchase what they want (can afford) at reduced prices. Needless to say the quality of collections varies widely. Some, such as that of the Westminster Public Library near Leicester Square in London, are very good.

Information Policies

The nature of national information policies will be largely obvious from what has been written above about government practice. The topic is examined at length in two monographs [25, 26] and in the proceedings of a conference [27]. It is a fact that the policies do very largely have to be inferred: there is no national information policy in either the UK or the USA or for that matter in most other countries. Where there have been attempts to formulate one, as in 'old Commonwealth' countries [28], the content has been fairly limited in scope and even then progress has been blocked by the number of interests involved [29, 30]. In the UK even an attempt to create a Minister with responsibility for information matters [31] was firmly refused [32] and one of the less influential Ministries given a 'good offices' role.

Despite such discouraging practice from the industrialized countries, UNESCO has tried to motivate developing countries to formulate information policies. In doing this it is concentrating attention in developing countries on the need to give the use of information, the building and stocking of libraries and documentation centres and the creation of facilities for accessing online services a degree of priority which local urging by librarians and documentalists would never achieve. Documentalists, like prophets, lack credibility and status in their own countries.

The Concise OED defines policy as 'a course or principle of action adopted or proposed by a government, party, business or individual'. It is often confused with strategy which the OED defines as 'a plan of action or policy in business or politics'. It is probably simplest to think of strategy as being the plan of campaign to give substance to the policy.

Official policy is often expressed as an intention, e.g. to equip all schools with computers and network them. The strategy may be to get private sector sponsorship and cooperation to fund purchases of computers and to connect them to the Internet. Often policies and strategies involve finding an acceptable balance between conflicting goals, interests and demands on resources. Frequently there is conflict between policies. An example occurs in copyright where a policy of encouraging authorship and the publishing industry conflicts with one to promote the information industry and the application of information.

Were there to be a national information policy it would have to cover issues such as:

- the extent of citizens' rights to seek, receive, store, use and communicate information and to restrict such rights by others rights of ownership of information;
- the extent of government's right to demand information from individuals and institutions;

- the extent of official right/duty to keep acquired information confidential;
- the extent and timing of public right of access to official information;
- the extent of duty/need to publish and disseminate information;
- policy on ways of publishing official information;
- policy towards transborder data flow;
- ways of ensuring official information needs can be met;
- ways of co-ordinating the information seeking practices of government departments and agencies;
- ensuring efficient information management practices in all official bodies;
- policies towards generating new information through research, commissions of enquiry etc
- policies towards the information industry including global information mining companies, the publishing industry and the media including ensuring the reliability of published information
- policies towards providing information sources such as libraries, museums, archives and Web Sites;
- policies towards encouraging and enabling the efficient and proper use of information in industry and commerce, in health, consumer and social services, in environmental protection and in law enforcement;
- policies towards educating students in the use of information and equipping individuals and organizations to play a full role in a learning and information society;
- policies towards the information technology and communications industries including regulating use of their products.

There is no doubt that this list is not complete but its sheer length serves to illustrate why there is no national information policy. Another reason is that in all policy matters there is a hierarchy of policies and lower level ones have to be adjusted whenever higher level ones change. Thus a few years ago, when the then government decided that market forces must be allowed to reign wherever practicable and that public sector services should, if possible, be privatized, the policy of providing information services from national libraries had to be modified to co-operate with the private sector in the provision of services or to provide only those that would not compete with the private sector.

The USA has long had a National Commission for Libraries and Information Services (NCLIS) which acts as a very pro-active link between the Federal Government and the library and information communities. It has, inter alia, organized the series of White House conferences on LIS matters and represented the US in relevant international meetings such as the Glenerin initiative [34]. The UK government appears to have followed suit in setting up a Library and Information Commission 'to be a national focus of expertise in the field of library and information services' [35] though it has been rather slow getting going. However, the issuing of its 2020 Vision document in 1997 indicated that it has clarified and established its role.

Not surprisingly in view of the all embracing nature of information, the field of action of the Commission is limited. Its core objectives [36] are stated as:

- to provide a single coherent and efficient source of advice to Government on all issues in the field of LIS;
- to draw Government's attention to emerging issues and to suggest appropriate responses to them;
- to provide all advice on the basis of as full a process of consultation within the library and information community as necessary and as time allows.

It also has a remit to develop a UK wide research strategy for the library and information field and to advise the government on the development of a national information policy.

The aim of keeping the LIS community quiet is apparent in the third core objective and the remit on national information policy. The care with which the Commission has to deal with other government departments (it is under the aegis of the Department for Culture, Sport and the Media, previously called the Department of National Heritage) is shown in the purposes stated in the 1995 statement to Parliament [36]: advise Government Departments representing the UK ... develop, in association with the relevant government departments ... advise governments which so request on co-ordinating ...

Nor was there any evidence of significant influence on the plans to develop the teaching of IT skills in schools and the plans to link all schools to the Internet (a Department of Education and Employment initiative) or on the proposals published at the end of 1997 for a Freedom of Information Act (handled by the Public

Services Minister). Nevertheless, appropriate advice may have been given, even if it is not publicly acknowledged.

Obviously the Commission will be the main player where policy towards national and public libraries is concerned. Its scope for impact on academic library policy has yet to be seen. Its main scope for involvement with all manner of libraries would seem to be in facilitating and ensuring that there is a coherent record of the contents of all UK libraries accessible through the Internet. In the field of information services there must be doubt about its scope for influence since the great majority of these are within the field of interest of other Departments (financial information, business information, health services, social services).

The remit to develop a research strategy stems from the Department of Scientific and Industrial Research whose interests in scientific and technical information (STI) were passed in the 1960s to a new organization, the Office for Scientific and Technical Information (OSTI) which was guided by an Advisory Council (ACSTI). One of its major roles was funding research into STI and its uses. Shortly after the British Library was established OSTI was transferred to it and became its Research and Development Department (BLR&DD, now renamed the Research and Innovation Centre). As part of the British Library its field of interest was expanded beyond that of STI into libraries in general and also from science into the humanities. The other UK research councils also funded some research in the information sector on topics of relevance to them (e.g. the Programme on Information and Communication Technologies, PICT) and there can be little doubt that there was some overlap. This, as most research workers know but governments rarely admit, is no bad thing provided it is kept within bounds. Two research teams pursuing the same task can report quite different results, sometimes contradicting each other because one is in error, sometimes complementary because they pursued a different line of investigation. This sometimes applies even in the field of applied 'bread and butter' research.

The new Commission has taken over from the British Library responsibility for devising the research strategy in the LIS sector and its mandate suggests it will keep itself aware of what other Research Councils may propose. Already the Commission has commissioned a research mapping exercise and initiated a consultation exercise on what the national research strategy should be. No doubt there will be consultation with the bodies involved in the previous Government's Technology Forecast Initiative.

A major information policy requirement for government is to look hard at the impact and potential of the new technological, especially networking and communicating, capabilities and deciding whether they are merely a beneficial new tool which does not require any change of policy or whether they create 'a whole new ball park' for which new policies are required.

For example, up to now the UK Government has put out news through the private sector media and the BBC despite its policy of allowing freedom of the press. It has only one newspaper of its own, the *London Gazette*, (some departments, the Patent Office for example, have highly specialized news journals) which is not a vehicle for giving news to the general public. It has published documents through HMSO, now the Stationery Office Ltd. It is not much over 20 years ago that policy changed and allowed Departments and agencies to choose whether to use HMSO or charge for copies. Thus putting publications direct onto Web sites raises no policy problem but whether issuing news that way does is an interesting question. There will be an internal question of whether and who will be allowed to put information onto the Internet and if answers to requests for information under the Freedom of Information should be placed there.

On the face of it there are likely to be more serious policy issues over the generation, gathering, access to, use and release of information in general than over channels for publishing government news. The main priority must surely be stimulating the information economy.

References

1. McGrath, M. (1997) *Hard, soft and wet; the digital generation comes of age.* London: Harper Collins

2. Bierce, A. (1996) *Devil's Dictionary.* Ware, UK: Wordsworth Editions Ltd

3. Uhlig, R. (1994) 'Should big brother hold the key to your secrets?' *Daily Telegraph, Connected.* p.3. 19 February 1998.

4. de Tocqueville, A. (1994) *Democracy in America.* 2nd part, p.316ff. London: Everyman (original text 1835/1840)

5. Berlin, I. (1979) *Against the Current: essays in the history of ideas.* London: Hogarth Press

6. de Tocqueville, A. *Ibid.* p.289

7. 'St. Pancras welcomes its first readers' (1997). *Library Association Record,* **99**(12), 634

8. National Libraries Committee, (1969) *Report of the National Libraries Committee.* (The Dainton Report). Cm4028. London: HMSO

9. The Prime Minister (1991) *Citizen's Charter.* Cm1599. London: HMSO

10. Department of the Environment, Transport and the Regions (1997) *Developing and integrated transport policy: an invitation to contribute.* London: Stationery Office

11. Board of Trade, Treasury et al. (1995) *Competitiveness: Forging Ahead,* Cm2867. London: HMSO

12. Hill, M.W. (1994) *National Information Policies and Strategies,* pp.35–43. London: Bowker-Saur

13. Commission of the European Communities, DGIII (1994). *Europe and the Global Information Society* (The Bangemann Report). Brussels: CEC

14. *Idem.,* DGXIII. (1994) *Europe's way to the information society. An action plan.* COM(94)347. Luxembourg: CEC

15. Royal Society of Chemistry. (1996) FP5 framework shapes up. *Chemistry in Europe,* **4**(5), 6

16. *G7 Information Society. Pilot Projects Progress Report.* (1995) Halifax, Canada: G7 Secretariat

17. *British Library Act 1972,* Chapter 54. London: HMSO

18. *Public Libraries and Museums Act 1964,* Chapter 75. London: HMSO

19. Commission of the European Communities, DGXIII (1995). *Information 2000. Proposal for a programme to stimulate the development of a European multimedia content industry.* COM(95)149 final. Luxembourg: CEC

20. Department of Trade and Industry, (1994) *Creating the Superhighways of the Future: developing broad band communications in the UK*, Cm2734, London: HMSO

     See also: *CCTA Report on Information Superhighways* (1995) London: CCTA

21. Library and Information Commission. (1997) *New Library: the People's Network*. London: Library and Information Commission Commission

22. Standage, T. (1997) All schools set to be wired by 2002. *Daily Telegraph, Connected,* 7 October 1997

23. Auger, C.P. (1994) *Information Sources in Grey Literature* 3rd edn. London: Bowker-Saur

24. Nurcombe, V.J. (1997) *Information Sources in Official Publications.* London: Bowker-Saur

25. Hill, M.W. *Ibid.*

26. Hill, M.W. (1996) National Information Policies. *Information UK Outlooks* 15

27. Rowlands, I. (1997) *Understanding Information Policy*. London: Bowker-Saur

28. Australian Department of Science (1985) *A National Information Policy for Australia*. Canberra: Department of Science

29. Judge, P. (1988) Questions of Information Policy. *Journal of Information Science*, **14**(6), 1988, 317–8

30. Sandow-Quirk, M. (1994) Information policy in the new world: the case of Australia. In: *New Worlds in Information and Documentation*, eds. J.R. Alvarez-Ossorio and B.G. Goedegebuure

FID 705. Amsterdam: FID Elsevier

31. House of Commons' Education, Science and Arts Committee (1980) *Information storage and retrieval in the British library service*. HC767. London: HMSO

32. Minister for the Arts. (1981) Same title. Cm8234. London: HMSO

33. Montviloff, V. (1990) *National Information Policies: a handbook on the formulation, approval, implementation and operation of a national policy on information*. Paris: UNESCO

Revised edition by F.W. Horton Jr. to be published.

34. Institute for the Research of Public Policy (1987) *Access: information distribution, efficiency and protection* (the Glenerin Declaration). Ontario: Insitute for the Research of Public Policy

35. House of Commons. *Hansard*. p.618, 31 January 1995. London: HMSO

36. Library and Information Commission, (1997) *2020 Vision*. London: Library and Information Commission

CHAPTER FIFTEEN

The information society: are we now part of it and where is it heading?

Whether or not we are entering a new age and whether or not we should claim that we live in an Information Society may be thought a matter primarily of concern to the image specialists and those who like to feel at the forefront of progress. One may well ask, does it matter what label we give the present or immediate future society? On reflection, I think it does. We live in a period when the degree of support and the resources one can command depend on whether the image presented is one that catches the public's attention. The recent adoption of the term 'knowledge management' for what is really little more than a subset of information management practices is a case in point. It has created a stir of interest among senior management and staff are encouraged to introduce it into company offices. However, rather than just calling this the dawn of the Information Age and labelling us members of an Information Society, I think we should explore whether there is a meaningful reality behind the words.

In previous chapters we have seen that both in terms of output and of employment, we have moved from an industrial to a service economy. But a service economy is not necessarily an information economy, even though manipulating and exploiting information is the major activity involved. In his 1994 paper, 'What information society?' [1], Webster examined the criteria that might be used to define an information society. After considering technological, economic, occupational, spatial and cultural factors, he concluded that the arguments that we are entering an information society were unconvincing.

However, nothing daunted, in 1997 the National Working Party on Social Inclusion in the Information Society, set up by IBM, defined the Information Society as, 'A society characterised by a high level of information intensity in the everyday life of most citizens, in most organizations and workplaces; by the use of common or compatible technology for a wide range of personal, social, educational and business activities; and by the ability to transmit and receive digital data rapidly between places irrespective of distance' [2]. While one might need forgiveness for thinking that the definition pre-eminently suits their task and their sponsors, it does in fact summarize very well what most people mean when they refer to the information society:

- greater availability and use of information;
- greater use of new computer and communication technologies;
- quite new applications of packages of information and of ICTs.

A definition does not of itself answer Webster's doubts about whether we are entering the new society but it may be that in the four years since his paper enough has happened to give substance to the popular belief that we are doing so. So let us list what we have reviewed in the previous chapters, together with some additional matter, as evidence for or against the proposition and also list some of the other changes that have occurred which do not fit with the concept of an information society.

Information intensity

1. That there is ever more information around is beyond doubt. Some merely replaces, corrects or updates earlier information but there is also a huge amount that is new emerging all the time revealing new truths and creating new concerns.

   This creates its own concerns: one learns that some people are so desperate to ensure that they have every possible scrap of relevant information that as a result they cannot reach decisions; that some people spend all day, every day, glued to the Internet; and that an average middle manager receives or sends about 180 messages every working day. Well balanced people find their own solution to such pressures.

2. A great amount of effort is being expended in generating, collecting, recording, consolidating, repackaging, interpreting and disseminating information. The way it is done may differ; armies of clerks are no longer needed. But large numbers of higher calibre staff are required to keep government, institutions, industry, commerce and all manner of activities running and supplied with the information they need in the form they can best use it.

3. Traditional sources of information (people one meets, expert contacts, books and magazines, filing systems, information services) and the traditional ways of accessing them (telephone and letter, meetings, libraries, personal assistants) remain and are still in heavy use. Indeed more books and magazines are being published now than ever (60 per cent more book titles were published in 1996 than in 1991 [3]).

   At the same time electronic sources (CD-ROMs and multimedia) are multiplying and the use of electronic channels of access is growing rapidly. Already some people are communicating exclusively by e-mail. Consequently, we can expect a new balance to be established between the patterns of use of the traditional and the modern sources and means of access.

4. For a variety of reasons, one can no longer learn most of the information one needs early in life, i.e. from one's parents, at school and in apprenticeships. Everyone needs to keep learning, adding new information, developing new areas of knowledge throughout most of one's life. For some of us, life has always been like this; the change is that lifelong learning and reskilling will, for the foreseeable future apply to everyone. One source of pressure is the ever increasing demand from employers for higher qualifications, even for jobs previously thought of as purely manual.

5. As was discussed in chapter 10, social changes have also resulted in an increase in the numbers of people who in one way or another are isolated and need means of access to information or means of establishing personal friends. The growth of matrimonial agencies, even partner seeking via the Internet, is one illustration of this. The increasing problems of coping in a changing world may give further impetus to the growth of community resource centres and local electronic kiosks as they have done to advisory and counselling services.

6. At work the value some information can have, the importance of treating it as a resource and of properly managing its acquisition, storing, access and dissemination is increasingly well understood. The practice of charging for information is growing especially by devising ways of access for which payment has to be made.

7. A major cultural change has been the increase in the degree of openness which the public expects. People and companies are much less secretive than they have been in the past. There is compulsion to publish many details and the Government is expected to introduce a Freedom of Information measure soon. There is considerable opposition to any attempts to censor or otherwise restrict the free flow of information.

8. However, at the same time personal privacy and the right to see, and if necessary correct, files of information about ourselves have become important issues. So to has the balance between the rights of ownership of information and the opportunity to reap reward from exploiting it on the one hand and, the freedom for others to be able to build on that information in order to create yet further information on the other.

9. We are having to adjust to situations in which biassed or slanted use is made of information, and those in which only information is published selectively to prove a case. This has always happened but it seems to be occurring nowadays to a far greater extent than in the past. If this subjective impression is correct, it may be a consequence of the greater attention paid to media reports and the outpourings of pressure groups.

10. More information is needed for almost everything we do. Whether it be assembling a piece of DIY furniture, cooking a prepared dish, matching clothing materials to washing machine programme, operating the PC, or fertilizing the garden, detailed instructions have to be read and followed. This constant need for new information about something which in slightly different form we have done many times in the past, is one of the reasons for some of the complaints about information overload and a feeling of inability to keep up.

Communicating and computing

11. At the personal level we network more, but some, at least, seem to have greater difficulty communicating with those who

should be their nearest and dearest. Although we may communicate less with our neighbours, we communicate more with those at a distance from us. The majority of homes have a telephone. Domestic/personal use of mobile phones, fax machines and e-mail is growing. We telephone rather than write personal letters. We do much personal business by telephone, though telephone shopping for goods is increasing only very slowly and then mainly as an alternative to posting a catalogue-chosen order. Those on the Net order goods direct from a Web site and download copies of documents. At work there is an increasing demand for communication skills, not only in the service sector but also in the factory where the ability to discuss technical problems and review the available information is an increasingly important part of many more jobs.

12.   In organizations computer terminals are at almost every desk and at the factory control system, linked via networks to other terminals and to the central or integrated computer systems. More and more the world around us is computer controlled. 'White collar' work has been transformed. Messages and instructions go when necessary, not when the next post goes, to staff and offices anywhere they may be in the world. Communication is instantly global and, as a consequence, global business can be conducted much more efficiently than before.

13.   It is claimed that the combination of PC and telecommunications has opened the opportunity of working from home. It is also claimed that this will not become popular because people will feel isolated. Both are, as is usual with generalizations, too sweeping but both contain some truth. Some people such as artists have always worked from home. But ICTs open up an opportunity for yet more people to do so if it suits them and, as happens quite often, to take work home and work there for several days while still in contact with the office as and when necessary. On the other hand, it is claimed that most home computers are used only for game playing.

14.   The ability to control the communication of information through networks will continue to be an important issue. There is the need to restrict illegal, criminal, subversive or immoral communications, and there is the need to keep sensitive personal, commercial, financial and political information confidential. Firewalls, encryption, V-chip and other devices will be a source of much argument. There can be little doubt

that both satellite and terrestrial surveillance techniques will become more and more sophisticated and so will the means by which we identify ourselves. One undoubted trend that will continue is that towards less and less real privacy.

15. The more recent era-shaping advances are, as has so often been said, the combination of computers with telecommunications and the development of the PC which serves as both computer and terminal and whose cost is within a domestic budget. Already millions are communicating from their PCs through the Internet and many more are similarly communicating via Intranets and orally via telephones. Nevertheless, the software is still, for many, complex to use and there is some way to go before PCs and searching the Internet are as simple as the using telephone and finding the required TV programme.

16. The modern communication systems are replacing or working alongside traditional ones. Postal correspondance courses have largely given way to the Open (i.e. TV and radio) University and to distance learning by computer and telecommunication. Social service information is available on the networks as an alternative to the telephone call or personal visit. The press and the entertainment industries have together taken full advantage of radio and television and now of CD-ROMs and multimedia.

17. New ways of carrying out many of our traditional activities have emerged. For example, 'mail ordering' on the Internet is growing apace; a service has opened a virtual cemetery, which carries memorials, an alternative to the carved gravestone; meetings (we may have to change that word) of people can be held without their having to leave their offices.

18. Credit cards, debit cards and smart cards have changed considerably the way we carry money and undertake paying for goods and services. The use of 'plastic money' has caught on; such cards are easy to carry and simplify transactions for the owner. Loyalty cards which assist information gathering will probably be developed into a restricted smart card in the future.

Social, cultural, economic and political change

These topics have been reviewed in detail in previous chapters. Though new information has led to, been part of or reinforced many of the changes that have occurred, it is often the way it has been disseminated and used, and the timing of it, that is the main reason for its having a considerable impact.

In society many changes have taken place which are not particularly information or ICT driven as well as many that were. Attitudes have changed. Many old values have vanished or are under attack. The degree of trust that once existed in public and professional organizations (MPs, the police, hospitals) has fallen sharply. Loyalty is arguably a thing of the past (loyalty cards are only discount cards). It seems as if the virtues of self-discipline and responsibility for one's own life and actions are no longer has widespread as they used to be and that we now have to legislate to maintain what, like 'my word is my bond', was once normal behaviour. To some extent it is the widespread awareness of defects and misfortunes that information about them has brought that is the cause.

We are increasingly a dissatisfied society, not just because we have been urged to complain and have learnt to sue if something goes wrong. Has information content made us contentious? Pressure to be upwardly mobile has led to disappointment for many who had only limited talents and who previously would have been satisfied with undemanding work.

There is a lack of stability that is encountered not only in jobs and personal relationships but in daily life in the community and in the worlds of the arts and entertainment. A new label does not always mean change, far from it, but the widespread use of the term 'networking' to describe the way one is interacting with other people is indicative of an impersonal approach where before there was personal camaraderie if not comradeship.

One field in which new information has grown rapidly and is having a dramatic impact is information about ourselves, our genetic makeup and how our minds and bodies work. Information about genetically transmitted ailments could eventually lead to their control.

Is it ironic that while we are learning that our mental processes are essentially electro-chemical, in our day-to-day life our actions are controlled more and more by machine rather than by our using our own judgement. In other ways too the need to use judgement is being whittled away and everyday skills are becoming redundant or the subject only of hobbies. Culinary skills are an example.

Not only have we moved to a service economy rather than an industrial one, but we have also learnt to harness information so that its wealth creating potential can be fully exploited.

The extent to which we communicate via telecommunications networks with people both far and near has also increased enormously and, an important development, machines can be programmed similarly to communicate with other machines. In the course of all this it has become necessary for most people of a working age to be able to operate at least some of the information and communication technologies.

At the political level, governments have become information conscious. One change with important information consequences is that the government and other authorities seek people's opinions on various topics. Normally, when you seek someone's opinion on an important topic, you choose someone whom you believe to be knowledgeable. You do not seek their views, except as a social courtesy, on topics of which you suspect they are ignorant. Lord Emsworth sought his pig keeper's views on pigs but not on any other topic. Today, the government seeks the views on almost every policy topic of even those who are pig-ignorant. If enquiries of this type are to have any value rather than being merely cynical political gimmicry, then it is vital that the public are presented with all the necessary facts, including those of the side effects. Yet, the facts are complex and often require a good standard of numeracy as well as an ability to take a balanced rather than biassed approach. If the public are to take part in decision-making, more thorough and unbiassed presentation of information than the media can provide becomes essential. Yet, only those with the will to do so will read and digest it. The solution is not obvious but one fears the outcome is.

In fairness, government is only responding to a public demand to be consulted on major issues and also it has put education at the top level of its agenda.

The political policy of privatization, allied to insistence on a market economy, has put the private sector/public sector balance of ownership of organizations back roughly to the pre-1940 situation. However, the post-1945 Welfare State has resulted in a population that is State dependent, that very often looks to the authorities to supply a solution to problems rather than individuals helping one another as used to be more common. That does not overlook the growth of self-help groups for those with special problems.

What do we conclude and where are we heading?

First, whether or not we choose to call this the Information Age and our way of living an Information Society, the information component, however important, is only one of several major influ-ences. I will risk sticking my neck out and forecast that it will not be long before enthusiasm for information this and information that falls out of favour, becomes unfashionable, and we shall be able to return to treating it, as we always used to, as part of the furniture of life.

This does not mean that information, especially new, exploitable information and that which creates new awareness, will not play an increasingly important role in the future. Its impact has been growing century by century and there is no obvious sign of any slowing down of the trend.

Certainly this is the age of change, accelerating change. Ironically, it is evidenced by the almost obsessive urge for conservation. It is an era when technology has had an enormous impact on the way we live. Undoubtedly it is an electronic age. The marvels of the computer, the microprocessor, radio/TV and digital communica-tions are entirely modern and have had far reaching consequences both literally and metaphorically. Was Shockley's invention of the transistor even more important than that of the wheel?

There is no question but that maintaining, perhaps increasing, existing standards of wealth will require effective creation and exploitation of information. To this end new skills for manipulating it, human or computerized, will be increasingly in demand. So too will new information, not merely that which is the product of scien-tific, technological or market research but also that about everyday life and leisure and especially about friends and family. At one time, before the need for an information search was recognized, there was much money wasted on duplicated work. Now the need is to make sure that the results of research are sound before they are acted upon. Duplication did occasionally disprove the earlier work.

Some information is immutable. The Second World War ran from 1939 to 1945. Dickens did write the *Pickwick Papers*. But much infor-mation is ephemeral and much does get changed. Some of it can be superseded just as theories can be superseded. Much informa-tion is valid for only a short while and is only expected to be. New athletic records are set at almost every major gathering; new discov-eries keep putting back the time life has existed on earth; share prices change by the minute. It becomes important to judge not only the accuracy and reliability of information when you receive it but also the probable period over which each piece of informa-tion will remain valid and not to use it, if usable it is, after its 'sell by' date. An important need is for the public to understand how knowledge advances so that news of information which modifies earlier 'facts' does not lead to cynicism.

We must not forget that information is not usually handled as isolated pieces. It comes as a package, sometimes termed 'content', and we must look forward to the package being better designed, better in quality and depth and more readily usable and memorable.

The need to generate and utilize more information, and its increasingly complex nature, will increase the pressure to educate people to higher and higher standards and to maintain a lifelong appetite for learning.

Alongside this I think the the present trend towards trivializing everything will end abruptly. What will cause the abrupt change I cannot even guess but I feel sure that the realization that issues must be looked at in depth will become general. What gives me hope, in an age in which superficiality and 'sound bites' are increasingly prevalent, is the way that our so-called caring society no longer forms instant prejudged views of the way people behave but examines individual circumstances and motives carefully before reaching its verdicts.

For some people, the more information that is available the greater attention they give to detail. At the right level this is crucially important, but it often seems to impede the ability to stand back and see the big issues more clearly. This is when there are complaints of information overload. An important part of education is showing us how to plan when to give close attention to detail and when to let the detail digest while we assess the objectives.

Information-based awareness is spreading about the amount of damage that results from many individuals acting carelessly or irresponsibly and that the cure is for each individual to behave in a thoughtful way. The particular example is that either we care for our local environment or the world environment will suffer. Information about what is happening to the environment and the forecasts based on extrapolating the information (unreliable though extrapolation is) have brought about a growing recognition that some current modes of development must change. Among them is that our high mobility society must restrict its freedom to travel by whatever means it chooses. There is an increasing sense of becoming fearful for the future.

There is little doubt that, more and more, new information as it comes along will influence other aspects our lifestyle. At present much emphasis is placed on adopting healthier and risk-free practices. Other information, on its own or in combination with ICTs, will require us to rethink the way we carry out commonplace tasks. Usually the result is we devise a better way but the pressure to rethink does upset some people, especially those who prefer the comfort of stability to the excitement of the new. Especially it will be more and more vital to take early action if new technologies or new applications impinge significantly on our liberties.

In most fields of activity there will be the usual set of contradictions. Some people, perhaps most, will communicate more and more using the new ICTs, which will progress far beyond their present crude forms. At the same time we shall hear more about the problems people experience as a result of being unable to communicate. Some people may be able to pour their heart out to a computer terminal but it is difficult to believe that the most cleverly programmed expert system will give the comfort another human being present at the time can.

At heart the difference is that we can communicate information and advice and instructions ever more easily to colleagues and acquaintances. But we live more emotionally isolated lives, working less closely with our workmates and too rarely forming those close, lifelong friendships (including that of marriage) in which we can share intensely personal information, hopes, ideals and ideas.

Information is the form in which we convey a part of our knowledge of a topic to other people. It is also the mind's way of expressing what it has observed through one or more of the senses. Despite the growth, which will continue, of pictorial communication, the principal means of communicating information will be words. But, as Humpty Dumpty said [4] 'When *I* use a word it means just what I choose it to mean – neither more nor less', which is all very well provided the listener understands what that meaning is. Technology allows us to communicate more readily but changing language makes it more difficult except between specialists who develop their own jargon with each term clearly and precisely understood. This situation was discussed in chapter 5.

Human beings achieved their present place in the world by virtue of their greater brains and their greater ability to use tools. We have used them to defeat Darwinian selection. The unfit can and do survive. One curious result is that the physically supreme are becoming show pieces, top sports stars especially. The physique required for labouring work is no longer a premium. The real stars are those with top class brains, not just intellectuals but those other sorts of acumen and the power of judgement.

In the future we can expect the genuinely well educated, those who know themselves and the world around them and who can discriminate between the imaginative and the trivial, to hold their place. The technically well educated, those who are literate, numerate and able to communicate, will also do well whatever the future society may be like. But for the poor and those who are but poorly educated the outlook would seem to be increasingly bleak. The new ICTs may help in a few cases but for the majority inspired action of some sort is needed and, at present, inspiration is lacking.

Frankly I doubt if we are approaching an Information Age. It would be better by analogy with the Industrial Age to consider it the Electronic Age since it is electronic devices and their products that affect our lives and how we earn our living. Or we could call it The Age of Awareness as a successor to the Age of Reason.

However, whether or not we are becoming an information society is quite a different matter. We have vastly more information than ever before and it continues to increase and, in respect of each field of information, gradually to become more reliable. We have increased very rapidly our ability to manipulate, communicate and use it. We are exploiting information more and, in general, untenable beliefs are dying away. However, despite the marvels of the Internet, which will be very influential, the principal forces shaping society will continue to be cultural and social in origin. Information will play a part in shaping these influences but it will be only a part, albeit a principal part in a play with many more characters.

Information is a gallimaufry of raw materials from which today we can conjure up new products (services) just as in the past iron ore, bauxite and cotton were converted into new products. It will make some wealthier, it will improve life for many, it will add problems for many and it will make some poorer. Referring to industrial disputes Annan wrote [5], 'It was one of the misjudgements of the dons of our age to imagine that one had but to analyse a problem and come to conclusions and the problem was solved'. The problems that the content of information systems will lead us into need to be researched and the results presented as information which we ourselves, together with politicians and educators and all manner of professionals, can use to devise and implement solutions.

References

1. Webster, F. (1994) 'What information society?' *The Information Society*, **10**, 1–23

2. INSINC Working Party (1997) *The Net Result. Social inclusion in the information society.* London: IBM

3. Library and Information Statistics Unit (1998) *Library & Information Statistics Tables.* Loughborough: LISU

4. Carroll, L. *Through the looking glass*, Chapter 7.

5. Annan, N. (1991) *Our Age.* p.297. London: Fontana

Index

Abbreviating information 44–5, 104–5
Abstracts as an information source, abstracting services (see also databases and online services) 104, 219
Access to sources 145–6, 184
Acquiring information, ways of 17ff
Advertising (see also publicizing) 181ff, 200–21
Agenda 21, Local 229–30
American Library Association 127
Andersson, Claes 24
Annan, Lord Noel 285
Antarctic ice-cap 228
Aslib 94
Atkins, Peter 66
Audience restriction 74–5
Auditing information resources 108
Averages 53

Background knowledge and comprehension 65ff
Badenoch et al 11, 208
Barsoum, Kalil 175, 214
Bawden, D. 13, 25, 191

Belief 30, 47
Bell, Daniel 3
Berlin, Isaiah 24, 43
Best, D.P. 95
Bias 44ff
Board policy 94
Body language 79ff
Bradman, impact of information on recovery 1
Brain 16
British Computer Society, Code of Conduct 136
British Library Research and Development Department (Research & Innovation Centre) 269
Broadcasting 87, 179–80
"Bugging" devices 163
Business Ethics, Institute of 133
Business, exploiting and harnessing information 94ff, 212ff

Campaign for Learning 244
Carelessness in comprehension 70
CD-ROMs 102, 276, 279
Censorship, limits of 126ff
Charges, influence on access to information 146ff

CIRIA 88
Citizens Advice Bureau (CAB) 185–6
Citizens' Charter 260
Collapse of Communism, impact of information 253
Commodity model of information 207
Common language, value of 85
Communicating 78ff
  effects of ICTs 81ff
  freedom of 128ff, 141
  and computing, select list of current developments 277–9
Communication, social 78ff, 195–7
Communication systems, national government responsibility for 263–5
Community resource centres 184
Comprehending 60ff
Computers
  impact on employment 172ff, 201
  misuse 117
Computer publishing 102
Concept of information 21–3
Confidential information 8–9, 136–8
Conflicting data 47–9
Consultation documents as information source 261
Copyright 156ff
Costing information 208ff
Counselling services 185–7
Cultural and social changes 7–8, 279–81
Cultural policies 150

Dainton, Lord Frederick 2, 100
Data 20–1
  conflicting 47–9
  protection 165ff
  statistical 49ff
  warehousing 168, 214
Databases, database services 89, 102, 215

Definitions of information 11ff
Dehn, Guy 130
Demographic information 226, 228
DG XIII of the European Union 262
Diet information 191–3
Digitised manuscripts, copyright in 161
Disclosure of information 141
Dissemination of information 79ff, 128ff
DNA as personal information 177
Doctorates, education for PhD 244
Drucker, Peter 25, 212, 240
DSIR 269
Duty to clients 135

Earth, growing awareness of structure 36–7
Ecological studies 227
Educationally backward children 237ff
Educational standards, aims 238, 240
Electronic publishing and copyright 160ff
E-mail 81, 84, 177, 182, 276, 279
Employee right to information 124
Employment 172ff, 200ff
Encouraging information use 262
English, campaign for plain 68
Enser, P. 96
Environment and Climate Research Programme 229
Environmental information 225ff
EU Programmes 243, 263
EURONET 262
European Convention on Human Rights 112, 124
Evans, R.J. 21
Excessive information 130–1, 275

Facsimile, transmission (fax) 88–9
Facts, nature of 19–21, 24
"Fair dealing" 158, 160

Financial
impact of information
revolution 205
restrictions on searches 146
Finnis, J. 127
Food
labelling 194
scares 192–3
Formats of compilations of
information 23
Forum for Ethics in the Workplace
133
Franklin, Benjamin 48
Free
information 210–11
services, elimination in number
147
speech, right to 128–31
Freedom of information 121–4
Future educational requirements
(*see also* employment) 239ff

G7 information services
programme 263
Gardner, Howard 16, 61–2
General Medical Council 135, 137
Giddens, A. 190
Global communication of
information 8, 263, 278
Government
and information 112–13, 121–4,
134, 251ff
nature of 253ff
roles of 255ff
Graphical data 53–7
Greenfield, Susan 16, 37

Handy, Charles 50, 206
Hawley Committee 94, 212
Haywood, Trevor 143
Health information 191ff
Health records and data
protection 169, 177
Heine, Michael 207
History of communication
technologies 82–4

Hobsbawm, E.J. 201
Hoggart, Richard 52
Holland, Sir Geoffrey 239
Holocaust, denial of 129
Homeworking 204
Human rights, international
declarations 112
Hutton, William 212

Identity 176–8
Imaginary information 56–7
Imagination 31, 68–70
Impact
consequences of aiming for 45–6
of information, examples 1–2,
4–5, 172ff, 199ff, 225ff
Influence, consequences of aiming
for 46–7
Information and communication
technologies
examples 3
growth of 81–4, 276
impact of 81–4, 201–6, 277–9
origins 4–5, 82–4
right to use 116–17
Information and fashion changes
188
Information as a concept 21–3
Information
audit 108
disclosure 141
freedom of 121–4
gathering by Government 257
industry 214ff
intensify, examples of current
practices 225ff
management 95–8
overload 130–1
policies 265ff
rejection 73–4
Information rich-information poor
divide 142ff, 184, 188
Information
right to receive 126–8
seeking and research 32ff
skills 143ff, 234, 245ff

society
  defining 11, 274ff
  entrusted to private sector 264
Information Society Forum 184
Information Society
  House of Lords Report 3
  social aspects 7–9, 172ff, 274ff
Information
  superhighway 3
  Technology, Minister of 2
  unreliable 42ff
  uses of the word in phrases
    11–12
  work and workers 217ff
Insight 30
Integrity 140
Intellectual property 153ff
Internet 3, 89, 147–8, 215–6, 234–5
  and social communication 196–7
  fraud 221

Jepson, John 42
Judgement, component of
  knowledge 25
Junk mail 131

Know-how 31–2
Knowledge
  background information and
    comprehension 65–8
  incomplete and impermanent
    28–9
  relationship to information 23ff
  types of 26ff
Knowledge management 98–9
KPMG Impact Study 94, 212

Learning as a leisure activity 220
Leisure industries 220
Library and Information
  Commission, UK 268–9
Libraries as sources of information
  106–8, 147–8
Library Association, Code of
  Conduct 135
Library Bill of Rights, US 127

Lies 127–8
Lifestyle 187ff
"Limits to growth" 226
Loss of living species 227

Magazines 180, 185, 191
Malthus 226
Management attitudes to
  information 2, 7, 94, 212
Marchand, D.A. 96, 212, 214
Market research services 216, 220
Mason, R.O. and colleagues 13, 29
Media (The) and information
  178ff
Medical records and data
  protection 169, 177
Memory
  and imagination 68–70
  training 242, 245
Mind 16–18, 29–31
Minister for Information
  Technology 2
Ministries, information
  requirements of individual
  departments 257–8
Minitel 88
Monitoring devices and privacy
  163–5
Moroney, M.J. 50
Multimedia and copyright 162
Multiple intelligences 16, 61–2
Myers, J. and McClean, J. 185

National Commission for
  Libraries and Information
  Services, US (NCLIS) 268
National Grid for Learning 234
National information policies 265ff
Nervous system 15
Newspapers
  and the Internet 179
  and magazines 180, 185, 220
Nolan Committee 134

Oakeshott, Professor Michael 19,
  25–6

Office for Scientific and Technical
Information (OSTI) 269
Official
documents, publication and
access 265, 270
information gathering 257
Official Secrets Act 123
Online search systems (*see also*
databases and abstracting
services) 89
Open government 122
Open University 234
Openness in society 8–9, 114ff
Oppenheim, Charles (*see also*
Badenoch) 162

Pace and comprehension 71
Pace of social and technological
change 175
Parrinder, P. 156
Patents for invention 154ff
Performing Rights 154
Personal information
and privacy 163ff
computerised records 165–9,
176–8
DNA 177
skills 88
Physics of information 14ff
Physiology of information 14ff
Pinker, S. 61, 62, 75
Plain English Campaign 68
Poetry and painting, presenting
information 34
Politically correct language 129
Polls and surveys 52
Population information 226
Precis writing 104
Presentation of information 6, 44ff
Pressure groups 227, 230, 254
Pricing database services 208
Primary information, category of
17
Printed publications, development
of 100ff
Private sector and Government 256

Probability 51
Professional duty 133ff
Programme on Information and
Communication Technologies
(PICT) 269
Property rights, intellectual 153ff
Public libraries 106ff
access to Internet etc. 147
Publicizing government, PR work
260
Pupils, school, numbers of 232
Puttnam, Lord David 11, 74, 184

Radio 84, 234
Recording 82, 87, 100ff
Records, integrity of 140
Reed Elsevier, takeover of
LEXIS-NEXIS 217
References, inaccurate 42
Research Councils 269
Research
consequences of and growth of
information 5, 119
dissemination of results 119, 230
Research, Environment and
Climate Programme 229
Research
freedom to undertake 118
information seeking and
generating 32
Reuters 213, 217
Right to know 121
Rights and duties, list of 112
Rio Earth Summit 229
Royal Society, Scientific
Information Conference 2
RSA
Campaign for Learning 244
Forum for Ethics in the
Workplace 133
Russell, Bertram 20, 62, 69

Sampling 50
School populations 232
Science, confusion with
technology 34

Scientific
  Information Conference, Royal
    Society 2
  research 33ff
Secondary information, category
  of 17
Seeking information, right to do
  so 114
Sexual information, access to
  children 115
Shannon and Weaver 12
"Silent Spring" 227
Smart Cards 103
Social
  and cultural changes 7–8, 172ff
  communication 195
Social Services 183ff
Social status 188–9
Sources of information 17, 105ff,
  145
  diminution in personal 173
  ethical principles in use 138
Spain, information and defeat of
  attempted coup 253
Speech patterns 189
Stakeholders rights to information
  124
Standard English 85
Standards in Public Life,
  Committee on 134
Statistical data 49
Stock markets 206
Stonier, Tom 11, 19
Superhighway, information 3
Surveys 52

Tape recorders 83
Targeted information 74
Teaching 233ff
  teachers 236
Technologies in education 233ff
Telecottages 184, 203
Telefacsimile transmission (fax) 88
Telegrams 1, 82
Television 86–7, 179, 234
"Think tanks" 259

Toffler, Alrim 3
Tradeable information initiative
  123, 262
Trust 136–8
Typewriters 83

UK Library and Information
  Commission 268– 70
UNESCO and national
  information policies 266
UNGASS meeting 229
United Nations, Universal
  Declaration of Human Rights
  112, 126
US National Commission for
  Libraries and Information
  Science (NCLIS) 268

Valuing information 206ff
Vickery, Brian and Arlene 13
Videoconferencing 83
Videophone 83
Videotex 88
Virtual reality 87, 102
Vocabulary
  problems in comprehension 62ff
  size in use 64

Warnock, Lady Mary 68
Watson, I. 208
Webster, F. 274
Whistle Blowing 127
Williams, Bernard 111
Wilson, Tom 14
WIPO (World Intellectual
  Property Organisation) 154,
  161
Words, changes in meaning 63
World Wide Web (WWW) 90, 102,
  162, 215–16, 221
Wriston, Walter 205
Writing, impact of ICTs on style
  81–2

Zeki, S. 16
Zeldim, Theodore 64, 69